Egypt and American
Foreign Assistance, 1952–1956 ~

Egypt and American Foreign Assistance, 1952–1956

Hopes Dashed

Jon B. Alterman

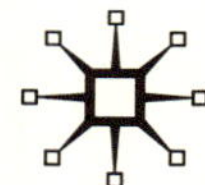

EGYPT AND AMERICAN FOREIGN ASSISTANCE, 1952–1956
Copyright © Jon B. Alterman, 2002.
All rights reserved. No part of this book may be used or reproduced in any
manner whatsoever without written permission except in the case of brief
quotations embodied in critical articles or reviews.

First published 2002 by
PALGRAVE MACMILLAN™
175 Fifth Avenue, New York, N.Y. 10010 and
Houndmills, Basingstoke, Hampshire, England RG21 6XS.
Companies and representatives throughout the world.

PALGRAVE MACMILLAN IS THE GLOBAL ACADEMIC IMPRINT OF THE
PALGRAVE MACMILLAN division of St. Martin's Press, LLC and of Palgrave
Macmillan Ltd. Macmillan® is a registered trademark in the United States,
United Kingdom and other countries. Palgrave is a registered trademark in
the European Union and other countries.

ISBN 0–312–29621–5

Library of Congress Cataloging-in-Publication Data
available from the Library of Congress

A catalogue record for this book is available from the British Library.

Design by Letra Libre, Inc.

First edition: October 2002
10 9 8 7 6 5 4 3 2 1

Printed in the United States of America

For my family

Contents

Abbreviations

CGF	Classified General Files
CSF	Classified Subject Files
DD Ops	Deputy Director for Operations
ECA	Economic Cooperation Administration
EARIS	Egyptian-American Rural Improvement Service
FOA	Foreign Operations Administration
HQ Off	Headquarters Office
IBRD	International Bank for Reconstruction and Development (World Bank)
ICA	International Cooperation Administration
MSA	Mutual Security Agency
NEA Ops	Near East and South Asia Operations (part of FOA)
NEADS	Near East and Africa Development Service (part of TCA)
NED	Near East Division (part of FOA/NEA Ops)
PCDNP	Permanent Council for the Development of National Production
RCC	Revolutionary Command Council
RG	Record Group (U.S. National Archives)
SWSASME	Social Welfare Seminar for Arab States of the Middle East
TCA	Technical Cooperation Administration
USOM	US Operations Mission (TCA, FOA, ICA missions in individual countries)

Currency equivalents:

1 Egyptian pound (£E) = $2.87
$1 = 0.35 £E
1 £E = 100 piasters

Area equivalents:

1 feddan = 1.038 acres = .42 hectares

A Note about Translation and Transliteration

Arabic is notoriously difficult to represent in English. The system adopted by the Library of Congress, for example, creates seven new characters and adds five two-letter combinations to the standard Roman alphabet. In the interests of simplicity, I have adopted a simplified system that should be accessible to the novice reader while only minimally annoying to the expert. Purists can consult the dissertation on which this manuscript is based, which leaves Arabic citations wholly in Arabic script.

Also, I have generally respected individuals' preferences for representing their own names in English even when such spellings do not comport with more orthodox transliteration schemes. I make an exception for transliterated bibliographic entries, which are done strictly on the Library of Congress's simplified scheme. Thus, Rashed Barawy, Rashid Elbrawy, and Rashid al-Barrawi are all the same person.

I have translated all of the Arabic materials into English myself, and I bear full responsibility for any errors that may remain.

Acknowledgments

In the course of writing this manuscript, I have accumulated many debts. Professor Roger Owen advised the dissertation on which this manuscript is based, offered excellent counsel, provided work space for two years, and, along with Margaret Owen and their children, became a good friend throughout the otherwise solitary writing process. I did not realize the depth of my debt to Professor Akira Iriye until I read through my dissertation for the first time and recognized so many of his ideas in it. He has been interested and helpful throughout this project as well, and I am very grateful. Also at Harvard, Professors Ernest May and Philip Zelikow organized several conferences on the Suez Canal Crisis from the various national perspectives that gave me the opportunity to receive feedback on some of the material in chapter 5 from distinguished participants.

The U.S. Department of Education Jacob Javits Fellowship Program, the Foreign Language and Areas Studies Program, and the USIA/American Research Center in Egypt Traveling Fellowship provided generous financial support for the work on which this project is based. At Harvard, I am grateful for the support I received from the Charles Warren Center for Studies in American History, the Center for Middle Eastern Studies, and the Department of History.

My work in the National Archives facility in Suitland, Maryland, was considerably eased by Miss Washington and Dr. Carey Conn. Mr. Robert French, formerly of the World Bank Archives, was unfailingly helpful. In Harvard's Widener Library, Middle East Division head Mr. Michael Hopper and the entire interlibrary loan staff were fantastic, and their efforts enriched this work significantly.

My time in Cairo was eased and enriched by my good friend Amir Abdel Hamid of the American Research Center in Egypt. Although I am still not sure exactly why I was allowed to be the first American ever to see the Egyptian Foreign Ministry Archives, I am sure the process had something to do with the efforts of Mme. Amira Khattab and Dr. Ibrahim Sadek of ARCE, and Ambassador Ahmed al-Messiri and Mr. Ala' Abdel Hamid of the Egyptian Foreign Ministry. Once I had gained access to the archives, Mr. Ibrahim

Fathallah Ahmed and Mme. Sawsan Abdel 'Aani did everything in their power to help me. In the archives, my colleague Ala' al-Din Abdel Ghaffaar patiently answered many of my silly questions. Outside of the archives, Ambassador Tahsin Bashir, Dr. Rifaat al-Said, and Mr. Salah Dessouki were very helpful in my efforts to meet former Egyptian government officials and generous with their time talking about Egyptian political history. I know that Dr. Rifky Anwar is unhappy with some of what I have written. I hope he will be more pleased when he sees it in a larger context. I enjoyed our conversations about EARIS immensely and I am grateful to him for putting me in touch with other veterans of the program.

The Department of Near Eastern and Judaic Languages and Literatures at Emory University provided a welcoming environment in which I was able to write much of the first two chapters of this dissertation. I am especially grateful to Emory Arabic Professor Kristen Brustad. Without her encouragement and support when she was teaching Arabic at Harvard, this dissertation would have taken a drastically different form.

Mme. Aziza Shukri Hussein was kind enough to share with me her husband's personal diary from 1956 to 1957, and Mr. Christopher J. Makins generously allowed me to quote from his father's unpublished memoirs, to be deposited at the Bodleian Library at Oxford. Dr. Pamela Johnson gave me materials from the evaluation of EARIS she led in 1983, and Professor Richard Dekmejian gave me permission to quote from his interviews with EARIS alumni. I am grateful to them all.

Professor John Waterbury, who taught my first course in Middle Eastern studies almost two decades ago, was kind enough to remember an old student, and sent along material that enriched chapter three. I shared ideas at length with my colleague Dr. Martin Malin, who passed on an invaluable list of contacts in Cairo. The late Professor David Bell and Professor Tom Knock offered very helpful comments on chapter four, Ahmed el-Gaili helped check translations of quotations in chapter five, and my colleagues Mona Mourshed, Professor Margaret Menninger, and Leslyn Hall's critical readings improved the overall manuscript considerably.

In more recent times, Dr. Robert Satloff's job offer kept me in Middle Eastern studies and reintroduced me to Washington, for which I am very appreciative. The United States Institute of Peace gave me a marvelous environment in which to grow intellectually. I am deeply indebted to my colleagues in the Research and Studies Program at the Institute, and especially to the former director of the Program, Dr. Patrick Cronin. Also at USIP, Dr. Peter Pavilionis made several helpful suggestions on this manuscript that add considerably to the finished product. He is a gifted editor, and I am grateful for his interest.

Any errors that remain after this tremendous outpouring of assistance are a result of my own shortcomings, rather than those named above. Also, as I write this I am on leave from USIP, being paid by the Council on Foreign Relations to work in the U.S. Department of State. This work represents only my own views only, and not those of USIP, the Council on Foreign Relations, the U.S. government, or the Department of State.

Throughout my life, I have enjoyed the extraordinary love and support of my parents, Morton and Rita Alterman. For the last ten years, my wife Katherine LaRiviere has not only matched that love and support and more—she has done so through long separations at the beginning, and while juggling an ever-growing brood of children at the end. Sam, Bella, and Jed have thus far shown no interest in the subject of aid to Egypt in the 1950s, and perhaps they never will. It matters much more to me that they can know the same extraordinary level of love and support from their family that I have enjoyed throughout this project.

—Jon B. Alterman
Bethesda, Maryland
January 1, 2002

Introduction

April 10, 1956, was to have been a glorious day for American aid officials in Egypt. Twenty-six highway engineers and 81 laborers and equipment operators were graduating from an American-sponsored Highway Training Center in a Cairo suburb. The capstone of their graduation ceremony was to be the distribution of U.S.-donated highway construction equipment to provincial authorities. American and Egyptian officials had planned a festive celebration. They inspected the new equipment an hour before the ceremony began, and they found it all in place and in excellent condition. In the light of the bright Cairo sun, the American aid personnel and contractors took their places in a large reviewing tent erected for the occasion and prepared to celebrate the fruits of their cooperation with the Egyptians.

As the new equipment passed by the reviewing tent, however, the Americans grew increasingly dismayed. On each and every vehicle, the trademark symbol of American aid—two hands clasped in partnership—and legends indicating the American source of the equipment in Arabic and English "had either been rubbed off, painted over, or covered with paper." The United States received no mention in any of the speeches delivered that day. None of the subsequent press reports indicated that Americans had either donated the equipment or were even in attendance at the ceremony. When U.S. officials inspected other American-donated equipment at the Highway Center, they found that the American insignias had been removed from all but two vehicles. Those vehicles' insignia had been welded onto the front grilles.[1]

Four months later, American officials inspecting 20 American-donated General Motors locomotives found that Egyptians had removed the clasped-hand insignia plates that had been bolted to the trains. For the 12 locomotives still to be delivered, American Embassy officials asked GM either to weld the insignia on or to take other measures "in order to make removal as difficult as possible."[2]

The U.S. government had donated tens of millions of dollars to Egypt in the four years following the Egyptian revolution of July 1952. Yet in the spring and summer of 1956, it found itself embroiled in petty battles to force the Egyptian government to acknowledge that aid publicly.

In the months immediately following the Egyptian revolution, American economic assistance had been fairly small—a smattering of programs costing several hundred thousand dollars—and directed at discrete efforts to boost the Egyptian economy. Such aid was fairly closely tailored to Egyptian needs, and Egyptians had wide latitude in determining its disbursal. The aid program quickly grew, as Americans and Egyptians looked toward a larger and more dramatic program to highlight Egyptian-American cooperation. They soon established the Egyptian-American Rural Improvement Service (EARIS) as a prototype for cooperative land reclamation and resettlement in Egypt and around the world. The American government committed $10 million to EARIS, and the Egyptian government committed the local equivalent of about $15 million. American technicians with EARIS hoped to stress the political goals of the program—aiding the establishment of a yeoman farmer class in the Egyptian countryside that would politically mobilize the peasantry on the local level—but they were unable to motivate their Egyptian counterparts to shift their sights from the technical aspects of land reclamation. While Americans had a large role in drawing up initial plans for EARIS, the program was "captured" by its Egyptian bureaucracy. Americans regarded EARIS as a partial success for American foreign assistance, while Egyptians to this day regard it as one of Egypt's most successful land reclamation programs.

The final stage of American assistance to Egypt was funding for the Aswan High Dam. Plans for the dam approached completion in the winter of 1955–56, and total costs were estimated to exceed $1 billion. In their enthusiasm for the project, Egyptian government officials did not appear to have realized that Western funding for the dam—a project judged absolutely vital to the economic survival of the country—had become subordinated to American desires to reach an Arab-Israeli peace settlement. Accustomed to Americans' proclamations of interest in Egyptian economic development and the handling of such projects primarily out of American government offices in Cairo, Egyptian government officials appear to have been caught by surprise when Washington-based opposition scrapped American funding for the dam. Although Egyptian diplomats made generally accurate assessments of American thinking throughout this period, Egyptian government officials appear to have had difficulty conceiving of U.S. counterparts who did not care at all about Egypt's economic future. In fact, such thinking was rife among the strategic thinkers at the top levels of the U.S. government.

The traditional explanation for the cancellation of High Dam funding is that the United States had lost patience with Gamal Abdel Nasser and that he was finally being punished for his recklessness and adventurism in foreign policy. A more careful study of the history of the Egyptian-American relationship creates a fascinating picture of missed messages and mutual frustrations. It suggests that the relationship was in some ways a victim of its context: uncertainty on both sides about how to promote economic development, uncertainty over the roles that Egypt and the United States would each play in the post-colonial world, and the intervention of third countries—the UK, the USSR, and Israel—into that relationship.

The Egyptian-American relationship in the 1950s is not virgin territory for historians.[3] American and Egyptian scholars have used declassified U.S. government (and to a lesser extent, British government) documents to chronicle that relationship's varying fortunes. Their accounts of the Egyptian-American relationship in the early 1950s all essentially argue that although the U.S. government was cautiously optimistic about the Egyptian revolution in 1952, the Egyptian-American relationship took a decisive turn when Egypt bought East-bloc arms from Czechoslovakia in September 1955. According to this version, the relationship then became a personal battle, pitting Gamal Abdel Nasser's flirtations with Communist countries and his assertions of independence against John Foster Dulles' vehement anti-Communism. In the event, Abdel Nasser's gambit failed, the U.S. government withdrew funding for the High Dam at Aswan, and what might have been a productive relationship was spoiled. Like the documents on which it is based, this scholarship is primarily concerned with politico-military matters and dwells predominantly on issues of weapons, regional influence, and Soviet penetration of the Middle East. As such, they portray the Egyptian-American relationship almost wholly as an expression of developing Cold War tensions in the Middle East.

Orienting the relationship around Cold War considerations, however, results in a skewed understanding of the period. It is helpful to conceptualize the Egyptian-American relationship as consisting of three intersecting spheres. The Cold War represents one, the policies of the Egyptian government another, and the U.S. government's policies the third. Some issues, such as Egypt's quest for arms, fell into the intersection of all three spheres. Other issues involved the intersection of only two spheres, such as Egyptian efforts to attract more U.S. investment or U.S. cotton-import policy. Some issues are specific to only one sphere, because they involved either wholly domestic issues or third countries with no bearing on U.S.-Egyptian ties or to the Cold War.

It is important to remember that the Egyptian-American relationship is part of each of these spheres but central to none of them. Egypt was not the primary concern for leading American government officials, nor was the United States the primary concern of those officials' Egyptian counterparts. While the areas of intersection of the three spheres is an important matter for study, concentrating solely on that intersection is misleading if one wishes to understand the goals, perceptions, and motivations of each party.

Economics is a valuable prism through which to view the U.S.-Egyptian relationship for several reasons. First, economic assistance was the first expression of the new Egyptian-American relationship after the revolution, and it continued to be a source of interaction through the next four years. Economic concerns were also at the forefront of the Egyptian leadership's thinking. Finally, economic assistance was a dynamic variable in the period under study, going from small scale to large scale, moving from bureaucracy to bureaucracy, and proving highly sensitive to external conditions. Negotiations over arms assistance, by contrast, were far more static and mostly got bogged down in Washington resistance. While the military relationship was a constant source for frustration for the Egyptians, it cannot serve as a wholly satisfactory example of how the relationship worked.

The other advantage of viewing this relationship through the prism of economic assistance is that it represents one of the incentives that was supposed to build a close relationship with the Free Officers in Egypt. While some maintain that Gamal Abdel Nasser's nationalist ambitions made U.S.-Egyptian cooperation a doomed enterprise,[4] contemporary documentation suggests that he and his colleagues were deeply pragmatic, not ideological. Had the relationship worked in the ways the Egyptians had hoped, there seems little question that Egypt would have nurtured it. As it transpired, the relationship was troubled on many levels, and Egypt believed it had few incentives for fostering it. The failure of economic aid to strengthen that relationship, then, is an important part of the picture that has thus far been neglected.

Previous work on Egyptian-American relations has imputed the Egyptian position almost entirely from American government documents. As such, Egyptian positions cannot help but appear to be in response to American interests or actions.[5] The present work attempts to reconstitute the Egyptian sphere as best as can be done from available Egyptian documentation. Some of that sphere was affected by the calculus of the Cold War, but, importantly, much of it was not. Indeed, the Cold War looked much different from Cairo than it did from Washington and Moscow. The life-and-death struggle in Egypt was not against a Communist menace but against the long arm of British imperialism on the one hand and poverty and disease on the other. Assigning primacy to Cold War explanations of Egyptian leaders' behavior is to read into those leaders an American sensibility that they certainly did not share.

From the perspective of international history, it is interesting as well how a reliance on American documents can subtly shift attention away from the United States. American government documents almost invariably assume that the U.S. government's position is clear, measured, and plainly communicated.[6] If a country fails to act in a manner consonant with American wishes, then such action becomes an intentional slight. Even a cursory examination of the Egyptian Foreign Ministry Archives undermines this perspective.

The extensive use of American government documents also leads one to reduce international relations to conflicts of individual personalities. The presidential library system and the *Foreign Relations of the United States* volumes ensure scholars access to much of the high-level thinking surrounding critical decisions, but excellent record-keeping and archive management gives the researcher a false sense of the comprehensiveness of their studies. What of the environments that conditioned the choices that policy makers faced? High-level records rarely indicate any of the low- and mid-level day-to-day successes and tensions that enable or constrain high-level action. It is true that decisions such as withdrawing funding for the High Dam at Aswan can only be understood by examining the records from the very high level at which those decisions were made. However, examining only the records of high-level officials does little to illuminate how conditions reached the point at which such a decision was taken. To understand the background to high-level decisions affecting the relations between governments, one must divert at least part of one's attention away from the high-level archives of a single country and toward the low- and mid-level contacts between those two governments and their peoples.

In addition to the ways in which the nature of the archives has steered historians of this period, subsequent events have also weighed heavily on them. This is especially true of Egyptian historians, since a subsequent turn toward Arab Socialism after the Suez Crisis led most scholars and memoirists to dismiss the possibility that a long-lasting and close relationship ever could have evolved between the Egyptian and American governments.[7] On the American side, historians have examined the early years of the revolutionary regime with an eye toward determining where the roots of Arab Socialism and military authoritarianism—characteristics of Egypt in the 1960s—lay.[8] Such accounts elide the true optimism that existed in some circles for friendship between the two countries and take the victory of forces skeptical of U.S. motives to be a foregone conclusion.

Revisiting the history with a fresh eye highlights that there were forces on each side that very much wanted U.S.-Egyptian cooperation to proceed, and forces that wanted it to fail. There was no single Egyptian attitude to the United States, nor was there a single American attitude toward Egypt. It is important to recall as well that nongovernmental actors played a significant role in inter-governmental relations of the period. Private and institutional investors, corporations, and interest groups in both countries all made decisions which strongly affected the Egyptian-American relationship. The period under study—1952 to 1956—is best understood as a period in which forces in both countries favoring and opposing close cooperation clashed. Leftists and vehement nationalists in Egypt shared a cause with American anti-Communists, farming interests, and pro-Israel forces in seeking to head off close Egyptian-American ties. Meanwhile, a collection of internationalists on both sides of the Atlantic labored against increasing odds to put the Egyptian-American relationship on stable footing.

The present work is, to a large extent, a record of the efforts of those internationalists. Americans and Egyptians both saw economic aid as an avenue for cooperation and mutual benefit. The U.S. government in particular saw its nascent foreign assistance apparatus as a way to win friends across the globe through good will, American know-how, and a relatively small amount of money. A group of Americans and Egyptians shared the hope that American economic development efforts would provide far greater benefit to recipient nations than the efforts of the colonial and mandate powers had previously.

In previous studies, economic assistance has played a smaller role in accounts of the Egyptian-American relationship than military assistance. There are several reasons for this. One is the popularity of CIA memoirs, which recount some of the military aid negotiations.[9] Another is the relatively discrete nature of an arms deal (be it from the United States or Egypt's subsequent acquisition of arms from Czechoslovakia) as opposed to broad-based attempts to affect social and economic change. Finally, Egyptian government officials have sought to justify their turn to non-U.S. sources for arms in 1955, and in so doing have downplayed how deeply disappointed they were with the progress of the American economic aid program. Revealing the depth of that disappointment would suggest that Egypt was incapable of independent economic development.

Recounting this tale in a balanced way is not an easy task, primarily because Western countries tend to have well-maintained archives that facilitate the type of research Western historians are trained to do. Other countries' archives often present special challenges. In the present case, the available Egyptian archives were not equivalent to the American sources. No records of Egyptians' daily contacts with Americans in Egypt could be located, and records of internal Egyptian governmental discussions remain mostly unavailable. In the present work, the Egyptian side is pieced together from three sources. The first is a set of records from the Egyptian Embassy in Washington that had been previously closed to researchers. The Embassy's records cast important new light on internal decision making in the Egyptian government, on Egyptian assessments of American policy, and surprisingly, on the conduct of American policy itself. The second source is Arabic periodical literature from the period. Egyptian periodicals reflect a fascinating, changing picture of the Egyptian domestic scene, and they reflect well the uncertainty and hope for positive change that dominated the early post-revolutionary period. The third source is a series of interviews I conducted with people high and low in the Egyptian system—from former diplomats and ministers to farmers and engineers. From them I learned a great deal about how Egyptians perceived and interacted with Americans and American assistance.

On the American side, I examined previously untouched project files from the sequence of bureaucracies concerned with aid to the Middle East, as well as from the Foreign Operations Mission in Cairo. I also interviewed several individuals who had worked on American aid to Egypt during the period under study and obtained copies of interviews conducted in the early 1980s by an AID contractor for a study of EARIS. Finally, I examined the diplomatic correspondence between Cairo and Washington in order to understand the larger context in which these events took place.

This manuscript begins with a chapter laying out the various contexts in which the events under study unfolded. It includes brief discussions of Egyptian history and the Cold War context, and contains explorations of American and Egyptian attitudes toward each other. Chapter two examines foreign assistance in theory and practice. It contains a description of changing thinking about development in the period under study, a brief survey of the background of American thinking about foreign assistance, and a legislative history of American foreign aid after World War II. Chapter three analyzes Egyptian-American cooperation on small-scale projects intended to put Egypt on the path toward capitalist development. Chapter four is a study of EARIS, a project that was to be a model for future cooperation but instead stood as a reminder of how difficult it is to encourage social change from abroad. Chapter five examines the High Dam at Aswan from the project's inception, highlighting especially the heretofore-unrecognized degree to which American assistance and advice played an important role in the project's planning. It also relies heavily on Egyptian Foreign Ministry documentation to change our understanding of American diplomacy with Egypt during the period. Previous writers have assumed that the State Department carried out such diplomacy, but Egyptian documentation suggests persuasively that the CIA took on a leading role.

This study seeks to deepen our understanding of the Egyptian-American relationship in the early 1950s. Equally importantly, it suggests that the Cold War prism through which scholars have viewed this and other relationships during the same period can be distorting. While the Cold War may have shaped American policy makers' thinking during this period, the Egyptian-American relationship faltered largely for reasons specific to the Egyptian context. Egypt's leaders were impatient to strengthen their country economically, yet they shared the uncertainty of the period over how such growth might be achieved rapidly. When they came to the conclusion that American support was soft, they turned away from a policy of close cooperation with U.S. government authorities. Egyptian goals remained remarkably stable through the period under study, although Egyptian government tactics shifted several times. The same might be said of the American side as well. It is here that the nub of the problem lies.

Reexamining the history of this troubled relationship reveals a far more interesting story than the conventional narrative would suggest. Rather than representing a stock tale of two-timing and treachery, it more closely resembles an account of a failed—and perhaps always doomed—courtship between a young girl and her older suitor. Both sides approached the relationship with good intentions but ultimately succumbed to the difficulties created by their differences. While there are many aspects of the Egyptian-American relationship which are *sui generis*—especially the rapidity with which hopes rose and fell—the fundamental problem of creating a durable partnership predicated on economic assistance was repeated around the globe, and continues to be encountered to this day.

Chapter 1 ~

Contexts

Egypt

After World War II, the climate in Egypt began to shift against the old ways of doing business. This drive was partly driven by the image of King Farouk, whose excesses of the flesh seemed to reach ever-greater heights. Additionally, the privations of the war years, subsequent inflation, and a devastating malaria epidemic in Upper Egypt "shocked some social consciousness into the rulers."[1] Criticism of the economic basis of the British occupation led to an awareness of the no-less-benign economics of Egyptian domestic rule, causing the author Mirrit Butros Ghali to write in 1946 that "the basis of true independence" was internal reform.[2] The army, which had been embarrassed by its performance in the Palestine War in 1948, blamed its losses on the surfeit of defective arms with which they had been supplied by corrupt leaders, who had accepted the second-rate weapons in exchange for handsome bribes.

Finally, Allied propaganda during the war, which had been intended to bolster support for the war effort in the Middle East, also had the effect of spurring nationalism. Constant Allied calls for self-determination and freedom in Europe led to calls for the same freedoms in the region. In their Egyptian manifestation, these calls took the form of virulently anti-British propaganda from all stripes of Egyptian politicians—from the leading Wafd Party to the Socialist Party (actually fascist and the offspring of the Young Egypt party of the 1930s), the Communist party (which was Levantine and Jewish in leadership and had shallow roots in Egyptian society), and the Muslim Brotherhood.

As Egyptian politics descended into a spiral of anti-British feeling in the autumn of 1951, Egyptian commandos attacked British troops in the Canal Zone with the tacit approval of the Egyptian government, and Egyptians refused to have any economic dealings with the British troops. On October

15, 1951, the Egyptian parliament unilaterally renounced the 1936 treaty with Britain that legitimated the latter's presence in Egypt. The act had no basis in international law, and outside observers dismissed it as being more of an adolescent rant than a serious policy position.

Agitation reached its peak when anti-foreign riots broke out in Cairo on January 26, 1952, and roving mobs destroyed some of the most visible symbols of foreign society in Egypt: the Turf Club, Shepheard's Hotel, the TWA office, four night clubs, seven department stores, eighteen cinemas, and seventy other commercial establishments downtown.[3] The riots ostensibly responded to a British attack on the Egyptian police headquarters in the Canal Zone where commandos were being protected. Yet the proximate instigation for the riots has never been clear—the Palace, the Wafd Party, the police, and the Muslim Brotherhood have variously been blamed. In any event, the Egyptian authorities waited for seven hours after the riots began to impose martial law and move against the rioters.[4]

More lasting than the physical damage from the riots was the feeling that Egypt was truly adrift. Cabinets changed increasingly rapidly in the spring of 1952, and the invective became more frenzied. The Palace and the British Embassy believed that they faced a common foe in the populist calls of the mob. The American Embassy took a more circumspect position, and in the months following the riots sought to deepen its contacts with a broad range of groups on the Egyptian political scene.

In late July 1952, the king insisted on appointing Isma'il Shirin as Minister of War. Shirin had no military experience whatsoever, and his only qualification for the position was his status as the king's brother-in-law. His appointment was significant more as a symptom of the dysfunction of Egyptian politics rather than as a proximate cause for what followed; on the next night, a small group of army officers calling themselves the Free Officers implemented a long-simmering plot and moved to overthrow the king.

The nearly bloodless revolution did not start as a revolution at all, and was not called one for some time. At first it was known only as a "movement" whose immediate goal was the removal of the king and the eradication of corruption from Egyptian society. The nominal leader of the officers was General Muhammad Naguib, a modest, middle-aged, half-Sudanese officer who had acquitted himself well in Palestine. He quickly won the support of the Egyptian public. The officers asked veteran politician Ali Maher to stay on as Prime Minister, but Maher resigned after six weeks over a dispute on land reform. The movement's deeper roots were unclear. Naguib was known to represent a group of officers (later to emerge publicly as the Revolutionary Command Council), but their identities and their number were not publicly known.[5] In particular, 34-year-old Colonel Gamal Abdel

Nasser, who had masterminded the coup and personally recruited its leaders including Naguib, stayed deep in the shadows for several months. In October, one Egyptian newspaper with CIA connections suggested that he was the true power in the Egyptian government, but it would be several months before Abdel Nasser's prominence was an accepted fact.[6]

There has been much speculation as to whether the CIA was behind the Egyptian coup, particularly in Egypt. Stories abound in Egypt about how CIA operatives met Abdel Nasser several months beforehand, knowing him only as "Maurice," and how Ambassador Jefferson Caffery used to call the Free Officers who ran the coup "my boys." Caffery's posting to Cairo has also aroused suspicion, since his previous posting was as Ambassador to Paris, from which Cairo appeared to many to be something of a demotion.[7] There undeniably were contacts before the coup between David Evans, the Embassy's Air Force liaison, and Ali Sabri, the head of Egyptian Air Force intelligence and one of the Free Officers. Yet, declassified Embassy records consistently show a lack of definite foreknowledge that the coup was underway.[8] Further, the Embassy's political officer, William Lakeland, told this author that Muhammad Hassanein Heikal, an Egyptian journalist who was close to the coup plotters, suggested vaguely to him several days before the coup that "something might be happening." Lakeland's reporting cable to Washington suggesting a possibly imminent coup was toned down significantly by the Ambassador, who thought it unlikely. Lakeland thought it highly improbable that the CIA had any contact with the Free Officers before the coup; however, he thought it quite possible that the American Embassy had contacted the British Embassy at about the time the coup took place, asking that the British army not intervene and thus allow the coup to unfold.[9]

While the Embassy seems not to have been behind the coup before it happened, it quickly swung behind the Free Officers in the immediate aftermath. Ambassador Caffery personally guaranteed the king's safe passage out of Egypt on July 26, 1952, and saw him off at the shore,[10] thereby gaining Caffery credit both for ensuring that the abdication took place and that the coup was as peaceful as it was.[11] Naguib wrote that at the time of the Revolution, Caffery was "one of the few foreign diplomats whom we believed we could trust."[12] Embassy officers struck quick friendships with the Free Officers. Lakeland, the Embassy's then–32-year-old political officer, recalls spending evenings watching Esther Williams films with Gamal Abdel Nasser in the Embassy canteen and enjoying dinner parties at the officers' houses.[13] Just as the American Embassy had served as an alternate locus of power in Cairo to the British-linked palace before the coup, the Free Officers took advantage of American offers to be an "honest broker" in relations with the British Embassy.

Ambassador Caffery became a prominent personality on the Egyptian scene, and his social and political functions were frequently reported in one of the leading Egyptian news and satirical magazines, *Rose al-Yusef.* Support from the American Embassy served at least two functions for the Egyptian leadership: It lent strength to Egyptian efforts to steer a political course independent of Britain, and it served to snub the British Embassy, which was witnessing a general decline in British influence throughout the region.

The Free Officers spent their first month in office cleaning house and propounding the "six principles of the revolution": the end of imperialism, the end of feudalism, the elimination of monopoly capitalism, social justice, a strong military, and a return to parliamentary rule. Newspapers and magazines sympathetic to the revolution filled their pages with reports of the scandalous excesses of the previous government. A new magazine that was a mouthpiece for the Free Officers, *al-Tahrir* ("Liberation"), reported in its first issue that the dogs of large landowners lived better lives than "ours." They enjoyed "a private bathroom, a physician, and each were given daily six pounds of milk and three pounds of meat."[14]

The officers who seized power in the summer of 1952 did so with some degree of urgency. Since the turn of the century, Egypt's living standards had been in decline.[15] The cause was not a long-term contraction of the Egyptian economy, but rather the economy's inability to keep pace with rapid population growth.[16] The indicators were not just starving peasants in the countryside. As the tools of statistics and social science improved in the 1930s, analysts began to fear a looming Malthusian disaster in Egypt. Writing in 1936, one sociologist estimated that in the period 1886–1927, "population increased almost seven times as fast as the land on which it lived, and over two and one half times as fast as the crops raised."[17] The problem only worsened as the century progressed. Rapidly declining death rates brought on by improvements in health care caused the Egyptian population to grow at 1.1–1.2 percent per year in the decades before World War II, and 2 percent or more per year in the decade after.[18]

Although Egyptian and international economists pinned their long-term hopes on industrialization to promote prosperity and employ the expanding population, improving the agricultural sector was agreed to be a prerequisite to improvement in the industrial sector for several reasons:

1. Agricultural products represented 96 percent of all exports, and contributed 60 percent of the annual income of the country. Without an improvement in agricultural income, Egypt would be unable to finance industrial development.[19]
2. 68 percent of the Egyptian population in 1952 was rural.[20] A boost in rural incomes would provide vast local markets for the sorts of sim-

ple manufactured goods that light (that is, labor-intensive, capital-extensive) industry could turn out.

3. The agricultural sector provided many of the raw materials for light industry: cotton and wool, oil seeds, hides, and so on, and uncertain supplies of materials of varying quality would severely hamper manufacturing efforts.

4. Egyptian industry had already capitalized on the "easy" import-substituting projects, making likely industrial growth in the coming decade or two lower than the rate that had prevailed in the previous decade.[21]

5. In the eyes of many, rural economics were partly responsible for sluggish industrial development. Widespread land speculation among the wealthy meant that money for industrial development was scarce.[22]

In response to the challenges listed above, the Free Officers adopted a three-pronged attack on the country's economic problems. The first was land reform, which raised incomes among poor farmers and that many expected to free capital absorbed by speculative land investments for industrial development. The second was a program of technical improvements via drainage projects, transportation enhancements, hybrid seed dissemination, and breeding programs intended to raise rural incomes.[23]

The third, and in many ways the most important, was land reclamation. The area of cropped land per capita had been falling steadily in Egypt since 1898, and was projected to be half as much in 1975 as at the turn of the century.[24] A rising pool of tenant farmers and laborers lived on an annual per capita income of only 12 £E (approximately $34.50), 63 percent below the national average of 32 £E, which also happened to be the average per capita income among families farming their own land.[25] Land reclamation would not only boost rural incomes, but would do so by creating wealth out of the approximately 97 percent of Egypt's land that was not presently arable. In a single sweep, land reclamation could increase the size of the economic pie, ameliorate the poverty of landless peasants, and create a vast number of consumers for the products of Egyptian industry. On another level, land reclamation could create political support for the new government among the peasantry by demonstrably increasing their wealth. The urgent need for land reclamation required an ambitious plan to control the waters of the Nile. Although a plan to use African lakes circulated in the Egyptian government since the late 1940s, that plan gave way to the vision of a massive High Dam at Aswan in Upper Egypt—a dam so monumental that it would be 17 times the size of the pyramids at Giza. Its execution became tied not only to the survival of the regime, but to that of the country as a whole.

The Cold War

While most Egyptians' appreciation of global politics extended little beyond the ongoing British occupation and the Egyptian army's ignominious defeat in Palestine, change in Egypt coincided with upheavals around the globe. Great Britain had stood as the primary power in the Middle East after World War I. Although it theoretically shared power with France, Britain's control over the heart of Arab world—Egypt, Palestine, Transjordan, and Mesopotamia—as well as its ties to most of the sheikhdoms ringing the Arabian Peninsula gave it the preponderance of influence. The discovery of oil in many of these areas in the first half of the century made Britain's political dominance strategically even more important. British hegemony in the region became far more than an effort to protect imperial communications, and became one to safeguard access to vital petroleum reserves.

In the aftermath of World War II, however, the model began to crumble. Exhaustion from the war, restiveness from nationalists in areas under British control, and international impatience with the persistence of colonialism combined to spell problems for continued British rule. At the same time, rivalry between the Soviet Union and the Western powers surged, creating a feeling of crisis. Western strategists feared that British withdrawal might create a dangerous vacuum in the Middle East, which at the very least would lead to instability and at worst open the door to Soviet expansion. The way out of the conundrum was a hand-off of some of the responsibility that Britain had mostly borne alone. The United States, which had emerged strongest out of the war, would support the British presence in the Middle East while assuming responsibilities the British could no longer bear. The proclamation of the Truman Doctrine on March 12, 1947, in which President Truman pledged to assume the heretofore British responsibility of protecting Greece and Turkey, was the beginning of this transfer.

In the event, the transfer was not always smooth or clear. While British and American officials shared the same strategic goal—checking Soviet expansion into the region—their tactics sometimes differed. American officials often felt that their British counterparts had never quite shaken their imperialist convictions, while some Britons believed that "the Americans were attempting to curry favour with the nationalists by leaving the British in the lurch."[26] British officials sought to maintain maximum British prestige and influence, while Americans sometimes bristled at Britain's old Middle East hands trying to preserve a world that no longer existed. Overall, the partnership was sometimes trying, but a partnership nonetheless. While some individuals remained highly skeptical of their ally's intentions, the overwhelming importance of the region to what was increasingly called the Free World overrode most considerations.

The outbreak of the Korean War in June 1950 made the perceived need for a stable security regime in the Mediterranean basin all the more urgent. In October 1951 the American and British governments approached the Egyptian government with a proposal to establish a Middle East Command. The British-built military base in the Suez Canal Zone would be turned over to Egypt in name, and the base would be used to defend the region from outside attack. As originally envisioned, the United States, the United Kingdom, France, Turkey, and Egypt would be the command's first members, and other Arab states would be expected to follow Cairo's lead. Egyptian politicians treated the idea as poison, and the Egyptian parliament rejected the proposal two days after its receipt, and concurrently unilaterally renounced the Anglo-Egyptian Treaty of 1936 and the Sudan Treaty of 1899 for good measure.[27] The Middle East Command idea was quickly dropped.

American Attitudes Toward Egypt

In 1952, Cold War concerns seemed much more pressing to most Americans than the dramatic events in Egypt. Preoccupied with the fall of China and the Korean War in Asia, and McCarthyism and defense reconversion at home, Cairo seemed distant from the living rooms of most American families. While the Pyramids and the Sphinx were fixed as images in the public mind (as they had been in America since the nineteenth century), the political and social conditions in the lands surrounding those images remained dim points on the American compass.

Before the 1952 Revolution, American magazines published several articles that catalogued the dysfunction of Egyptian politics. In some cases, American news magazines seem to have reflected a British viewpoint and relied at least partly on the British Embassy in Cairo for their information,[28] thus supporting the king if not the agglomerations of Pashas and Beys whose corruption was the grease of Egyptian politics of the period.

The *New York Times Magazine* published an article by a British author in 1951 that stressed the need for continued British influence in Egyptian affairs. Characterizing educated Egyptians as suffering from "psychological confusion," Philip Toynbee noted:

> He would like to be as cultivated and as "modern" as the European; he would like to be sufficiently African to justify his claim to brotherhood with the Sudanese, yet sufficiently Arabic to lead the whole Asiatic area of the Middle East. He is aware of his country's social backwardness and of her damaged reputation among her neighbors. He resents the humiliation of having British troops in the canal zone, and yet he knows that his own army is incapable of safeguarding that vital area. He is not to be envied.[29]

Such articles, however, were unlikely to resonate with Americans whose core values were firmly anti-colonial, even if they were blind to the imperialistic aspects of their own foreign policy. Other articles reflected Americans' growing discomfort with tottering Third World monarchies.

King Farouk's steady descent into unrestrained self-indulgence with liquor, food and women drew gasps of incredulity from *Life,* whose article, "The Problem King of Egypt," brought protests from the palace. Calling the king a "moody, petulant, headstrong man,"[30] the author wrote, "Unfortunately, most of [Farouk's] waking hours are devoted to self-gratification."[31]

The magazine related a story of a recent high-stakes poker game in which the king was betting heavily on his hand of three kings. His opponent showed four jacks, but Farouk began to rake in the pot. "I have four kings. I am the fourth," he said.[32] The king's gluttony—both for food and women—shocked the American public. *Life* published a photograph of one of Farouk's "typical" lunches: peaches, lobster, roast chicken, pomegranates, mangoes, chicken fricasee, mutton chops, sole, bouchée à la reine, potatoes, peas, rice, and artichokes. The article noted that Farouk recently had embarked on a diet, thus necessitating having oysters air-expressed to him from Copenhagen at a rate of 200 to 600 per week.[33] Farouk often ended his days of self-indulgence at the Scarabee, a semiprivate club with a "lush, 20 year-old French singer" as its main attraction. Sitting in the dark after 2 A.M., "His eyes are hidden, his thick, sulky lips seldom smile and his fleshy body hardly moves."[34]

The folly of Egyptian politics would have been easier for Americans to take were there not a sense of imminent change in the air. American journalists saw the Cairo riots of January 26, 1952, as a scapegoating of the West for the failures of the Egyptian government. Their articles were rife with rumors that the government intentionally let the riots go on longer than they had to. One tale commonly circulated placed Interior Minister Fouad Serag el-Din in meetings sealing a profitable land deal the Saturday morning of the riots rather than directing his government's response to the chaos. A *New Republic* editorial immediately following the riots blamed American government policy toward Egypt as much as "Farouk and the fast-living wealthy Egyptian cliques around him" for the downturn there. Under the British aegis, the editorial stated,

> No stable Arab middle class has grown up. What is new is the emergence of an Arab intellectual proletariat, a class of small clerks and government officials, half-educated, underpaid, whose resentment against the "Old Gang" has been diverted into nationalist fury against the West. . . . If anything is certain, it is that the future in the Middle East belongs not to the "Old Gang" of Pashas but to these same nationalists.[35]

American writers in 1952 were concerned with the future of the Middle East and the need to develop a "new middle class"[36] not only for reasons of equity and advancement in the region. The spectre of Communist influence, even during this period of relatively little Soviet activity beyond Europe, loomed large in Americans' minds, as did the fear that American influence in the region would be crippled by American support for Israel and a perception that the United States was too close to Britain and her colonial policies.[37]

When the revolution came in July 1952, it was met with little alarm. General Naguib was a reassuring presence to many Western observers, who saw the revolution as an opportunity for "Kemalist" change[38] and saw Naguib himself as "a sort of Egyptian Abraham Lincoln."[39] Reporters commented favorably on his piety, simplicity, and apparent honesty. Naguib, described as "a paragon of middle-class virtues, hardworking, sober, and economical to the point of puritanism, and a family man,"[40] was a welcome relief from the "slothful, greedy and capricious" Farouk.[41]

Americans, who had won their own freedom from a king almost two centuries before, shared Egyptians' awe when the splendor of Muhammad Ali's clan was revealed. Palaces were seen to be stuffed not only with priceless art and coin collections, but also a staggering collection of nude portraits and lush beds for the king's many exploits. Americans seemed to feel a unity with Egyptians over this point—that somehow the British had allowed this situation to persist, and now that the world was under the aegis of American power, the extravagance of tyrannical rulers no longer had a place.

The Revolutionary Command Council's policies, although mistakenly attributed to Naguib's personal leadership, also drew praise. The RCC was careful to present itself as pro-American, at least to Americans. Gamal Abdel Nasser insisted even before the revolution that the epithet "Anglo-American Imperialism," which had appeared in Communist publications in Egypt, be sharpened to "British imperialism"[42] in order to gain support in American quarters. The RCC's repeated assurances that they were anti-Communists brought great forbearance from Americans, who were willing to excuse martial law in Egypt because "a mild dictatorship is just what this country needs."[43] Correctly noting that "parliamentary systems hastily adopted from the West . . . have generally operated only in the interests of the landowning class . . . [that] effectively preserved a vestigial feudal system and prevented all social change,"[44] writers on Egypt welcomed the young officers and their agenda for land reform and an end to pervasive corruption. The revolution's slogan of "Unity, Discipline, Work," offered hope for the rest of the region. 'For the first time since the Prophet Mohammed the Moslem world has produced a man whose claim to leadership is based on social justice," one author gushed. "It is beginning to seem possible that, with the proper assistance from the United States, the blessed movement will provide an effective answer to the Russian challenge in every Moslem country."[45]

After an initial flurry of stories about the new regime, however, Americans' interest in modern Egypt waned. Aside from a few travel articles, which concentrated on the Egyptian Museum and the treasures of ancient Egypt,[46] and several small articles during the political crisis in 1954, in which Abdel Nasser finally toppled Muhammad Naguib from his figurehead position, Egypt mostly retreated from American view. Americans were growing increasingly concerned with domestic affairs, tax rates, and the Army McCarthy hearings. The stunning allied defeat at Dienbienphu took up much of the energy that was left for foreign affairs.

Beginning in late 1954, Egypt began to loom in some quarters as a hostile force. The repeated deferral of elections and increasing tensions on the Israeli border dissipated much of the good will that had accumulated after the revolution, at least among writers sympathetic to Israel. For the first time, journalists used "dictatorship" as an epithet against the Egyptian leadership and warned of Egypt as a destabilizing force in the region.[47] Part of the concern over Egyptian militarism, paradoxically, may have resulted from Egypt's having successfully negotiated an agreement mid-year with the British over the Suez Canal Base. The negotiations over the terms of a possible British withdrawal from that base (and thus the end of the 70-year British occupation of Egypt) had begun under the king and been a persistent source of tension. The American government had played a role through the negotiations as an honest broker and had dangled the prospect of significant American military and economic assistance to Egypt upon the completion of the deal. Israel's supporters believed that Egypt would use any increased strength to attack Israel and that the evacuation of British troops from the Canal Zone would destabilize the region. The new coolness to Egypt in the American press, then, may have been part of an effort to preempt close American-Egyptian relations and head off an American arms agreement with Egypt.[48]

While American attitudes toward Egypt were at least mixed through much of this period, the shipment of Soviet arms to Egypt in October 1955 marked the end of warm feelings toward the revolution. Writing in March 1956, *Life* referred to Egypt's "dangerous eminence," and asserted that Abdel Nasser gained his influence in the region by "championing the Arab crusade against Israel, by prodding neutralists against the West and by cottoning to the Communists."[49] Indeed, journalists ceased writing elegies to the new middle class or on the fruits of limited dictatorship, and instead turned their thoughts to Gamal Abdel Nasser, the charismatic leader who not only led his country but seemed to many to be the only thing that mattered about it.

Egyptian Attitudes Toward America

While it is difficult to talk of a definitive American attitude toward Egypt during this period, it is similarly difficult to talk of a definitive Egyptian attitude toward the United States. America played only a small role in the lives of most Egyptians. To the parochial *fellahin,* or peasants, conceptions of international relations seemed remote indeed to their daily life.[50] While opposition to the British occupation was widespread in Egypt throughout the late nineteenth and early twentieth century, exactly what that meant remained somewhat fuzzy to the majority of the Egyptian population. Among urban dwellers and those in the Canal Zone (who had more contact with the foreign community), the population was split between those who sought to cultivate contacts in the foreign community and those who eschewed such interaction. These groups were somewhat defined by class, with the upper class—many of whose members were foreigners themselves—tending to be more international in outlook, and the middle class showing more support for nationalist and, at times, xenophobic causes.

In this context, the United States was something of a puzzle. Without a history of colonialism in the Middle East, the United States represented, to some, a savior from the clutches of the British. After World War II, opposition parties sought out the American Embassy in Cairo for a sympathetic ear and a hopeful "in" to balance against British influence over the crown.[51] To others, particularly leftists in Egypt, the United States was part and parcel of the European colonial project. To both the middle and upper classes, the United States was a fount of consumer goods, from Coca-Cola to Hollywood films, both of which could be enjoyed at the American-owned Metro Cinema in downtown Cairo. The image of the United States found in the Egyptian press of the period is one of both prosperity and informality. Americans were "easy going and gum-chewing"[52] and appeared to enjoy an unselfconscious, carefree lifestyle that stood in stark contrast to the starched collars of Egypt's British residents.

Egyptians shared a fear, however, that deep down, Americans and Britons were not so different from one another. The leftist press advocated this idea most openly, echoing—perhaps by design—the propaganda line of the Soviet Union. A young Free Officer and propagandist named Anwar Sadat[53] wrote in 1953 of American and Britain: "Between you two is a bond of blood . . . and blood will not change to water, as our fathers the peasants say . . . ! But I want to tell you that Britain—as she rocks you in the cradle of politics—is making from this [cradle] a funeral bier . . . !"[54] To be sure, the Americans were not willing to snub the British totally. Washington certainly did not approve of doing so, nor did Ambassador Caffery. While the activities of the British Embassy in Egypt met with some opprobrium from

Americans, and especially those resident in Cairo, the essential unity of American and British interests in the Middle East was never far from the minds of American and British embassy officials. For Egyptians, though, the American Embassy was a more palatable partner than the British, and one could claim to be both anti-British and pro-American without compromising one's nationalist credentials.

A year before the revolution, the leftist Egyptian writer Ahmed Baha' al-Din published *The New American Colonialism, or the Point Four Program,* a small 92-page book critiquing Point Four, which had not yet been implemented in Egypt.[55] The first half of the book summarized the program from an American perspective, stressing the importance of exporting American expertise, particularly to regions of strategic importance to the United States. The second half of the book, however, criticized the "true purpose" of the program, which Baha' al-Din saw to be facilitating the export of American investment capital. Seizing on Truman's claim that American technical assistance overseas would increase opportunities for profitable American capital investment in the undeveloped countries—essentially a selling point for the program in the United States— Baha' al-Din asserted that the American program was fundamentally self-interested, and, further, that it would operate against the interests of countries accepting such assistance. Long-accustomed to colonial patterns of investment, which he saw as a zero-sum game in which the power and benefits accrued to the colonizing nations, Baha' al-Din asserted that the only innovation in the Point Four program was the use of "treaties and agreements and surveys before taking a single step with capital."[56] Despite the investments in Egypt, profits would still be repatriated overseas, and constitute a net drain on Egyptian resources.[57] As proof of his claim that America was little better than other colonial powers, he pointed out that Latin America was still relatively poor despite more than a half century of American investment and interest.[58] He wrote, "There is nothing new under the sun, except for honeyed words and tempting propaganda connected with this new colonialism."[59] The Embassy dismissed Baha' al-Din's book as Communist propaganda, but translations and analyses of the work that circulated within the Embassy suggest that it was taken seriously.

Baha' al-Din was unusual for his time, for most Egyptians and Americans looked upon each other with few preconceptions. They had no long history of either conflict or cooperation. When the U.S. government indicated its support for the 1952 coup in Egypt, cautious optimism prevailed on both sides. From the Egyptian perspective, rising American power in the world was almost certainly preferable to that of the British. From the American perspective, if the new government could ameliorate the grinding poverty of many Egyptians, then the threat of Communist-inspired unrest would recede. Neither side anticipated the rapid flux the relationship was to go through in the coming years. Not only were there the problems of creating a new kind of Egyptian government and adjusting to a new U.S. role in the world. Great changes were also occurring in thinking about geopolitics and global strategy. While there was some agreement on the importance of economics to the global struggle, the new field of post-colonial development economics was going through revolutionary changes itself.

Chapter 2 ∾

The Economic Origins
of a Partnership

Given the importance that both Egyptians and Americans ascribed to economic development in 1952, the economic policies of the new revolutionary government have received surprisingly little attention from historians. One judged, for instance, that "The regime was in its first three to four years totally occupied with the political issues of consolidating its power and negotiating an evacuation agreement with Britain. Much of its economic policy was one of holding down expenditures and inflation."[1] A leading political economist, for his part, suggested that the RCC followed a naïve policy of import substituting industrialization, "however rudimentary its understanding of economics,"[2] and modeled its experience on the successes of Turkey under Atatürk. On the Egyptian side, there is almost no scholarship at all on the economic policies of the government before the nationalizations that began after the Suez Crisis; Ahmed Hamrouche's *Story of the July Revolution*,[3] which is one of the most comprehensive accounts of the Revolution, barely mentions economics at all.

The Egyptian government's economic policies in this period were unremarkable to contemporary observers because they were directly in step with mainstream academic and governmental solutions to the problems of poor countries, not because they were poorly thought out or poorly executed. Rather than exhibit a stumbling naïveté, those charged with establishing an economic development program in Egypt followed relatively orthodox, capitalist models for economic development.[4] A confidential World Bank report from 1955 observed favorably that the "present government is tackling the problem of economic development with great vigor."[5] Egyptian economic development was indeed slow to take off, but at least part of the difficulty lay with frequently changing advice offered by consulting economists.

When the Revolutionary Command Council came to power in 1952, experts framed much of the debate about development as the challenge of alleviating widespread abject poverty. As the decade advanced, however, the terms of the debate shifted to considering development as a larger process. No longer concerned solely with raising per capita incomes among the poor, economists shifted their sights to questions of how much total capital needed to be invested in a poor country before the economy would blossom and deliver benefits across the entire economic spectrum.

This chapter explores the changing state of development economics in the early 1950s. It goes on to discuss the background to evolving American ideas about overseas technical assistance and the ongoing congressional debate over how Americans would be involved in the post-colonial world in the years after World War II. In each area, the ideas were in a high state of flux in the early 1950s, making it difficult even for astute observers to predict the course of the next policy twist or turn.

The Economic Milieu

After World War II, economists were generally optimistic about their abilities to foster growth in poor countries. Emboldened by their confidence in social science to solve the problems of the modern world, economists believed that they could make a significant difference in the short term in the economies of poor countries. Combined with their expertise, "a breathing space of a generation may be all that is needed to break the vicious circle of poverty and population pressure in which some of the areas are caught."[6]

Nevertheless, there were some fundamental problems in the way of those seeking to promote world development. The first, of course, was defining exactly what "development" meant. Indeed, there was not even a consensus that development was the goal or that the countries targeted should properly be described as "underdeveloped." The Burmese economist Hla Myint favored the term "backward" because in many poor countries, the available resources—agricultural and mineral commodities, mostly—were fully developed while the mass of people remained poor. The problem was not better exploitation of extant resources but, rather, how to change the peoples' way of life. A comprehensive United Nations report of the time favored using the word "poor" countries because of the theoretical possibility that some countries would be poor not because they were "underdeveloped," but because they had fully developed the resources that they had and, nevertheless, remained poor.[7] One anthropologist even suggested that poor countries be referred to as "overdeveloped," because they were characterized by "too many techniques . . . too exhaustively applied by too many people to too little land."[8] For most social scientists, however—and the economists battled mightily throughout the 1950s to assert the primacy of their role in economic development—the term "underdevelopment" had the most intellectual currency. To their minds, it best captured the interconnected aspects of life in poor countries that had to change in order to industrialize and modernize those societies.[9]

The primacy of economics arose at least in part because of the apparent precision of measuring cash compared to other variables. Many economists recognized that the absence of money was merely a symptom of poverty rather than the totality of the problem.[10] Also, measuring capital in poor societies was a harder problem than it first appeared. Economists had to grapple with issues like measuring the value of farmers' own labor in improving land when the labor market was extremely weak and labor might not otherwise be employed in the economy. Another problem was how one could measure the cash value of barter transactions for commodities or services that were never exchanged for cash.[11]

Even when one accepted the premise that "backwardness" was primarily an economic problem, uncertainties persisted. Capitalist economics place primacy on the market mechanism, but it was precisely this mechanism that had failed to promote development in poor countries. Economics also did not have an obvious answer to the problem of establishing the optimum mix between improvements in agriculture and industrialization. Because all advanced economies of the day were primarily industrialized economies, was the answer promoting industrial projects that would draw people off the countryside and into cities? Or should primary emphasis be on increasing the food supply and improving conditions in the countryside, where the population could provide a vital market for the manufactured goods of the cities? The economist Joseph Schumpeter's work emphasized the role of individual entrepreneurs in economic growth, but how was entrepreneurship to be encouraged?

The first economist to address the issue of the "development" of poor countries in a concerted way was P. N. Rosenstein-Rodan. Writing in 1943, Rosenstein-Rodan advocated a massive, coordinated infusion of foreign cash to Eastern and Southeastern Europe to promote "balanced" development. He stressed that a broad variety of development projects would have a complementary effect on each other and would be more effective and less risky than either a few large, capital-intensive projects or reliance on individual entrepreneurs.[12] In his famous example, he pointed out that the workers in a newly established shoe factory would not use all of their newfound wages only to buy the shoes that they themselves made; they would also purchase other manufactured goods. The establishment of a single factory, then, created opportunities for other domestic industrial projects.[13] Labor intensive and capital extensive light industry was optimal in this model: it maximized the symbiotic relationships between newly established industries while minimizing the need for capital.[14]

Rosenstein-Rodan stressed that the market was not always a sufficient engine of development, especially when fundamental structural changes were being sought in developing economies. In particular, some investments might be "profitable in terms of 'social marginal net product' but do not appear profitable in terms of 'private marginal net product.'"[15] In other words, such activities benefit the society as a whole but may not necessarily benefit the individual entrepreneurs who undertake them. The construction of a transportation infrastructure is one example of an investment of this kind, as is the construction of an electric power plant (that in turn creates a market for electric appliances). Education and training often falls into the same category, because a single firm cannot always recover its costs.[16] The importance of Rosenstein-Rodan's contribution was its novelty in suggesting a mode of massive state intervention along non-Soviet lines. Within a generally capitalist framework, Rosenstein-Rodan highlighted the limitations of pure capitalism for inducing broad economic change. His suggestion of a brief period of state-sponsored capitalism to be followed by a more prosperous, laissez-faire intermediate term certainly seems to have been an inspiration for Egyptian planners shortly after the Revolution.

Another strong voice for state capitalism in the early 1950s came from the left. Paul Baran advocated the institution of highly progressive tax systems in poor countries to accumulate state capital, which could then be put to productive goals.[17] An unapologetic socialist, Baran believed the differences between rich and poor to be capitalism's *problematique,* the solution to which was socialist development. The problem with his plan, as Baran himself noted, was that governments in poor countries were often too corrupt to administer accumulated state capital efficiently and were generally composed of people sympathetic to (if not members of) the dominant capitalist class. In order to push for development, Baran argued, the United States would have to forge wholly new alliances with peasants and workers and push for political and economic change. Without such an alliance, the status quo would be insurmountable.[18]

The most ambitious study of economic development to emerge in the early 1950s was a United Nations report entitled *Measures for the Economic Development of Under-developed Areas.* The report was written by an international committee of economists that had been charged with addressing a rather narrow set of issues: "unemployment and underemployment in under-developed countries, and the national and international measures required to reduce such unemployment and underemployment."[19] Their response, consisting of some 90 typeset pages, was far more encompassing and addressed the entire issue of underdevelopment, as well as domestic and international measures necessary to alleviate poverty and promote development. In brief, the United Nations report was strongly pro-capitalist, pro-industrialization—especially in countries with overpopulated rural areas like Egypt—and pro-land reform.[20] The overarching goal of the study's recommendations was the creation of an urban consumer class that would monetize poor economies, reward entrepreneurship, and relieve overcrowding in the countryside.[21]

The two primary ingredients of development, the authors suggested, were capital and technology. "We cannot overemphasize the fact that capital and technology are joint inputs in one process," they wrote, "the use of either of which necessarily involves the other."[22] With regard to capital, domestic sources were clearly insufficient. Even raising taxes and improving the availability of savings institutions in poor countries would leave them less than halfway toward the estimated $19 billion of annual investment required to boost the per capita national income in poor countries by two percent per year.[23] The remainder would have to come from foreign capital, partly through grants and partly through foreign investment, the latter of which was primarily directed toward oil-rich countries during that period.[24] A founding purpose of the International Bank for Reconstruction and Development (the World Bank) was to lend to poor countries. Yet it had been doing so at "a rate well below $300 million annually, and expects not to exceed this figure in the next few years. In view of the need of the underdeveloped countries for capital, the Bank cannot be said to be meeting the challenge of the circumstances," the authors concluded, their understatement indicating their displeasure. They suggested a target lending rate of at least $1 billion per year.[25] The UN study also came down harshly on the upper classes in poor countries whose members had been hoarding their profits rather than investing them in national development—particularly in the Middle East and Latin America. In some of these countries, the hoards were estimated to represent perhaps ten percent of the national income. The study stated the urgent need to put these funds into productive investments in the national economy but was realistically pessimistic that the hoards could either be found or put to productive use.[26]

With regard to technology, the authors noted that the technology gap between rich and poor countries had widened over the past two centuries. The possibility of quickly and cheaply transmitting that knowledge and closing the technology gap offered significant hope for closing the economic gap as well: "[H]ighly productive methods and processes . . . open wide opportunities for the underdeveloped countries to profit from experience already gained and results already well-established."[27] The authors recommended vast efforts to disseminate new knowledge through agricultural extension programs—expending as much as one percent of the national income—and detailed surveys of nations' resources and capabilities so as to better plan their economic development.[28] The downside of technological improvement, however, was the possibility that, *ceteris paribus,* increased efficiency would result in the employment of *fewer* individuals rather than more. To prevent this, economies should be expanding while technological improvements are introduced, so those who lost their jobs to efficiency could quickly find new ones in the expanding employment sector.[29]

Along similar lines, improvements in health care tended to boost population growth. While some advances like the treatment of malaria or better nutrition improved productivity, lower infant mortality rates and lower death rates for adults caused many countries' populations to expand without any immediate productivity gains.[30] Ominously, the UN experts expected the population to increase with or without economic development, because medical information was transmitted independently of industrial and agricultural technology. Because population growth was inevitable, the question became not whether but *how* to accommodate larger populations. On the question of how to regulate population growth, the report was silent except for a suggestion that experts in the field apply themselves to the problem.

The UN report broke new ground in development economics in that it presented an integrated plan for the development of poor countries based on the coordinated and integrated efforts of those countries themselves, wealthy countries, and international organizations. It was highly progressive in that it appeared to call for dramatic social change to ameliorate the great disparities between rich and poor in many of the poorer countries. Liberal in its viewpoint, it suggested that the state had a large role to play in development projects, both in creating an environment in which development could take place and, in many cases, carrying out programs that private capital eschewed. Ambitious in scope, the report could have been written only after the Marshall Plan had enjoyed as much success as it did in Europe; the huge capital transfers of the type the report envisioned were unprecedented.

In the years following the UN report and the success of the Marshall Plan, economists began to consolidate their primacy in the development process. One consequence of this consolidation was an increasing tendency in the debate over development to focus on capital and capital processes rather than on social or technological change. Discussion shifted to issues of how much capital was required for a given amount of development, and how it could be made to act productively in countries where capitalism had not led to development. Subsequent discussions of wealth formation tended to downplay the concentration on the alleviation of poverty on the microeconomic level that had characterized earlier work.

One of the pioneers in this field was Harvey Leibenstein, who largely developed an approach called "equilibrium theory." Leibenstein's theory centered around the idea that a poor country was one in which the economy had settled into an equilibrium, while a wealthy country was one in which the economy was in dynamic disequilibrium. The disorder that characterized disequilibrium was in fact creative and led to progressive improvements. The society in equilibrium, however, had a stagnant economy that discouraged both economic and cultural change. Expanding populations, for example, offset any advances in income.[31] Although Leibenstein did not use the example, Newton's First Law of Motion seems apposite: a body at rest tends to stay at rest, and a body in motion tends to stay in motion. The developmental imperative for poor countries, then, was for a "big push"— a massive capital influx—provoking a change so fundamental that it would overcome the countervailing forces depressing development. While Leibenstein's approach gained great currency among economists in the 1960s, it was less influential in the tight budgetary climate of Washington in the 1950s. Large outlays for economic development overseas enjoyed little support in Congress or the Executive Branch.

The History of Technical Assistance

Overseas technical assistance, broadly defined, did not begin in the 1940s, and it did not necessarily originate in the United States. Beginning in the latter part of the nineteenth century, foreign governments began to hire European and American experts for advice and administration of specific civil and agricultural programs in their countries. American experts contributed to the advancement of Japan during the Meiji Restoration in the fields of agriculture, geography, engineering, and public administration. The Chinese viceroy Chang Chih-t'ung of Hunan and Hubei sent for an expert from the Agricultural Experimental Station at Cornell for advice on improving Chinese agriculture in 1897.[32] In 1872, a 25-year-old American named Samuel Bryan led the modernization of the Japanese postal service, stayed for a decade, and headed Japan's efforts for admission to the International Postal Union in 1877.[33] American expertise extended to financial fields as well. In 1922, the State Department sent economist Arthur C. Millspaugh to reform Persian government finances and thereby attract foreign investment, and Professor Edwin Kemmerer of Princeton led an economic mission to spur Chinese modernization and reform.[34]

On a broader level, much of the technical assistance in the nineteenth century was transmitted by soldiers and missionaries. Egypt, among many countries, received its share of technical assistance through the nineteenth century from both. When Napoleon invaded Egypt in 1798, he brought with him a printing press (printing in French and Arabic, both firsts for the region), modern hospitals, and the plans for a sewer system.[35] His forces' expeditions to the South also set the stage for later archeological expeditions and their outgrowth, tourism, which lent support to the Egyptian economy beginning in the 1850s and continues to this day.

American missionaries' involvement in the Middle East began with Pliny Fisk and Levi Parson's trip to Smyrna in 1819, and by 1900 missions were operating throughout the Ottoman Empire and in Persia, the Persian Gulf, and Egypt. The phrase, "The evangelization of the world in this generation" gathered increasing support for overseas missionary activities in the latter part of the nineteenth century. But in the twentieth century, American missions in the Mediterranean and the rest of the world became more educational than evangelical in their thrust, "hoping to bring people and societies to Christ by environmental influences and a kind of spiritual osmosis."[36] In these efforts, missionaries established schools throughout the region, the most famous of them being the American University of Beirut. One American faculty member described AUB in the 1930s as "a nursery of good men and a perpetual fountain of good will."[37] Other similar institutions of higher education included Robert College in Constantinople (1863) and the American University in Cairo (1920).

More numerous by far were the many primary schools the missionaries established. By 1901, Presbyterians claimed to operate 200 schools in Egypt with 14,000 pupils; in 1933, the number of schools appears to have declined significantly, but the number of students increased to 19,000.[38] The effects of these schools were not evenly spread throughout the native population, however. In Egypt, enrollment in the missionary schools was overwhelmingly Christian, and it was a cause for some pride that the American University in Cairo was able to draw almost 50 percent of its student body from the Muslim population in 1920, compared to 15 percent for most other missionary schools then operating in Egypt.[39] Further, many of the elite institutions charged tuition, which put them beyond the reach of the vast majority of the populace.

The effect of the missionary schools was more cultural than religious, in any event. They were popular among parents because they afforded advantages to their pupils, exposing them to Western modes of thought in a world in which progress seemed increasingly to come from the West. Teachers were aware that proselytization among Muslim students would jeopardize their entire educational enterprise in Egypt, and thus the religious content of the schools remained rather low. Practically all of their new co-religionists converted from Coptic Christianity to Roman Catholicism or Protestantism.[40]

Beginning in the twentieth century, the affiliates of secular American philanthropic organizations entered the international scene. The Rockefeller Foundation, chartered in 1913, established an International Health Commission only six weeks after its founding and funded health projects throughout Latin America and the rest of the world.[41] The Near East Foundation, continuing the work of missionaries, instituted projects from Albania to Ethiopia. While none was comprehensive in its scope, they were distinctive in that their aim was purely humanitarian and their resources sufficient to have lasting effects on the areas in which they worked.

The immediate precursor of the United States' Point Four program was the Institute for Inter-American Affairs (IIAA), part of President Franklin Roosevelt's "Good Neighbor" policy. Intended in large part to stem insurrection and anti-Americanism in the hemisphere during World War II, the IIAA—under the leadership of Nelson Rockefeller—established joint projects between the host governments and the U.S. government in health, education, and agriculture. These projects were known as *servicios cooperativos,* or *servicios* for short, which roughly translates to "cooperative bureaus." They combined American seed money and direction with local currency, manpower, and support.

The *servicios* were by design extra-ministerial in the countries in which they operated, which aided in hiring the most qualified personnel, streamlining operations, insulating the organizations from "pork-barrel" pressures, and stabilizing them against the swings of changing governments.[42] Many were also excluded from the fiscal rules and regulations under which the ministries had to operate.[43] By the end of the war, 25 *servicios* were operating in 18 Latin American countries.[44] *Servicios* had initiated "over 2,800 projects in health and sanitation alone" by 1951,[45] and the U.S. portion of their budget was in the neighborhood of $7.5 million per year. Official estimates stated that by 1950, 28 million people had benefited from IIAA programs, and that the ratio of local to U.S. spending was three to one.[46] Counting only the contributions to local activities and not the administrative and travel costs of sending Americans overseas, that ratio increased to eight to one.[47]

Point Four

The famous fourth point of President Truman's inaugural address in January 1949—his call for an ambitious program of technical assistance to the developing world—was not the result of a long, drawn-out planning process. More than anything, it was the product of happenstance. A State Department aide named Ben Hardy tried to incorporate a high-profile technical assistance program into a version of Truman's speech that he was helping draft. Higher-ups in the State Department clearance process deleted it, because they felt it was too vague and optimistic. Not to be defeated, Hardy passed the language to George Elsey, a young assistant in the White House, who in turn put it into a version of the speech shown to the president. Truman liked the idea—over the objections of Undersecretary Robert Lovett and Ambassador Charles Bohlen—and it stayed.[48]

In the final version of that speech, Truman outlined four "major courses of action" for American foreign policy: support for the United Nations, encouragement of world economic recovery and an accompanying reduction in impediments to trade, defense of countries facing aggression, and "a bold new program for making the benefits of our scientific advances and industrial progress available for the improvement and growth of underdeveloped areas." The last point—Point Four—was the only one of those principles that was new, and it resonated among the post-war American public. In his speech, Truman intertwined the triumph of American technology and the nation's mission in the world. "For the first time in history," the president said, "humanity possesses the knowledge and the skill to relieve the suffering" of the world's poor. "The United States is pre-eminent among nations in the development of industrial and scientific techniques. . . . Our imponderable resources in technical knowledge are constantly growing and are inexhaustible." While Truman allowed for international cooperation in this mission, the flavor was to be distinctly American. "The old imperialism—exploitation for foreign profit—has no place in our plans," he said. "What we envisage is a program of development based on the concepts of democratic fair dealing."[49]

The idea of technical assistance was immediately appealing to Americans in the early 1950s for several reasons. First, it seemed intuitive. One congressional report on the origins of technical assistance began simply, "Technical assistance began when the man who invented the wheel told somebody about it."[50] The exchange of knowledge and techniques had built the Industrial Revolution and spread it throughout Europe, and similar exchanges had aided agricultural development in the European countryside. If the rural poor in underdeveloped areas grew meager crops using antiquated methods, surely introducing them to hybrid seed and modern farming techniques would alleviate their suffering without posing a threat to the highly industrialized societies of the West. The idea's appeal was not simply naïve. The development economist W. Arthur Lewis wrote in *The Nation* that "Asia and Africa and large parts of Latin America remain poor mainly because the information about how to increase production which has been accumulating for two centuries in the Western World has not yet been applied to their problems."[51]

Second, agricultural extension was something Americans already understood. Starting in the nineteenth century, Grange Societies across the country organized the dissemination of agricultural information to its 800,000 members, and the Smith-Lever Act of 1914 institutionalized federal sponsorship of agricultural extension through land-grant colleges. Americans were used to the idea that agricultural prosperity often emerged from universities and the county agents who acted as intermediaries between those universities and local farmers. This idea seemed to run particularly strongly among America's southerners, in whose states agricultural extension alleviated some of the country's most grinding poverty.[52]

Third, technical assistance seemed to fulfill Americans' altruistic impulses for a very small price. "It emphasizes the distribution of knowledge rather than money," one supporter wrote, which "makes it so infinitely appealing."[53] The idea was that a tiny investment of American knowledge would nourish the arid soils of the Third World, reaping results many times in excess of the initial outlay. At a time when the United States was spending billions on the Marshall Plan, to begrudge some small fraction of that amount for improving the lives of the impoverished majority of the world's inhabitants seemed exceedingly niggardly.

Finally, technical assistance seemed the perfect antidote to resurgent Communism in the late 1940s. Many in the United States believed that Communism's greatest weapon was hungry peasants who had been duped by Marxist-Leninist promises of economic advancement. Technical assistance could provide examples of economic betterment under a capitalist framework that emphasized individual liberties and democratic cooperation. The widely popular 1958 novel *The Ugly American,* based on field experience in Southeast Asia earlier in the decade, provides an example of the appeal of technical assistance to a broad American audience.[54] Set in the fictional Southeast Asian country of Sarkhan, the novel lampoons protocol-obsessed, out-of-touch American diplomats and their Sarkhanese elite counterparts. Its heroes are people like the ugly American, a heavy construction engineer named Homer Atkins, who cares little for diplomatic niceties and has the true interests of the Southeast Asian people at heart. In the novel, Atkins is initially assigned to Vietnam, where he argues with American and Vietnamese officials over the superfluity of building extensive networks of roads and dams in Vietnam. "You don't need dams and roads," Atkins argues. "Maybe later, but right now you need to concentrate on first things—largely things that your own people can manufacture and use. . . . You ever hear of a food shortage being solved by someone building a military highway designed to carry tanks and trucks?" The political officer in the embassy cuts him short, and says, "Mr. Atkins, I think that's a political decision that goes beyond your province."[55] Atkins is transferred to Sarkhan, where the American ambassador is more receptive to his ideas. He proceeds to the countryside and designs a pump irrigation system out of bamboo, a discarded jeep engine and a bicycle—all supplies in abundance in rural areas, and all replicable by ordinary Sarkhanese. With a tinkering Sarkhanese partner, whose "fingernails were as dirty as Atkins' and [whose] hands were also covered with dozens of little scars,"[56] Atkins perfects the pump and convinces village men to build a series of them. After 24 pumps are built, Atkins dispatches members of the village into the countryside to sell them. They return loaded with orders. In one swift motion, a micro-enterprise has been launched, the villagers have been won over to capitalism, and the United States has saved the Sarkhanese peasants from the clutches of Communism.

In a triumph over the well-educated elite that constituted the American diplomatic corps, the Ugly American and his counterparts (among them a Burmese-speaking Irish-Catholic priest who retreats to the countryside to fight Communism, "the devil's face, put on earth to test again the morality of men"[57]) represent the triumph of Main Street America in the Cold War. In the mood of the time, the Cold War was to be fought by and for ordinary citizens. In the non-fictional realm, this spirit was captured by a prominent businessman who ran the Economic Stabilization Agency under President Truman and who later played a major role in the Eisenhower administration. He wrote in 1948,

> I have been backstage in the global drama of today and talked with men and women who have flesh-and-blood parts. I didn't rely for my impressions on just the heads of states—the Stalins, the Blums, the Churchills or the Roosevelts; I also saw and talked with people in less exalted positions—with people in labor, agriculture, in the professions and with small shopkeepers. The flavor of the play is sampled better on those levels, and the acts to come are being written there."[58]

Supreme Court Justice William O. Douglas shared the same assumptions and wrote a number of travelogues in the early 1950s detailing his meetings with people in remote areas. In one such book, Douglas suggested that it would take almost a willful effort for the United States to "lose" such countries to Communism:

> [The peoples'] suspicion of Soviet communism is so great that a real program of social reform would rob the Communists for all time of any popular following. . . . [The Communists] won in China against a corrupt and reactionary government which had liquidated the liberal movement. Those are the conditions under which Soviet communism threatens to win countries in the Middle East and southeast Asia. It is clear that it can win political victories in this region only when it operates in a political vacuum.[59]

To eliminate this "political vacuum," as he called it, Douglas advocated a politicization of the entire aid program. He wrote in 1952:

> Take all the American money that you can collect and all the guns and all the atomic bombs and keep your program sterile of these ideas of freedom and

justice and opportunity—and the Red tide of Communism will roll on and on and on. And that's what it's doing today. You can't stop it by talking about democracy and peace. You have to talk about it in terms that are understandable at the village level. We can't do that unless we are prepared to go into the villages of Asia and the Middle East with a program of political action. If you can't go in that way, stay out. When you go in, go in whole-heartedly the American way. With a few dollars and a few great ideas, you can save the world from this horrible spectre of Soviet imperialism.[60]

When President Truman introduced Point Four, he did not couch technical assistance in such stark Cold War terms. Rather, his swipe at Communism was indirect, stating that "Democracy alone can supply the vitalizing force to stir the peoples of the world into triumphant action, not only against their human oppressors, but also against their ancient enemies— hunger, misery and despair."[61] Even so, observers embraced the political goals of the program. The American Academy of Political and Social Science devoted two issues of its *Annals* to Point Four in 1950. The foreword to the first issue noted:

> Much that gives significance to Point Four of the President's address stems from the possibility and even likelihood that the judicious carrying out of a program for the widespread relief of human misery and the building up of underdeveloped areas elsewhere in the world will prove to be a real barrier to the insidious spread of totalitarian influences, and a source of strength—both moral and material—to the nations concerned with the worth of the human individual.[62]

It is worth recalling that this apocalyptic Cold War language preceded the outbreak of the Korean War by several months.

Several trends in American political thought suffused Americans' development work overseas in the years following World War II. The first was a sort of Jeffersonian idealism about the role of the yeoman farmer in American history. The assistant secretary of state for economic affairs told an international conference on land reform in 1951, "We in the United States have been firm believers in the farmer-owned family-size farm. We consider it one of the bulwarks of a healthy agriculture and a vigorous democracy."[63] The latter goal was as important as the former, although it would be rather difficult in the American mind to separate the two. Property's connection to citizenship and the state was not only that land ownership implied a certain respectability in the community, but also that ownership promoted vigilance against an overreaching arm of state power. Applied to developing societies in which the state apparatus lay heavy on an impoverished peasantry, broader distribution of land ownership would compel the state to pursue the interests of the mass of its subjects rather than those of the landed classes only.

The larger implication of land reform was that it could calm countrysides thought ripe for agitation by Communist propagandists. Drawing on the example of land reform in Japan, an American official responsible for implementing the program there said:

> The Communists of Japan tried hard to exploit the agrarian difficulties of the country and to use them as a base from which they would infiltrate the entire Japanese economy. However, in opposing the program on the ground that it was just another capitalistic device to enslave the farmers, they lost all popular support in the rural districts. By strengthening the principle of private property where it was weakest, i.e., at the base of the social pyramid, the reform has created a huge class of staunch opponents of the Communist ideology. . . . By multiplying the number of independent land-owning peasants, there came into being a middle-of-the-road, stable, rural society and a barrier against political extremism.[64]

The idea that land reform could "inoculate" potentially restive peasant societies against Communism recurred in discussions of the era and was certainly on the minds of those forming American policy toward Egypt.

Broader patterns of land ownership were not to be the end of the story, however. The Egyptian-American Rural Improvement Service (described in chapter 4, below) and a broad variety of other American-sponsored agricultural programs around the world had at their cores a goal of "community development." That is to say, they sought to create conditions which nurtured the growth of grass-roots self-help organizations among peasants.[65] These organizations had three main purposes: to enlist the efforts of peasants in improving their environments, to instill in such people a belief in democratic processes, and to begin to bridge the chasm between rich and poor that was characteristic of developing societies. In the long term, its advocates hoped, community development would economically invigorate peasant communities and lay the foundation for broad-based democracies throughout the formerly colonial world.[66]

The roots of community development as an idea in the United States are somewhat difficult to discern.[67] The concept seems, at least in part, to have drawn on the American experience of a broad variety of voluntary associations undertaking purposeful change in local communities. Out of the models of settlement houses, school centers, institutional churches and local charity organizations grew an idea that organizations—aided by professional social workers—could vest poor or "maladapted" individuals with the tools to improve their lives and the lives of their families. Going beyond simple "relief," social workers sought to educate and empower individuals to make positive change in their own lives. As an author of the period stated: "[The] social work method recognizes that the individual has the right and responsibility to determine his own course of action and to accept its consequences. To satisfy his own needs and interests he participates through voluntarily formed groups in activities directed toward social goals."[68] The attraction of the "social work method" to those working in overseas development projects in the 1950s was considerable. Villages were breeding grounds of disease far more vicious than those plaguing the tenements and slums of turn-of-the-century urban America. Filth and garbage in the streets, wholly unsanitary conditions within peasant homes, inadequate diets, contaminated water supplies, and swarms of parasitic insects created an environment in which disease was rampant, infant mortality extraordinarily high, and life expectancy decades less than in the industrialized West. Yet, even if filth and disease were eliminated, development workers believed that the lethargic and often obsequious behavior believed to be characteristic of peasants would still persist. The peasants would maintain a mindset that was antithetical to self-improvement, let alone entrepreneurial activities. Illiterate, uneducated and largely unskilled, peasants around the world had adapted to a life of few opportunities and grinding poverty. Because peasants lived so precariously on the margin of subsistence, they avoided risk-taking out of fear that any negative outcome would be catastrophic.

Development workers believed that social work, however, held out the opportunity for meaningful change. Agricultural extension, medical care, and education and literacy programs could radically change the life possibilities of peasants. Combined with efforts to transform villagers into political actors, the effect could be dramatic. The once-lethargic peasant, with proper guidance, could be transformed into an entrepreneurial being, striving for the improvement of his family and his community. Legions of the rural poor could be enlisted not as corvairs laboring for the interests of the state but as members of a community helping their neighbors. In an editorial about the vast Tennessee Valley Authority in 1943, Alabama's *Duluth Daily* opined:

> We can write of great dams . . . of the building of home-grown industry and of electricity at last coming to the farms of thousands of farm people in the Valley. Yet the significant advance has been in the thinking of a people. They are no longer afraid. They have caught the vision of their own powers. They can stand now and talk out in meeting and say that if industry doesn't come into the Valley from other sections, then we'll build our own industry.[69]

Carl Taylor, a leading U.S. government expert on community development, wrote in the early 1950s,

> It is my repeated observation . . . that people living in these extremely cultur-
> ally isolated rural communities are either not aware of some of their basic
> needs, or if aware of them often live in the belief that fate has destined them
> to continue to live with unsatisfied needs. When, however, these people are
> helped to meet and systematically discuss their common needs and offered
> technical assistance in meeting their needs something approaching miracles
> begins to take place. They build roads and schools, clear their streets of ani-
> mal manure, build latrines, make compost piles, etc. etc.[70]

The benefits of such efforts for the state were twofold: First, given the huge
rural population of many developing countries, directing the labor power of
the peasants would result in vast amounts of labor being unleashed. Second,
much of that labor would be free, because peasants would be working for
their own benefit.

The political effects of such efforts, U.S. officials thought, would be no
less dramatic. In most developing countries, the state was respected and
feared in the countryside but did little to improve the lot of the peasantry.
Tax collection and conscription were its most evident functions, and neither
won it much allegiance or affection.[71] Community development would for-
ever change that equation, banding peasants together to press for services
and representation. The roots of government would be thrust into the rural
communities themselves, and ideas and funds would flow back and forth;
under the extant system, ideas always flowed down while funds always
flowed up. The change would be revolutionary, and it would be global. At a
1954 conference in Tehran, Carl Taylor quoted with pleasure the comment
of a Pakistani Minister of Health: "We must shift gears. We have tried to
build Pakistan from Karachi. . . . Now we must begin to build Pakistan from
the villages."[72] In addition, community development would create a network of "local leaders by the thousands [who are] essential not only to the
effective and efficient operation of local governments but for the management of Cooperatives, the operation of local schools and the promotion of
every other type of local undertaking and programme."[73] Such leaders
would serve two purposes: They would be powerful catalysts for change in
their own communities, and they would help shape local institutions to be
more responsive to local conditions.

The creation of a rural leadership would help bridge the gap between
urban elites and the rural peasantry. Sharply divided by custom and outlook,
and often by language, the "gap between the two strata is wide, and the
means of communication are meagre."[74] To some extent, the separation was
necessary to maintain the extant political structure. Lucian Pye, an MIT political scientist who had a prominent voice in development theory, wrote in
1957: "These leaders in one sense must be 'out of touch' with the masses

since they are the prime source of political change in these societies. If they were to submerge their differences and accept the outlooks of the village people, something they could not possibly do, then much of the political drive for change would be eliminated from these societies."[75] At the same time, however, the split between the cities and countrysides was severely anti-democratic. Westernized elites—many of whom had gained education and experience under colonial rule—controlled the governmental apparatuses. While they might take action to improve peasant life, in such cases they did so paternalistically rather than empathetically. Neither anxious to share power with untutored peasants nor truly understanding of the social structures extant in the countryside, the division was, in the 1950s, likely to grow wider with the passage of time. Such a trend would retard democratization, undermine political stability, and preclude the sort of peasant mobilization envisioned under the rubric of community development. Consequently, community development programs consistently sought not only to develop rural leadership, but also to prepare cosmopolitan physicians, educators, engineers, and other professionals to work in the countryside in partnership with the peasantry.

As suggested previously, the international context in which these programs were devised was formative. U.S. government officials not only perceived a need to relieve rural poverty so as to make peasants less receptive to Communist dogma. They also felt a competition was under way "between the Communist and non-Communist worlds to demonstrate which political system is most likely to produce rapid economic and social progress."[76] State Department official Norman Mieklejohn stated baldly,

> Ideological considerations, distinguishing between Communism and Democracy, will not be the governing factors. The choice for the masses will be made largely in materialistic terms. If the issue is to be drawn on materialistic lines, so our activities must be along those lines. . . . Any program we undertake must be designed to have a quick tangible impact on the masses of the people in terms of their elementary requirements—namely, food, clothing, and shelter—adding up to an improved standard of living, greater security, and concomitant reluctance to accept revolutionary change.[77]

U.S. ambassador Loy Henderson made a direct connection between community development and national security in a speech to regional U.S. diplomatic personnel attending a community development conference his embassy in Iran hosted in 1954:

> If you work in such a manner as to create a desire among all elements of the village, including religious leaders, landlords, and peasants, to serve their

community, every structure which you help them to build and every institution which you assist them to create will serve as real demonstration projects and will be reproduced many fold by their own efforts and ingenuity; the position of the free world will be infinitely strengthened; free institutions will be made more secure, and the ideas and ideals of freedom and the dignity of the individual will be preserved.[78]

In such an environment, then, it was important not only to promote long-term change, but also to have something to show for one's efforts rather quickly.

Establishing an Aid Program

When it came time to implement Point Four, the U.S. government had been caught flat-footed. As was mentioned earlier, Point Four had not risen out of the bureaucracy but had been imposed upon it from above. The spring of 1949, therefore, was a time of hurried decision making and bureaucratic infighting as agencies designed plans to implement the presidential initiative. It was not until late June that President Truman submitted legislation to Congress implementing the Point Four program. In the accompanying statement, Truman more explicitly explained Point Four as an antidote to Communism than he had in his Inaugural Address. Recognizing that modernization had aroused expectations in the poorer nations, Truman said, "If [the poor] are frustrated and disappointed, they may turn to false doctrines which hold that the way of progress lies through tyranny. For the United States the great awakening of these peoples holds tremendous promise. It is not only a promise that new and stronger nations will be associated with us in the cause of human freedom, it is also a promise of new economic strength and growth for ourselves."[79]

The administration's first bill, the International Technical Cooperation Act, arrived on Capitol Hill some nine months after President Truman's speech.[80] Short on specifics (and criticized by conservatives for being so), the bill sought broad authorization for governmental activities to "promote the development of economically underdeveloped areas of the world.[81] The act provided for, but did not require, the appointment of a coordinator of technical cooperation, to be nominated by the president and confirmed by the Senate, as well as the establishment of an "Institute of International Technical Cooperation" within the Department of State.[82]

While the proposal to engage in technical cooperation enjoyed broad bipartisan support, the bill itself did not. In particular, Rep. John Vorys (R-Ohio) continually attacked administration witnesses in Foreign Affairs Committee hearings for merely restating the status quo. He challenged Undersecretary of State James E. Webb, saying:

Frankly, looking this over, it looks to me as though all you want to do is to get another $16,000 man up there in the State Department to coordinate and cooperate with the set-up that is already created for this specific purpose. . . . Your presentation points out a lot of swell things the United States and its people and its Government could do, but for the life of me I cannot see where you have made any case at all for new legislation.[83]

Business groups were also wary of the administration's bill, which made little mention of the role of private capital in the development of poorer countries. The National Foreign Trade Council objected to the legislation on these grounds, as did the U.S. Chamber of Commerce. In a report on Point Four that was entered into the hearing record, the Chamber wrote, "American private enterprise must form the cornerstone of the program for economic advancement in the underdeveloped areas of the world. . . . The profit motive, the mainspring of the free enterprise system, should assure desirable incentives and results which experience has demonstrated are unlikely under Government loans or grants."[84]

Overseas aid to poor countries was never able to marshal the popular support necessary to ensure its well being. Its warmest support came from somewhat "soft" lobbying groups—the League of Women Voters, Friends Committee on National Legislation, and the Women's International League for Peace and Freedom. These organizations, which supported foreign aid for its humanitarian impact, sponsored letter-writing drives and lobbied their representatives. They formed an umbrella organization called the Point Four Information Service to coordinate their efforts.[85] Business lobbyists never embraced the images built up around Point Four that the citizen groups did. The more influential lobbies—organized labor, the National Association of Manufacturers, the American Farm Bureau Federation, and others—had discrete and self-interested concerns. Particularly, they hoped to find new markets for American goods overseas while restraining the import of cheap goods. Businessmen also sought federal guarantees against the loss of investments in more volatile overseas environments, although Congress proved resistant to indemnifying private industry.[86] Despite public enthusiasm in some quarters, Capitol Hill continued to view foreign aid skeptically in the late 1940s, and Congress reduced presidential foreign aid requests every year, in some cases despite intensive lobbying by the White House.[87] The image of American county agents spreading throughout India and lending American know-how to villagers—like the hero of *The Ugly American*—never truly caught the imagination of corporate America, although it enjoyed considerable support among church groups and liberal-thinking activists.

Business found a more sympathetic approach in the bill put forth by Representative Christian Herter (R-Mass.), the Foreign Economic Development

Act of 1949.[88] Herter's bill was more explicit than the Truman Administration's, both in terms of diagnosing the problem and prescribing a solution. Whereas the administration bill had talked in general terms of the "promotion of international understanding and good will," the Herter bill set as its goals "creating new sources of wealth [in poor countries], increasing their purchasing power, and strengthening them in their struggle against communism and other forms of statism."[89] Herter's bill featured a number of organizational innovations. One was that it established a 12-member advisory board to oversee the operations of the technical assistance organization (in his case to be named the Foreign Economic Development Administration—FEDA—that would operate in the Department of State). Another was the bill's call to establish joint commissions in each country that FEDA would operate, composed of equal numbers of Americans and foreign nationals. The commissions would survey the local needs, and then propose projects to both the U.S. government and the host country government.

Herter's bill also called for the extension of legal protections to American businessmen doing business overseas, shielding them from uncompensated expropriation of property and ensuring the convertability of currency. While Truman mentioned that such protections were under negotiation in his message to Congress on technical assistance programs, no mention of these protections was included in the legislative language in the White House bill.

While the House did not pass Herter's bill, Foreign Affairs Committee Chairman John Kee (D-West Va.), introduced a significantly amended bill on January 17, 1950 that incorporated many of Herter's innovations. For example, the new bill, the International Economic Development Act of 1950, called for the establishment of a 12-member advisory board.[90] The new bill was lukewarm on the joint commission concept, and merely authorized the establishment of joint commissions if the foreign nation wished one, whereas Herter's original bill had required it. Finally, the new bill included a section on the importance of investor confidence, although the language was significantly weaker than Herter had it. Herter called for the guarantee of certain investor rights by treaty, whereas the new bill incorporated those guarantees in a "finding" that mutual confidence between investors and the host country contributes to development and progress.

This new bill became the Act for International Development in June 1950, with one significant change.[91] While all of the previous administration bills had included language *requiring* that "the participation of the United Nations, the Organization of American States, and their related organizations shall be sought whenever practicable,"[92] the enacted law merely *permitted* the president to contribute limited amounts of money to those programs if their goals were consistent with the purposes of the act. This change was the beginning of a long effort to minimize the role of international organizations in the American development effort overseas.

Changing Organizations

Under the terms of the new law, a new organization arose within the Department of State called the Technical Cooperation Administration (TCA). The new organization was charged with implementing the development policy in poor countries not served by the Economic Cooperation Administration (ECA), which operated in Europe and East Asia. In many cases, the TCA and the ECA engaged in similar projects. However, the two programs were administratively separate, and ECA operated under an explicit aegis of security concerns, which TCA did not.[93] Further, the TCA's budget was just under $35 million in FY 1951, while the ECA's budget was $2.76 billion.[94]

In the midst of the Korean War, President Truman's budget message of 1951 explicitly linked economic and security assistance. He wrote, "A program of economic aid to Europe must with few exceptions be directed to support the European [defense] buildup rather than general economic expansion," and the goal of economic aid shifted more and more to enabling countries to afford the heavy armaments that the new security situation seemed to require. The economic aid previously administered by the ECA was transferred to the newly created Mutual Security Agency (MSA) under the terms of the Mutual Security Act of 1951, thereby allowing for increased coordination of economic and military aid. Economic aid was retitled "defense support." TCA remained autonomous from the larger aid apparatus, at least for the time being.[95]

More than one analysis of technical assistance programs from the early 1950s saw the infiltration of security concerns into technical assistance as an ominous development. "The chief danger to the long-term *economic* effectiveness of U.S. Point Four policy would appear to lie in the possibility that, because of pressures from Congress, it may insidiously be submerged in a program centered on military production and strategic materials requirements," one author suggested. The chief culprit in this creeping militarism was the fact that under the terms of the Mutual Security Act of 1951, the president must find that proposed aid would "strengthen the security of the United States" regardless of whether the program was military in nature. The author suggested that this requirement revealed "how the mood of Congress and the country concerning the objectives of foreign spending [had] changed since the 'bold new program' proposal of 1949."[96]

In terms of size, the ECA and MSA programs were vastly larger than those administered by TCA (which were sold to Congress as inexpensive yet highly effective). In Fiscal Year 1952, the newly created MSA programs, which combined military and economic aid, totaled $7.48 billion in spending authority worldwide, while TCA remained small at $85 million. Significantly, too, the security-conscious ECA and MSA programs were of strictly limited duration. The initial termination date for recovery aid was 1952, and although that date was pushed back in 1951 and 1955, Congress continued to insist on maintaining a grip on the program through annual appropriations. Because appropriations bills rarely passed before July, which was also the beginning of the new fiscal year, uncertainty over appropriations levels and possible restrictions in authorization language kept many programs off-balance during the annual funding cycle.[97]

Although Point Four was a Truman administration program, General Eisenhower proclaimed his support for technical assistance during the 1952 presidential campaign, when he told a newspaper forum, "We should intensify the extension of technical assistance to underdeveloped nations."[98] Eisenhower reiterated his support for economic development programs for poor countries after his election. In his foreign aid request for Fiscal Year 1954, he noted, "To guard against the external military threat is not enough; we must also move against those conditions exploited by subversive forces within."[99] The environment in which Eisenhower voiced his support, however, differed from the one in which Truman introduced the program. McCarthyism, the animus against what were perceived to be pallid State Department responses to the Communist threat and the ongoing war in Korea, led to calls for a proactive American policy to battle Communism. In comparison, Point Four's somewhat holistic, evolutionary approaches to help build stability in post-colonial countries seemed both too passive and too diffuse. While the long-term goals of Point Four may have sufficed in more peaceful times, the immediate threat of Communist activity all over the world seemed to require a more focused, results-based approach than technical assistance could offer.

Just as significantly, the technical assistance program had its share of growing pains. Program administrators had persistent difficulties staffing overseas projects,[100] and unexpended balances ran high, prompting congressional critics to wonder aloud why any new appropriations were necessary. In addition, representatives and senators criticized what they perceived to be the meager contributions of host governments compared with the U.S. contribution.

Finally, technical assistance was drawn into the circle of criticism surrounding U.S. foreign aid in general. Multi-billion dollar programs for overseas assistance drew fire from fiscal conservatives bent on reducing the federal budget and lowering taxes, and from isolationists seeking to curtail overseas entanglements in whatever form.[101] The Randall Commission, whose study of America's foreign economic policy was commissioned by

Congress in August 1953, sought to balance internationalism with fiscal conservatism.[102] Its conclusions were not far from those Congress reached on its own, although they were slightly more tight-fisted. Thus the commission counseled an end to grants of overseas aid and resistance to the impulse to augment technical assistance programs with capital assistance. "It need not and should not become a 'big money' program, and should not involve capital investments," the commission stated, despite the fact that new American private investment overseas—particularly in poor areas—was rare indeed, and virtually non-existent when one excludes petroleum company investments in the Middle East.[103] The recommendation to press forward vigorously with technical cooperation "within the limits imposed by congressional appropriations, the need for selecting only sound projects, the availability of trained technicians, and good administration" read as the sort of overqualified, tepid endorsement that it was.[104]

In an environment of congressional ambivalence over foreign aid and in a bid to increase government efficiency, the Eisenhower administration created, on August 1, 1953, the Foreign Operations Administration (FOA). It was a new bureaucracy that would consolidate all of the foreign aid functions of the U.S. government. Led by unsuccessful presidential contender Harold Stassen, the cabinet-level agency erased the line that had existed between big-money security and economic assistance programs and the small-money projects that characterized the TCA approach. It also took technical assistance programs out of the Department of State, which had supervised the TCA since its inception. Consequently, aid missions overseas (now known as U.S. Operations Missions) no longer reported to the Department of State, but to an entirely separate organization. More important, small, technically oriented economic aid programs were considered alongside larger, more politically urgent programs, and thus began to pale in comparison.

During the summer of 1955, the worldwide American aid program once again changed. Congress abolished the Foreign Operations Administration and created the International Cooperation Administration within the Department of State to take on the development tasks with which FOA (and its predecessor, TCA) had been engaged. The move was widely perceived to be a demotion for those involved in overseas aid: FOA chief Stassen had held cabinet status and sat on the National Security Council, and the head of ICA would be under the direction of Secretary of State Dulles. Adding to the concern of aid boosters, the man President Eisenhower nominated to lead the ICA, John Hollister, had no previous experience in the field. A long-time friend of Ohio Senator Robert Taft, Hollister had served in Congress in the 1930s where he was, in the words of the *New York Times,* "staunchly Republican, bitterly anti New Deal." Hollister professed no concrete views on foreign aid at the time of his appointment, although he did deny that he thought it should be abolished. The *Times* suggested he gained the appointment in "a bid for support of the right wing of the Republican Party."[105] While Hollister did not represent the end of the ICA, he would not lead the organization to prominence either.

Hollister's appointment to head the ICA captured how much American thinking about aid changed in the early 1950s. No longer the province of do-gooders and agricultural extension agents sent overseas, foreign aid had become part and parcel of the foreign policy establishment. The change held out both a promise and a threat. On the one hand, the amount of money available for foreign assistance increased; on the other hand, aid programs were closely tied and often subordinated to larger U.S. foreign policy objectives.

The increase in U.S. resources for foreign assistance coincided with a shift in economic thinking about development. Economists began to frame the underdevelopment debate in the mid-1950s not so much in terms of the pervasiveness of poverty as the absence of capital. The United States, as the wealthiest country in the world, thus had the tools to lift many countries out of poverty.

The early 1950s, then, was a time of flux for American foreign assistance. While governmental assistance to foreign countries was relatively new, Americans' involvement in the world was not. The Egyptian-American aid relationship began at a time when the terms of American aid in general were still evolving, and that placed its own strains on the larger relationship. Certainly, Egyptians and Americans expected that results would be quicker and easier to achieve than they proved to be. Neither side quite anticipated, either, how much external factors would intervene. The story of how those early hopes were dashed is the subject of the next few chapters.

Chapter 3 ~

Chicken Aid

In the years immediately following the July 23, 1952, coup in Egypt, the new government took actions that sought to have broad effects on the economy. The economic strategies pursued by the regime were by and large capitalist ones, and most observers have pointed to the broad continuities between the economic strategies of the pre- and post-revolutionary governments.[1] Such capitalist solutions were short-lived, however, and some scholars suggest that the public sector economies of the 1960s in Egypt were somehow implicit in and foreshadowed by the early economic policies of the revolutionary government. In this formulation, it was simply a matter of time before the military officers who assumed power in 1952 extended their control to the economy.[2]

Such analyses miss the energy with which the new government pursued capitalist solutions to Egypt's economic problems in the early years of the revolution. Egypt's leaders talked often about the need to "increase production" and pursued a wide variety of programs to do so. They did so despite an ambivalence toward capitalism, which was associated in their minds with the corrupt and rapacious reactionary forces that their coup had removed from power. Egypt's leaders resolved their ambivalence by establishing a technocratic structure to guide development. Through such a structure, capital could be enlisted for the common good while it remained at arm's length from political power. Most of the initial programs were modest in scope and covered disparate areas of the economy, as many economists of the time prescribed.

The following chapter investigates the framework under which economic development was sought in the years following the revolution. It concentrates particularly on the national planning body, the Permanent Council for the Development of National Production, and a representative joint U.S.-Egyptian activity, the Poultry Improvement Project. The failure of these kinds of activities to boost domestic investment and produce dramatic gains in a short period of time drove Egyptian officials to pursue a more vigorously state-led development strategy beginning in the mid-1950s.

Previous Efforts at Economic Development

The Egyptian economy had experienced significant growth in the nineteenth century, primarily as a consequence of improvements in irrigation and agricultural techniques. According to one historian of the period, "between 1821 and 1872–78, the volume of agricultural output rose twelve times and per capita agricultural production increased six-fold."[3] By World War I, however, economic growth had slowed. Further, the economic boom had left foreigners holding much of the economic power in the country. The banking sector was entirely foreign, and concentrated its activities in short-term agricultural loans and trade financing rather than developing the industrial capacities of the country. Tala'at Harb's founding of Bank Misr in 1920 (and its subsidiary businesses beginning in 1927) went some way toward steering capital toward domestic industrialization, but the onset of the Great Depression in 1930 dried up much of the world market for Egyptian cotton and with it some of the capital to fuel Egyptian development. Nevertheless, new Egyptian industries like sugar refining and textile production benefited from protective tariffs in the 1930s and were able to establish themselves somewhat.

Egyptian interest in industrialization did not penetrate all segments of society in the 1930s. A career in industry appealed to only a small minority of graduates of the Egyptian Higher School of Commerce between 1914 and 1936; fully two-thirds of those graduates whose activities were known in 1937 entered the safe preserve of government service.[4] Barriers to a successful career in large-scale industry were relatively high, since the foreign-dominated financial markets and the nature of the business community necessitated a degree of foreign-language proficiency and cultural skills that were beyond the reach of many Egyptians. As a consequence of this, a relatively small number of Egyptians became active in a wide variety of industrial activities. As these nascent industrialists gained influence on the domestic stage, they engaged in rent-seeking activities with foreign capitalist interests.

Rising nationalism on the domestic political stage heightened interest in "Egyptianization" of Egyptian industry in the 1940s. Legislation passed in 1947

> required that at least 40 percent of the board members of companies be Egyptian, 51 percent of the stock of new companies be held by nationals, 75 percent of white collar employees be Egyptian and receive 65 percent of the

salaries, and 90 percent of the workers be Egyptian and receive 80 percent of the wages.[5]

The beneficiaries of these restrictions were disproportionately those Egyptians who were already in positions of power and influence. Rather than open leadership opportunities for new generations of Egyptian businessmen, Egyptian industries evolved in a direction in which individuals served on multiple boards of directors and had only a diffuse interest in the operations of any single company.

As Robert Vitalis has described it, the consequence was a system that was resistant to entrepreneurship and rewarded rent-seeking behavior. A relatively small group of Egyptians and Egyptian-born foreigners held "cross-sectoral holdings in textiles, shipping, transportation, chemicals, services, food processing, etc."[6] Egyptianization resulted in the concentration of economic power rather than the dispersal of it.

The Pragmatism of the New Regime

Most of those who have studied the military regime that seized control on July 23, 1952, have agreed that the officers came to power without a well-developed economic plan in mind.[7] The junta's relative lack of ideology—either political or economic—derived from its origins as a nationalist movement in the army. Since the early 1930s Egyptian society had been riven by increasingly partisan political activity, but the Free Officers as a group had little stake in the platforms of the various contenders for power. They were, instead, united by the idea that united many Egyptians, which was to gain true independence for their country. Many of the officers maintained ties to several parties concurrently in the years before the Revolution.[8] Because they were united primarily by their discontent with the status quo, the military officers who led Egypt's government in 1952 had no immediate constituency upon seizing power.

Without a well-defined constituency and driven by a military brand of can-do pragmatism, the Free Officers set as their broad goal the "purification" of Egyptian life. They stated their intention of remaining in power for only a short time, until the Egyptian political system could again run on its own. In pursuit of "cleaning up" Egyptian politics, officials of the new government sounded the themes of populism. They made an end run around the deeply intertwined industrial, agricultural and political elites and publicly identified themselves with the ranks of the dispossessed and disempowered.

Less than a year after the revolution, Abdel Nasser told a holiday crowd in Alexandria that, upon taking power:

> We found two classes: a class of people who were dispossessed, and a class who were advantaged. They inherited us from their fathers and grandfathers, and they calculated that we had to serve them, and that it was their right to enslave us. They exploited the complete wealth of the country for their own gain, and they exploited the goodness of this people.[9]

Abdel Nasser sounded a similar theme in a rally with supporters in a working class district in 1953:

> In the past, we saw how capital held sway over the regime of the country and drove those in power to pursue the path favored by those who controlled capital. Now, my brothers, the owners of capital can protect their rights, but under no circumstances can they control the government. . . . I assure you that there is no person now who can exploit rule in pursuit of private gain.[10]

The junta felt compelled to do more than merely level the playing field, however. Eager for results and with power in their hands, many of the Free Officers wanted to employ government power for the common economic good of Egyptian workers. Later in his speech to the same crowd, Abdel Nasser told them, "You are responsible for increasing production. I am responsible for founding the factories which will give you work."[11]

The Free Officers did not hold uniform attitudes toward capital,[12] nor were their attitudes always manifested in official ways. President Muhammad Naguib, it has been widely reported, was concerned with trying to maintain a friendly public face for the Free Officers movement. Several members of the RCC maintain that it was he who pushed hard for identifying the Free Officers' coup only as a "movement" and not as a "revolution" for fear of frightening capital. In addition, "When dealing with old-regime figures, even those he ordered jailed, [Naguib] outwardly accorded them the proper respect due public statesmen. This in contrast to the gruff treatment described by Sayyid Marei and others who approached the officers after the takeover."[13]

Differences aside, in the words of one Egyptian writer on the revolution, "We need to distinguish between the presence of 'complete theory' behind the revolution, and the presence of a 'concept.'"[14] While the former was absent the latter was not, and that concept was to employ governmental power not only in the service of capitalists, but also in the service of the larger population.

Land Reform

The most dramatic manifestation of the new regime's attitude toward capital was the land reform law promulgated six weeks after the Free Officers came to power. The idea to pursue land reform was not of the Free Officers' invention. Egyptian Senator Muhammad Khattab led a fight in parliament in 1946 to bar acquisition of new land by those already owning 200 feddans. Conservative landlords in Parliament and their allies overwhelmingly defeated his bill.[15] Outside Egypt, land reform programs had been implemented in countries as diverse as Italy, Japan, India, Iran and Taiwan in the years following World War II,[16] generally with the support of the United States government as a barrier to Communist activity among the peasantry. Agitation in Egypt for land reform grew out of the fact that Egyptian land holding patterns reinforced great disparities between the rich and the poor. Just under two million Egyptians held less than one feddan, amounting to 12.9 percent of the total owned acreage. Meanwhile, 282 Egyptians maintained holdings of more than 800 feddans, totaling 9.8 percent of the owned land in the entire country.[17] Those with large holdings led lives of luxury, while those with small holdings mostly eked out a bare subsistence. Redistributing land from the wealthy to the poor, its supporters claimed, would improve the lives of the poor at relatively little cost to the rich.

Those advocating land reform also reasoned that forcing landlords to sell their land might boost Egyptian industry. Much of Egyptian domestic capital in 1952 was devoted to land speculation, making agricultural land a "'bottomless sink' which absorbed and dissipated the savings of the community."[18] Land reform would free that capital for use in Egypt's industrial sector, which had heretofore been dominated by foreign investors. In addition, it was hoped that agrarian reform would raise rural incomes, thereby increasing the market for domestically manufactured goods. Land reform also held political benefits. Many of the largest landholders were either members of the royal family or had close connections to it. Limiting the size of land holdings would at one stroke deal a blow to the tiny aristocracy while taking visible action to promote the well being of the more numerous peasantry,[19] who would thus feel some degree of loyalty toward the new regime.

All of this drew much interest from the United States government, which, as has been mentioned in chapter 2, was committed on a global basis to the idea of land reform. In the weeks following the coup, the Technical Cooperation Administration (TCA) quickly dispatched land reform expert Paul Maris to Egypt. The U.S. aid mission reported excitedly that the Egyptian Minister of Finance met with Maris "for almost four hours . . . within a day of his arrival" in Cairo.[20] To the Americans' disappointment, however, the Egyptians had no intention of letting American fingerprints appear on the land reform plan. Americans lobbied hard behind closed doors for the inclusion of favored provisions,[21] and the U.S. Information Service "fed general land reform articles to the Egyptian press," but the result was "by and large an Egyptian product."[22]

The land reform decree handed down on September 9, 1952, stipulated that land holdings would be capped at 200 feddans per individual, or 300 feddans per family. Landowners would be compensated at a rate of ten times the annual rent for expropriated land, and for such purposes the rent would be limited to seven times the amount of land tax paid.[23] Land so obtained would be distributed in lots of two to five feddans to Egyptian farmers who themselves owned less than five feddans at the time of land reform. The farmers would receive a 30-year mortgage on their property at 3 percent interest, the principal being the price paid in compensation to the original landholders plus 15 percent. Landholders would be compensated with long-term bonds.[24]

Whether the provisions of land reform were punitive to large landlords or not is unclear. Some authors stress that the price paid for land was only 1/2 to 1/3 of its current market value,[25] while others emphasize that land prices were artificially high in 1952 and were likely to have dropped 30 to 40 percent in the period following the Korean War even without land reform.[26] What is more clear is that land reform became a symbol of the military's intention to make sweeping changes in political and economic relations in Egypt, and that it intended to do so by championing the cause of the weak and numerous against the powerful and few.

The Need for Capital

The regime's proclaimed goal of social justice in no way impeded its more orthodox plans to promote economic development in the country. To a large degree, the discussion in the months following the coup centered on the need to dedicate more capital to economic development. The monthly economic magazine of the Egyptian daily newspaper *al-Ahram,* appropriately titled *al-Ahram al-Iqtisadi* [The Economic al-Ahram], ran an article in November 1953 calling for banks to invest their excess reserves in economic development projects.[27] In December, it published a long interview with the Minister of Finance and Economy, Abdel Galil al-Emary, who described Egypt's chief problems as declines in the standard of living, the amount of arable land per person, and per capita production. His solutions were to increase production, resettle populations from overcrowded areas, and cut the birth rate, with the first being the most important. He estimated the capital requirements for the needed economic projects to be on the order of 500 million £E (almost $1.5 billion 1952 dollars), an astronomical sum far in excess of what could be raised domestically, and thus requiring some combination of foreign capital and foreign assistance in addition to domestic investment.[28]

Such a large sum indicated a need to court private capital, and while the leadership of the Egyptian government never criticized private capital directly, it didn't particularly encourage it, either. The problem with private capital wasn't capital per se, but rather its identification with the corruption, feudalism, and "reactionary forces" which the revolution hoped to purge. The most egregious cases of perceived corruption from the old regime were brought before a highly publicized "revolutionary tribunal" and a "treason court" in 1952–53. While the regime put significant energy into identifying such individuals for ridicule and punishment, exceedingly little thought appears to have been given to how some of the capital of Egypt's wealthy individuals might be steered toward productive investment.

Throughout their rule, the RCC appeared to be attempting to promote capitalism without capitalists. The wealthy were regarded ambivalently, for they were both tied to the old system of power yet somehow necessary for the new. In a speech to labor delegates in April 1954—immediately after labor had provided him crucial support in wresting the last vestiges of power from Prime Minister Naguib—Abdel Nasser walked a fine line between labor and capital:

> We want workers and owners of capital to progress together shoulder to shoulder. If we deemed all the requests of the workers worthy and neglected the companies, the result would be an increase in unemployed workers. No companies would be founded and your children would not have jobs. We cannot require the owners of companies to agree to all the demands in one fell swoop because this will lead to capital disappearing. The national interest requires that we encourage investment of the owners' capital, so that such companies spread throughout the country.
>
> You know that the government does not have enough money to give rise to that industrial revitalization, and thus we need to encourage all who wish to invest their money, so that the country benefits and the workers benefit from that.[29]

As a prominent Egyptian historian of the revolution wrote:

> [The revolution] made clear to the peasants its resolve to free them from the control of the large landholders, but [the revolution] also revealed its resolve to protect the economic livelihood of those owners without infringement. [The revolution] made clear its determination to reform the relations between labor and the capitalists, but it also made clear its dependence on those capitalists in order to change Egypt from a backward agricultural country into an advanced industrial country.[30]

Rather than resolve its ambivalence toward capitalists, the new regime attempted to enlist them but keep them at arms length through the implementation of a technocratic planning process. The Free Officers believed that the pre-revolutionary economic system had been unfairly biased in favor of the privileged. A zealous pursuit of economic rationalism and technocratic detail, however, would serve to both increase the fairness of the system as well as reinforce the impression of competence that the junta sought to inculcate among the Egyptian populace. The consequence would be a more efficient and less corrupt system that would lead to economic prosperity and a national renaissance.

In part impelled by such a calculus, in part by the American government's urgings, and in part by an admiration for Soviet economic growth in the years following the Russian Revolution, the Free Officers quickly established governmental bodies which would survey the economic landscape and recommend opportunities for investment and advancement.[31] Just weeks after the Free Officer's coup, the head of the Technical Cooperation Administration program in Egypt, Dr. John Nichols, prepared a memorandum for Prime Minister Ali Maher. In that memorandum, he identified seven principal economic and social problems in Egypt, the last of which was "the absence of a national planning body to assess Egypt's economic potentialities and in relation thereto to chart a development program and to make recommendations concerning the organization and operation of government agencies for the most efficient and effective execution of this program." He went on to add:

> It is suggested that the Prime Minister invite those individuals whom he deems appropriate to form an interim planning committee looking to the establishment of a full-blown National Planning Board mentioned above. This committee should be in a position to marshal and call upon all available resources—local, national and international—for the undertaking of programs which it finds will promote economic development. It would not execute programs but should review all pending projects leading to economic development and have powers of decision action [sic] suited to the emergency needs for getting such projects rapidly under way.[32]

The memorandum listed 19 new areas of possible cooperation between the U.S. government and the government of Egypt, ranging from installing latrines in rural villages to developing Egypt's tourism industry. The overall intent was to lead Egypt away from a cotton monoculture which led not only to sharp differences in income between land owners and farmers, but also made the performance of the Egyptian economy subject to the vicissitudes of the international cotton market.

The Formation of the PCDNP

In the fall of 1952, the government of Egypt established precisely the sort of planning body that the Americans hoped it would.[33] Named the Permanent

Council for the Development of National Production (PCDNP), it served as a sort of super-ministerial coordinating council which would evaluate and co-ordinate a broad variety of economic programs intended to boost the Egyptian economy. PCDNP members represented a variety of viewpoints. The eleven original members named to the panel included a former Minister of Finance, a former Minister of Education, two professors, three directors who served on multiple corporate boards, and three members of the High Committee for Land Reform.[34] In addition, the Ministers of Finance and Economy, Commerce and Industry, Public Works, and Supply, along with a military representative from the Department of Mobilization and a member of the RCC, joined the council as *ex-officio* members. According to one of the three full-time members of the PCDNP, the "conservative and traditionalist" wing of the council represented the majority of members, while a minority was "rather more radical and called for more direct state intervention."[35]

The charge given to the council was extraordinarily broad:

> To explore economic projects whose purpose is to develop national production in terms of agriculture, industry and commerce, and related projects of reclamation of marsh and desert land, to diversify agricultural production and improve crop yield and agricultural methods, to develop animal production and electric generating projects, to build roads and improve other modes of transportation, to search for petroleum and other mineral wealth, to encourage existing industries and found new ones, to strengthen import-substituting industries, to organize internal markets and search for external ones, to look to establish the necessary mechanisms to fund these projects, to attract foreign loans to supplement Egyptian and foreign capital, to explore a tax and tariff system which will lead to an upswing in production, and to suggest what is necessary legislatively to attain these goals.[36]

Under the terms of the law that created the PCDNP, the council was to create a three-year integrated program of operations and give special priority to projects which involved the production of wheat, oil, sugar, animal products and fertilizers.[37]

It is unclear for whom exactly the PCDNP was created. One might look at its membership and determine that it represented some of the best civilian advice the military could obtain to promote Egypt's economic development. The board's membership might also suggest an effort to co-opt Egypt's economic elite to the new regime, or at least demonstrate the regime's lack of hostility to capital after the dramatic and sweeping program of land reform. In addition, the creation of an extra-ministerial body reporting to the cabinet extricated economic planning from the rivalries of competing ministries involved in economic development projects. Finally, it may have been created in part to please the Americans. Most likely the PCDNP was created in an effort to meet several or all of these goals.

The PCDNP set about its mandate with earnestness, but its tasks were immense. It divided itself into five committees: agriculture, industrialization, roads and transportation, finance, and minerals and petroleum.[38] With an initial full-time staff consisting only of the chairman, an economist, and an engineer, the council engaged in a flurry of studies covering its broad mandate.

Two question marks hung over the council throughout its deliberations. The first was the extent to which the council's activities would be connected to foreigners and foreign institutions in Egypt. Calls for the "Egyptianization" of economic activity had been endemic in Egypt for almost a century, and for many the presence of foreign advisers and foreign capital were simply another way of continuing the foreign domination of Egypt which the Free Officer's coup set out to eradicate. On the other hand, complete self-reliance would force Egyptians to "reinvent the wheel" time and time again, and to do so with relatively limited resources. Such self-reliance could delay Egypt's economic growth indefinitely, especially since booming population growth after World War II exerted strong downward pressure on per capita incomes. *Al-Ahram al-Iqtisadi's* lead article in its September 1952 issue stated, "It is clear that cooperation between foreign and Egyptian capital is among the desired means to provide for our economic renaissance."[39] In an interview a month after he assumed his position at the head of the council, Hussein Fahmy told the weekly magazine *Akher Sa'a*, "We need foreigners. There are two billion people in the world. Can we have distaste for two billion people? We are twenty million, one percent of the world's population, and it is in our interest to live with the other 99 percent and like them and cooperate with them."[40]

In repeated public statements and interviews throughout 1953, Fahmy and others involved in Egyptian economic planning emphasized the need to attract capital from abroad in order to push forward with domestic economic programs. The amount of money they were discussing for productive investment—500 million £E—simply was not available on domestic capital markets. Rather than call outright for large infusions of foreign capital, however, Fahmy and others tried to allay fears of foreign loans. For example, in response to a question as to whether it was possible for Egypt to rely on its own resources for development, Fahmy was cagey, telling *Rose al-Yusef,* "We want to make use of all money and means from a variety of sources, but of course we will not resort to distant things if those which are close are sufficient."[41] Fahmy tried to raise a homey example with another interviewer, telling him that people constantly borrow a few piasters from each other in their daily lives without losing their sovereignty, and asking why it was any different with foreign capital.[42]

Fahmy, however, was something of a minority among the leaders of the new government. As a member of the old elite, he had traveled widely, was comfortable speaking French in addition to Arabic, and felt at home among the international businessmen and foreign officials with whom he had been interacting for decades. Such surroundings made the young army officers in charge of the government feel uneasy, and they periodically lashed out against any international involvement in Egypt's economic development.[43] The persistence of debate over the advisability of foreign investment in the years following the revolution suggests that the efforts of Fahmy and others were never wholly successful.

The second outstanding issue was how the activities the PCDNP supported might be financed. At least five sources were available: taxation, confiscated land, foreign aid, private capital, and government capital. While the government did raise income and inheritance taxes as part of a general program of reform, tax receipts in the early 1950s were generally declining due to worsening economic conditions.[44] Assets confiscated from the former royal family represented a significant sum—in the tens of millions of pounds—but were non-renewable and committed by the regime to the social activities of the Permanent Council for Public Welfare Services. Some Egyptians hoped foreign aid would represent a significant sum, especially after the Truman Doctrine and the Marshall Plan had resulted in windfalls for countries in the Mediterranean basin.[45] Such aid too often proved elusive, however, as it became tied first to an Anglo-Egyptian agreement on the Suez Canal Base and later to Arab-Israeli peace (see chapter 5). Private capital (domestic and foreign) was welcome in Egypt during this period, even if the reception given to capitalists was cool. In point of fact, as is discussed below, private capital did not enter the markets in significant amounts.

As a consequence, the results-driven implementers of Egypt's economic policy turned toward government financing. In its published documents and public utterances, the PCDNP emphasized the fact that the budget it controlled was specifically targeted for projects which would boost GNP. Although its budget of 20–30 million £E/year[46] was relatively small in relation to the overall capital needs of the country, it represented "the first time in Egyptian history that an independent budget for projects to boost production was established alongside the general budget."[47] The practical importance of establishing a separate budget to boost GNP was to legitimize financing that budget via loans rather than government receipts. The Egyptian government was strapped for cash after the revolution, since the previous government had run a deficit of 38 million £E in 1951/52 and lost approximately 30 million £E in addition through its cotton-selling activities.[48] Although the government did not float a bond issue for development until it floated three for a total of 25 million £E in December 1954,[49] it was operating in somewhat precarious financial straits.

The projects put forth by the PCDNP were as broad as the council's mandate. The PCDNP's annual report of 1954 listed 19 projects in its agriculture section alone, ranging from hybrid corn projects to fisheries to irrigation. The council also put forth 15 industrial projects, as well as projects involving mining, electrification and improvements in transportation and communications.[50] In some but not all cases, these projects already had at least partial sponsorship from foreign governments. The U.S. government, for instance, was in a partnership with the Egyptian government in the Egyptian-American Rural Improvement Service, a large land reclamation and resettlement scheme (described in chapter 4). The Americans were also deeply involved in a desert grasslands project in the Western Desert, a hybrid corn project, and several animal husbandry projects.[51]

The PCDNP's efforts were in part coordinated with the U.S. government. In August 1952—months before the PCDNP was even founded—Egyptian Prime Minister Ali Maher wrote the U.S. Embassy requesting "the services of a team of economic and industrial experts . . . to assist in assessing Egyptian industrial potentialities and draw up a comprehensive plan in relation thereto for the further industrialization of the country."[52] The head of the U.S. Operations Mission in Egypt, John Nichols, considered the request one of the two most urgent projects TCA could undertake there, and he pleaded with Washington to approve funding for the study as soon as possible.[53]

Anxious to appoint an American businessman of some standing to lead the American mission to Egypt, TCA was able to attract Thomas D. Cabot, a scion of the Boston business family, as the titular head of the mission. Cabot, it was hoped, would both impress upon the Egyptians the seriousness of American intentions and possess enough standing in American markets to begin to attract the investment capital necessary to implement any suggestions that might arise.[54] The actual surveying was done by Arthur D. Little, a Cambridge-based engineering consulting firm which up to that point had little overseas experience. For the bulk of the work, the firm sent over two investigators who examined Egyptian conditions and establishments and then sent reports back to Cambridge. Analysts based in Massachusetts then made recommendations.[55] A. D. Little received $240,000 for their initial report, submitted on July 15, 1953, and $295,000 more for additional studies completed over the subsequent 18 months.

A. D. Little's final report contained 25 suggestions for economic projects in Egypt. Of these, eleven were explicitly intended to substitute domestically manufactured products for items that were currently imported, and six were intended to boost Egyptian exports. The balance generally involved improving the health and nutrition of Egyptians.[56] A. D. Little's report was less clear from whence capital to implement the projects might come, observing "There is at present a shortage of venture capital willing to assume the risks of new undertakings." Egypt now had to compete on international markets for investment capital, and Egypt had to "meet the competition, not only of other underdeveloped countries, but also of industrialized areas where investment opportunities as well as capital are plentiful, and where relative freedom prevails for the management of business and industry."[57] While the government of Egypt had indeed taken steps to encourage foreign investment—involving guarantees of remittability, exemption of investments from income taxes and regulations allowing greater foreign ownership of Egyptian companies—A. D. Little concluded that such steps were insufficient by themselves. They had to be accompanied by a further loosening of fiduciary requirements and a general improvement in the administrative climate in Egypt in order to attract the requisite foreign investment. The report estimated that Egypt's capital needs to double industrial employment over the following decade were approximately 220 million £E—less than half the Egyptian government's working assumption of 500 million £E—and that about 70 million £E should be from overseas.[58]

Poultry Improvement

A. D. Little's ongoing work in Egypt reinforced the Egyptian government's predilection for improving the economy by engaging in discrete development projects. Typical of this kind of project, and of the sort of Egyptian-American partnership that the American Point Four operation was seeking to promote, was a Poultry Improvement Project. In 1952, Egyptian hens produced an average of 75 to 100 eggs per year, weighing approximately 35 to 40 grams apiece. By comparison, American hens averaged 165 eggs per year of 55 to 60 grams a piece. Egyptian hens therefore produced only 41 percent of the eggs that American hens did every year, weighing only 26 percent of the total output of their American counterparts. Boosting egg production would raise incomes in rural areas while at the same time improve the diets of millions of Egyptian farmers.[59] In pursuit of this goal, TCA proposed a program to import 100,000 newly hatched American chicks to Egypt using cargo planes taking 25,000 to 35,000 in each trip. The chicks would be raised on Ministry of Agriculture farms for a month, and then traded with Egyptian farmers for their own stock of domestic-variety chickens. Each farmer would sign a contract to supply the ministry with three fertilized eggs for each chicken he took, and the ministry would hatch those eggs and distribute the resulting chicks more widely in the Egyptian countryside. By 1956 or 1957, the planners projected, there would be 12 million eggs of the new varieties nationwide, the "normal hatch number for the

Egyptian country during each spring."[60] The Poultry Improvement Project dovetailed with an extant program, the National Poultry Improvement Project, which sought concurrently to "establish health centers, develop superior seed stock, and modernize poultry husbandry practices as part of a nationwide improvement program."[61] In the winter of 1952–53, rural experts in the U.S. Operations Mission in Cairo set about translating American educational materials into Arabic for distribution to Egyptian peasants.

The two poultry improvement projects closely fit the objectives of Egyptian and American economic planners. On the Egyptian side, they were programs that promised to sharply boost rural welfare through "scientific" means. The results would be quick and dramatic and would have economic as well as nutritional benefits. The programs also would neither entail extensive foreign involvement nor ongoing management. Although American technicians would participate in transferring the chickens and establishing educational programs for farmers, most Egyptians would never come in contact with any of the foreign advisers, and thus nationalist sensitivities would not be inflamed. The program was originally financed through an agreement with the Egyptian Ministry of Agriculture, although in September 1954 the Ministry sought (and gained) 45,470 £E of funding from the PCDNP to continue the program.[62]

On the American side, the programs were quintessential Point Four projects. The United States government put up relatively little money—$150,000 for the first year and $100,000 thereafter—the programs were self-sustaining, and they involved the simple transfer of American knowhow. Americans had enjoyed substantial success with almost identical programs of agricultural extension in the U.S. in the early part of the century, and the program was understandable to both technicians and a broad American audience as a rather basic thing Americans could do to improve the world.[63]

The appeal of poultry improvement to a broad American audience was made clear by a large photographic essay appearing in *Life* magazine in March 1954, after the arrival of the fourth shipment of chicks. The accompanying text called the eggs "Easter presents" from American Sunday school students, who contributed a small part of the cost of transporting the eggs to Egypt. Throughout, the idea of simple American charity was stressed. The text stated that the "Moslem farmers in Egypt . . . will find more use for [the eggs] than the average U.S. child does," and a caption under a photograph of a group of children described how "Young philanthropists watch crates being loaded into an airplane at New York airport." The final photograph in the series depicts a young Egyptian in peasant dress giving a "welcoming kiss" to one of the new hatchlings.[64] The clear intention of the article (which, interestingly, appeared in the religion section of *Life*) was to demonstrate the Point Four idea that very small efforts by Americans could make all the difference in poor countries.

When the poultry improvement program got underway, it evidently captivated many of the Americans and Egyptians who were involved with it. One American wrote to a friend in Washington:

> This is small stuff, but it is fundamental and it is succeeding almost magically. In this village the first chicks were distributed—10 to each family. They went back today to give them five more (15 in all) and also to give 15 to each of several families who did not take them before or were new in the village. The umdah [mayor] and each of the 30-odd village men signed an agreement to dispose of *all* their old "belledi" chickens, making this a 100 percent improved-flock village. And you should see how they proudly show you their chickens and the progeny of the original birds. Nothing to do but you must go down the dirty little street, kicking dogs out of the way, into the dark little huts, perhaps up to the roof, to see the fine healthy birds. And they *are* healthy—good size, good feathers, fine yellow legs. . . .
>
> I've gone on at some length about this, because this is the most vital thing I've seen yet. It's a direct and immediate benefit to the individual peasant and his family which I don't believe can be matched by any other single thing we can do at low cost or a big scale. This is one of the things that keeps my spirits up in this otherwise discouraging place.[65]

The new chickens also enjoyed some prominence in the Egyptian press. The week of March 22, 1953 was proclaimed "Chicken Week" in Egypt. The College of Agriculture put on a chicken show that featured two Egyptians and an American Point Four representative as judges. Photos of the various chicken varieties covered the back page of *al-Ahram* on March 25, with the lead photograph showing the profile of a robust Rhode Island Red in mid-crow.[66]

The weekly photojournalism magazine *al-Musawwar* ran an article that week entitled "30,000 Chicks Arrive in Egypt . . . By Plane!" The article explained that 25,000 Rhode Island chickens were "a gift of Uncle Sam to Egypt, and an example of one of the Point Four projects." The article went on to describe the distribution program in some depth, and even suggested that President Muhammad Naguib himself intended to supervise personally the distribution of the first chicks in three weeks' time.[67]

A competitor to *al-Musawwar, Akher Sa'a,* followed a similar line, promising its readers "the complete story of Chicken Week." In contrast to the *al-Musawwar* article, the *Akher Sa'a* piece very much underplayed any relation between Chicken Week and Point Four. In fact, it made no mention of either Point Four or the American government until deep into the article, and then only in the context of talking about "foreign chickens" imported from abroad. As this magazine portrayed it, Chicken Week was a domestic response to a domestic problem, and the problem solving was being led by the Ministry of Agriculture rather than foreign bodies. In addition, the article bluntly raised two questions about the birds to be imported: whether exemplary foreign varieties would manifest their exemplary traits in the conditions prevalent in Egypt, and whether they would have the resistance that local strains had to endemic diseases.[68]

After the drama of Chicken Week faded, the Egyptians and Americans set about raising and distributing superior chicken varieties to Egyptian peasants. 135,000 chickens arrived in Egypt in 1953 and 1954. The chicks were among the best quality available in the United States, generally coming from flocks in upstate New York and Massachusetts with "exceptional egg-producing records" and with very low levels of disease.[69] After the chickens spent less than a month on government farms, the Egyptian government distributed them to selected villages, as well as to large farms and to societies and associations interested in poultry breeding. The largest distribution center for the new poultry was in Bahtim, an area just northeast of Cairo. More than 75,000 Rhode Island Red chicks were distributed there, reaching "every qualified farmer in the area."[70]

The arrival of the fourth batch of chickens in March 1954 was widely reported in the Egyptian media, and this time the source of the chickens was completely clear. *Al-Ahram* carried a photo of the chicks' arrival at Cairo airport and appeared to write its story entirely from a USIS press release.[71] *Al-Musawwar* printed a full-page photo of fluffy hatchlings above the headline, "Point Four Chicks" and a short paragraph praising the program for its success.[72]

The distribution of American-variety chickens was not an unqualified success for American diplomacy, however. Some in Egypt disparaged the aid as insufficient for Egypt's needs. As Abdel Nasser described the project to an interviewer from *U.S. News and World Report* in September 1954, "Everyone jokes about it. They all laugh about American 'chicken aid.' The saying is that, after all the talk about American aid, all we got were a lot of chickens."[73] The U.S. Embassy's public affairs officer reported, apparently without irony, that the programs had received "considerable favorable coverage in the USIS-published Arabic weekly, *Al Sadaka.*" However, that "favorable publicity [for the U.S.-sponsored program] has been overshadowed by the wisecracks including cartoons about American chicken aid."[74]

Six months after distribution of the new chickens, fewer than half of the Rhode Island Reds and about a quarter of the Leghorns were still with the families to whom they had been given. The decline was due to "culling of the flocks, numerous sales, and losses due to disease and accident." The aid mission reported that "the Egyptian farmer . . . reports no difference in the mortality rate of his imported chicks." It proclaimed victory over those who "predicted that all the chickens would die" and announced that "skepticism about the imported chicks has almost entirely disappeared."[75]

Such optimism proved premature when, in the autumn of 1954, many of the imported chickens on Agriculture Ministry farms began manifesting a disease previously unknown in Egypt. Diagnosed later by an American veterinarian as coryza, an infection affecting the mucous membranes of the upper respiratory tract, the disease swept through American-variety flocks. The disease affected some chickens so severely that it caused pneumonia and permanent lung damage. The veterinarian judged that the American chickens experienced low-level coryza infections with few ill effects at home in America. Overseas, however, coryza became more dangerous because the chickens were at the same time trying to battle "common tropical diseases and parasites" in addition to coping with "a generally insanitary and crowded environment." The combination of all these things was a debilitating if not deadly combination for the chickens. The veterinarian recommended slaughtering birds on government farms with suspected clinical cases of coryza and dispatching agricultural extension workers to the villages to assess the health of the American strains there.[76]

While the susceptibility of the American chickens to disease did not end the Poultry Improvement Program in Egypt, it certainly slowed American involvement in that program. Because of the disease outbreak among the imported chicks, an order for $100,000 worth of additional chicks was cancelled. The Americans administering the program wrapped it up, wrote a final report, and left Egypt in 1955. After their departure, the Egyptian government continued its efforts both in education and in distribution of improved varieties. In the eight years after 1955, the government distributed more than 2.8 million chicks on a similar basis to the original cooperative program.[77]

The Investment Climate

The problems encountered by the Poultry Improvement Project were not unique, and perhaps not surprising in the context of the Egyptian government's interest in initiating a large number of discrete projects in a short period of time. Concurrent with those efforts, the government also sought to improve the investment climate for the broad variety of industrial projects the PCDNP was investigating. The first area in which the government pushed forward with change was in the underlying corporate laws in the first years of the revolution. Some of these changes were meant to encourage the entrance of foreign capital, and others were intended to open up company directorships to new candidates by establishing new rules for who could serve in such positions and how many they could occupy at one time.[78] Still more crafted medium-term tax exemptions for approved economic activities directed at increasing national production.[79] Such changes appear to have been joint efforts between the PCDNP finance committee and the Ministry of Commerce and Industry, the latter led by Egyptian government veteran Helmy Bahgat Bedawi.

The Egyptian government's second area of activity was the erection of high tariffs to discourage consumption of luxuries and protect domestic industries. Under decree laws published in February 1954, the tax on chocolates, biscuits and sweets was raised to 100 percent, and on cigars and liquor to 70 percent. Duties on goods for which "local production . . . is or will be sufficient for local consumption such as soap, matches, textiles" and margarine rose from 20 percent to 50 percent. Raw materials that would be used either for domestic processing or re-export were exempted from taxation.[80]

Such efforts reflect the tools that the government had at its disposal—laws and decrees—but they were unable to address some of the underlying concerns held by capitalists with money to invest. The President of the Board of the National Bank of Egypt reported in 1954 that the lack of general economic improvement was being hampered by "the twin fears of spasmodic intervention on the part of the State and a growing economic recession." He added, "Some circles are discouraged by the profusion of regulations and laws, the latter sometimes promulgated with retroactive effect, as well as by the spirit in which, at times, they are interpreted. . . . The restrictions and administrative annoyances to which the economy is still subjected tend to deprive it of that impetus which is so indispensable.[81]

Conditions for commerce had indeed improved in Egypt since the months following the revolution, when the desire for broadly popular measures sometimes got the better of government planners. In October 1952, for example, the U.S. Embassy's weekly economic report included the story of a Greek importer who was "jailed for selling Italian macaroni above the new ceiling of 7 piasters. The macaroni had cost him 11 piasters plus the unchanged duty of 8 piasters."[82] Still, a World Bank report observed in the summer of 1955 that the Egyptian government's "actions have not always been consistent or free of the uncertainty which sometimes deters private initiative."[83]

How much the American government could do about this was unclear, although it seems certain that had American investors been more prominent, the economic and political landscape would have been different. The new regime's hope for a significant role for American capital in Egypt's economic renaissance is perhaps best expressed by the fact that the cable address of the Commercial Counselor in the Egyptian Embassy in Washington was "TAKADUM," the Arabic word for "progress." Equally telling, *Rose al-Yusef* reported two months after Dr. Ahmed Hussein arrived in Washington as Egypt's Ambassador that several ministers had sent "urgent messages to the

Egyptian Embassy asking for the responses of the government and American companies on the Egyptian projects the Ambassador had carried with him."[84] The American government appears to have preferred a more laissez-faire approach to encouraging private investment in Egypt than the Egyptian government might have liked. The American Ambassador, for example, explained to *Rose al-Yusef* in February 1953 that American investors seeking to invest in Egypt sought precisely the same things that Egyptian investors sought.[85]

Investors' economic confidence in the new regime appears never to have reached particularly high levels. In the aftermath of land reform, building speculation appears to have replaced land speculation as a repository for cash. Capitalists' ever-spiraling investments in real estate were troublesome to those on the PCDNP, who sounded a constant drumbeat to increase "production."[86] Indeed, despite the efforts of the PCDNP to identify opportunities for investment in Egypt, investment in productive assets represented a mere fraction of what they hoped it would. According to the National Bank of Egypt, only 6.9 million £E of new capital flowed to industry in 1954, and 7.7 million £E in 1955.[87] By comparison, Egyptian government planning ministries poured 23 million £E and 27 million £E into productive investments during those same years, respectively.[88]

By contrast, in 1954 20.6 million £E of private funds flowed into building projects, and 28.5 million £E in 1955. Throughout the economy, building activity accounted for 49 percent of gross capital formation in 1954 and 44 percent in 1955.[89] The Federation of Egyptian Industries estimated that Egyptians constructed about 40 million £E of new buildings in 1953, a figure representing 59 percent of new investments for the year and equivalent to the net rise in capital formation for that year.[90] Twenty percent more building permits were issued the next year, suggesting to economists at the National Bank of Egypt that new building represented 50 million £E in new investment in 1954.[91]

One consequence of the building boom was the creation of "an important black market in cement . . . where considerably higher prices prevailed" than the official fixed price.[92] But a larger problem was that while the buildings may have been profitable for individual investors, they had a relatively low rate of return for the economy at large. National Bank of Egypt economists estimated that the capital/output ratio[93] for Egyptian industry averaged approximately 2 to 1, but the ratio in construction was 8 to 1.[94] As Egyptian officials desperately sought to boost national income, individual investors' preference to pour capital into building rather than industry both soured the officials on the possibility of relying on private capital and convinced them of the need for the government to move forward on its own.

Foreign capital provided no relief for Egyptian government officials seeking investment. Despite far-reaching changes in the way foreign capital was treated under Egyptian law, including significant rollbacks in the "Egyptianization" laws affecting capital imposed in the late 1940s,[95] foreigners invested a mere 700,000 £E in Egypt in 1954 and 900,000 £E in 1955.[96] Paltry as domestic levels of productive investment were, foreign levels were even lower.

Problems attracting investment in Egypt can be traced at least in part to the prevailing political climate. The secrecy with which decisions were taken—and, initially, secrecy over who was making the decisions—had a chilling effect on capital. A recent historian captured the mood this way:

> The people heard about the Revolutionary Command Council, but they saw nothing before them except its public face, Brig. Gen. Muhammad Naguib. The people slept in peace and awoke to sudden decisions. . . . There was no open rule . . . and this led to the loss of trust in everything said and issued by those in power. And this led to a transformation in the leaders, the politicians, and the intellectuals, from a condition of passivity to a condition of paralysis.[97]

An example of the sort of activity investors found troubling concerned the establishment of a new constitution. The RCC unilaterally annulled the Egyptian constitution on December 10, 1952, and announced that it would appoint a committee of 50 leaders to write a new document. The RCC named a distinguished list of political figures, members of the intelligentsia, and jurists to the constitutional committee on January 13, and three days later it announced the dissolution of political parties. Days later, hundreds were arrested. The constitutional committee first met in February and made good progress. By late March its Executive Committee had adopted a resolution calling for Egypt to be a republic and proceeded to discuss the precise form that Egypt's new government should take. On June 18, 1953, sidestepping the constitutional committee entirely, the RCC unilaterally abolished the monarchy. It declared Egypt a republic and named the titular leader of the RCC, Muhammad Naguib, President of Egypt. The constitutional committee of fifty was left to wonder what role it had left to play.[98]

Immediately after the dissolution of the old political parties in January 1953, the RCC created what was essentially a single-party organization called the Liberation Rally. The goal of the organization, clearly, was not to act as a conduit for ideas from the populace to the RCC, but the opposite. It was created expressly to build popular support for the policies that the RCC had decided to follow. The Liberation Rally model reveals more than it was perhaps intended to. The RCC sought support for its policies, but it did not seek broad guidance on the policies themselves. The committees that the RCC established—the PCDNP and the constitutional committee, for example— although composed of esteemed experts, appear to have been conceived not so much to lead the government as to vet plans conceived in the secret councils of the military leadership. In all cases, the committees appeared to serve at the pleasure of the RCC, and they could be overridden with little forethought.

It appears ironic that a new government that sought to promote its "rationality" above all else would eschew the guidance of experts who might better be able to guide its policy. In the irony, however, lies a truth: that the RCC bore some degree of distrust toward those with needed expertise, since that expertise could only have been gained through compromising ties to the old system. The problem with experts replicated itself with regard to capital. While the army needed private capital for its economic program, it felt private capital to be tainted somehow. This explains the rather peculiar pursuit of capital in which the Free Officers engaged—hoping that some sort of arm's-length study founded on "rationality" would cause capitalists to come out of the woodwork without ever really forcing the new government to enter into discussions with them.

In the event, the capitalists never came. Egyptian officials believed that they had very little to show for its economic efforts. The $40 million American aid package that followed an Anglo-Egyptian agreement in November 1954 was fundamentally disappointing to Egyptians, who had been hoping for at least twice as much. Israel was forcing itself onto the Egyptian mindset, first with the Lavon affair in the summer of 1954[99] and then with an attack on an Egyptian border post in Gaza in February 1955. Egypt was beginning to pursue an outspokenly independent foreign policy that could not but chill foreign investment. Finally, and most importantly, the Malthusian dilemma which framed all Egyptian discussions of development was not going away. Despite Rashed al-Barrawi's caution that there was "no magic wand by which the projects would be executed in moments or hours,"[100] a magic wand was clearly what was desired.

A Change in Direction

The editorial content of *al-Ahram al-Iqtisadi* unmistakably changed in the winter of 1954–55. In the years immediately following the revolution, most issues had feature stories on entrepreneurial successes. Henry Ford, F. W. Woolworth, John D. Rockefeller and others figured prominently in its pages. Scientific advances abroad in pest prevention, crop improvement, and related fields also appeared. Finally, general articles surveying market conditions and business administration were a mainstay of the magazine. By the winter of 1954–55, such articles gave way to descriptions of government plans to build heavy industry. The magazine clearly shifted from a readership concerned with personal business affairs to a record of the state's progress in promoting economic advancement.

A special issue of *al-Ahram al-Iqtisadi* in April 1955 dramatized the change in Egyptian thinking. Published in both Arabic and English, the special issue described in depth the economic development plans of the new Minister of Production, Wing Commander Hassan Ibrahim. While the program Ibrahim outlined fairly closely followed the PCDNP's program in substance, it differed significantly in style, not least because it was taken from a speech he delivered at Air Force Headquarters in Cairo. Ibrahim's speech departed most dramatically from the PCDNP line as he talked about the role of the state. "Under present circumstances," the article said, "it is impossible to leave private concerns entirely to their own initiative, some sort of supervision is bound to be exercised by the State both in order to promote public welfare and to ensure the correct pursuance of the production policy."[101]

The preference for planning over the free market was clearly expressed in another article in the same issue, this one written by Brig. Samir Helmy. Helmy wrote:

> As a point of fact, Government intervention in the field of economy has become an accepted principle. It is applied in many countries of the world, in one way or another, alongside existing legislations designed to protect private enterprise. In Egypt, the principle is not only essential but vital if we accept the assumption that the State represents the best interest of the community in all its diverse elements and classes and hence, is responsible for the coordination of efforts, the organization and guidance of the economic and social activity of the nation.[102]

As the state expanded its role in the economy, two projects stood out. The first was the decision taken in the spring of 1954 to proceed with the construction of an iron and steel plant at Helwan. Of the 7 million £E required for the project, the government of Egypt committed 2 million £E in "machinery and tools already available," the PCDNP committed 1 million £E, two banks and two investment companies committed another 1.25 million £E, and 750,000 £E was left open for private investments. The German Demag Company (which contracted with the Egyptian government to supply and assemble the plant) was to contribute the remainder, with the amount capped at 2 million £E.[103] While the project represented a mix of private and public capital, the Egyptian government was clearly to be the largest shareholder and the impetus behind the company's formation.

The second large project was the Aswan High Dam (discussed more completely in chapter 5). It is significant that while most of the articles in *al-Ahram al-Iqtisadi's* special issue in April 1955 were identical in English and Arabic, the article on the High Dam differed greatly. The English version described a 1947 government plan for dam construction, and then laid out 13 benefits of proceeding with the High Dam project over the previous scheme. The article was almost terse about the Egyptian government's role. The author used the passive construction: "studies and researches, begun late in 1952, have made it clear that the construction of a High Dam six kilometers south of Aswan Dam is more advantageous than the abovementioned program in every respect"; further, he neither identified the studies nor those who carried them out.[104]

The Arabic article was a text of an address by Samir Helmy to an unspecified audience that began by identifying the High Dam as a "good opportunity to increase agricultural production and industrial production quickly." After a brief description of the project, Helmy went on to explicate the idea of over-year storage of water to compensate for years of heavy and light flooding. He did so in some detail, although he did not mention H. E. Hurst, the British irrigation engineer employed by the Egyptian Ministry of Public Works who conceived of the concept originally.[105] He then continued with a description of every kind of study carried out to investigate the feasibility of the High Dam scheme, from aerial surveys to mapping to hydrological studies. He identified most of these as having been carried out by Egyptian engineers, with the cooperation of the German firm Hochteif. Helmy scrupulously edited out any mention of American assistance on the feasibility studies—which was considerable—and of the preponderance of Americans serving on the international board of experts which gave final approval for the High Dam plans. The article concludes with a summary of the report of the international experts, essentially verifying the wisdom of the High Dam plan and the completeness of the subsidiary studies.[106]

Helmy's speech was clearly intended to rally support behind the Egyptian government as much as it was to rally support for the High Dam. He surely intended to impress his audience with his concentration on technical details. Further, his portrayal of Egyptian technicians as heroic and hard working, while omitting virtually any mention of foreigners (except to vouch for the soundness of the Egyptians' work), presaged the role the dam was to play—but had not played so far—in Egyptian nationalist thought. Helmy was announcing a different role for the government than it had played heretofore. It no longer merely governed, but now it executed vital projects that would change the face of the country.

The new mood was perhaps best expressed by a cartoon that appeared in *Rose al-Yusef* on May 9, 1955. The cartoon pictured Misri Effendi, a rotund, bespectacled character who was used in cartoons of the time to represent the Egyptian nation. In the cartoon, Misri Effendi is a woman nursing a baby labeled "projects." The woman is surrounded by competing wet nurses, clearly representing Britain and the United States, who are offering their breasts. The doctor (who resembles Abdel Nasser) waves off the wet nurses, telling them, "Excuse me . . . his mother will nurse him herself."[107]

The shift toward public sector financing was more than an institutional change. It is more accurately understood as the consequence of the Egyptian government reaching two conclusions: First, that the private sector was unwilling or unable to push forward with the economic development schemes that Egypt required, and second, that only centrally directed, "rational" development could produce the sort of rapid development Egypt needed. To say it another way, the Free Officers believed that they had tried capitalist development and it had failed (if not completely, then at least relative to Egypt's need for rapid progress).[108]

This begs a different question, which is whether the regime would have allowed a powerful private sector to develop as an alternate center of power to the military-led government. This question is harder to assess, because the regime's ability to extend control through the society rapidly evolved in the years after the revolution. At the same time, a consensus existed within the government and without of the primacy of economic development. What seems most likely is that if there had been significant economic development in the first years after the revolution, the military junta would have found some way to accommodate it. There were few in the government opposed to private capital in principle, and the military officers who held power were, above all, pragmatists.

In the first years of the revolution, the Egyptian government's approach to economic development was incremental, and legislation "more often than not represented extensions and additions to the existing body of legislation rather than definite innovations."[109] It was the failure of these incremental efforts—be they to amend a provision of the company law, to entice local or foreign investment in a paper factory, to improve the quality of domestic livestock, or to interest firms in prospecting for mineral wealth—that led to the triumph of those calling for large scale, coordinated efforts. The central organizing principle of the revolution's economic policy—"rationality"—was predicated on results, not ideology, and the results from small projects were difficult to discern.

Chapter 4 ～

EARIS

The New Deal in the United States represented an unprecedented use of governmental power to improve directly the lives of the general population. Massive irrigation projects in the American West and Southwest supplied employment for tens of thousands and expanded agricultural land dramatically. The Tennessee Valley Authority's scope extended far beyond mere irrigation and electrification work to battle endemic poverty in the Southeast. As the United States turned its face abroad in the 1950s, some officials thought that the ideas and approaches that the U.S. government had used to ameliorate the Great Depression might usefully be employed in poor countries. The American experience was a happy match for Egypt, especially since land reclamation and irrigation were so high on the Egyptian agenda. A partnership with American engineers and scientists held out the promise of vastly improving Egyptian agriculture, still the main source of national income.

The Egyptian-American partnership reached fruition in a land reclamation and resettlement program called the Egyptian-American Rural Improvement Service (EARIS). Although the program began amid much hope, its execution phase revealed just how difficult collaboration could be. To the disappointment of the Americans, Egyptians seemed single-mindedly interested in the narrow land reclamation aspects of EARIS to the exclusion of its broader, political, "community development" component. Although the two parties agreed on the overall goals of the program, differences over the administrative structure and execution persisted. The program was effectively "Egyptianized" by the winter of 1955–56, leaving the Americans to wonder what constructive role they could still play in the project. Equally importantly, the program never succeeded as a prototype either for Egyptian-American cooperation or for land reclamation and resettlement.

A New Aid Commitment

As the Revolutionary government consolidated its power in the latter months of 1952, the feeling grew in the American Embassy in Cairo and in the Department of State that some large, symbolic gesture of friendship by the United States toward the new government was urgently needed. Ambassador Caffery wrote Washington in early January 1953, "To date, [the] contribution made by [the] Point Four program has been negligible," but he added that the "outlook is encouraging if [the] present atmosphere can be retained."[1] The Department of State agreed with Caffery's assessment and sent an urgent cable back approving an additional $10 million in American aid to Egypt. The $10 million was to be used to purchase American wheat; the Egyptian government could employ the proceeds from the wheat's sale in Egypt to finance domestic development projects. The Department of State suggested investing the counterpart funds in irrigation projects and possibly road improvement, but allowed that the disposition of the funds depended on the outcome of negotiations between the Egyptian and American governments.[2]

Those negotiations quickly ran into difficulty when the Egyptian Minister of Finance proposed that Egypt spend the funds wholly on a project to reclaim 357,000 acres of land, without any ongoing oversight by the U.S. government. Such a proposal was unacceptable to Washington, which in early February dispatched to Cairo E. Reeseman "Si" Fryer, the head of the Near East and Africa Development Service.[3] Fryer, who had a reputation in the Technical Cooperation Administration as a man of action and a dynamo of activity,[4] arrived with a different agenda.

From the start, Fryer sought to use the American aid as an opportunity to sell the new Egyptian government on a concerted program of human capital development. Just before Fryer left Washington, one of his assistants sent him a lengthy memorandum on a proposal to strengthen an Egyptian program of Rural Social Centers already extant in the country. Constructed under a ten-year-old program operated by the Ministry of Social Affairs' Fellah Department,[5] the social centers were a network of meeting halls, health clinics, and school rooms, with each cluster serving approximately 10,000 peasants. Each center employed a full-time agricultural adviser, doctor, and nurse. Several centers in a single region shared the services of pharmacists, veterinarians, and craft instructors among them. The centers sought gradually to improve the quality of village life through an integrated program that addressed the misery of the poor from several directions at once. The Egyptian government, which had established 151 such centers by early 1953, planned to replicate them all over Egypt.[6] Fryer's aide suggested that the American government join the Rural Social Center program as a full partner, establishing a "Joint Village Improvement Board" to "formulate joint plans for a comprehensive rural improvement program and to mobilize and integrate the services available in the various ministries."[7]

The Rural Social Centers scheme was certainly waxing in the early 1950s. Originally proposed in 1939, only eleven were built from 1941 to 1946. In the next five years, however, the Egyptians built 115 new centers.[8] In each instance, the communities to be served were required to gather 1500 £E, or 15 piasters per capita ($4,320 and $0.43 respectively), as well as contribute a small plot of land and temporary housing for the advisers. Such efforts by the community, the planners hoped, would help enlist the enthusiasm and support of the beneficiaries and "make them feel that the centre is theirs."[9]

The social centers project aimed to change attitudes in rural Egypt as much as it aimed to change material conditions. A Ministry of Social Affairs report stated explicitly, "The Fellah Department from the first instance had as its goal the awakening of the rural population and educating them to their need for reform, so that they will harken to the call willingly, and participate morally and materially having once been convinced of the need for reform."[10]

The image of the peasant espoused by urban elites in Egypt, as well as by elites in other Arab countries, was that rural life in the Middle East was characterized by a complex mix of pathological behaviors which condemned peasants to live brutal, disease-ridden lives; their poverty was such that it made "them physically and mentally defective."[11] One aspect of their poverty, according to some, was psychological. A Syrian agricultural expert observed at a 1950 conference on social welfare in the Arab states held in Cairo:

> The farmers themselves have no self-respect. . . . Lack of self-respect causes many of the undesirable traits in the character of human society. . . . Before attempting material uplift in rural areas we should work on the moral uplift of the farmer so as to create in him ambition and the will to rise. He should feel in his spirit the dignity of man and realise that he is a human being endowed with all the good qualities of mankind and entitled to the enjoyment of life in its higher values. This is not revolutionary; it is elemental, and every cooperative or every social organization should begin by uplifting the soul of the farmer so that he may better work the soil.[12]

Members of that conference's Rural Education Committee evoked the same psychological goals in their final report, although they put a more political spin on them. They concluded that among the aims of rural education were:

1. The formation of the good citizen from a spiritual, moral and social point of view—a citizen who is able to think freely for himself, who can work in harmony with others, who can utilise his environment profitably, and who can work for its continued progress;

2. Inculcation of the spirit of democracy as a method of action, of social co-operation, and of working towards national and human ideals;
3. Preparation of a rural environment favourable to the rise of leaders who work with other countrymen for rural reconstruction, and for national public service in the country at large.[13]

In the Egyptian case, the means for instilling such values in the peasantry were through contact with educated Egyptian professionals, in particular with the agricultural and social welfare specialist who would work full-time in an individual Social Welfare Center. The position's job description was to

> help raise their cultural and social standard by combating illiteracy and encouraging adult education; settling disputes, and removing old-established bad practices and superstitions; he has to work for the cleanliness of the village, its inhabitants, roadways and alleys; to organize charity and help find a regular income for poor families—all in cooperation with the people around him.[14]

Preparation for this task, in addition to a degree from the College of Agriculture, was a 14-week course in rural sociology.

Standards for selection were quite rigorous. An aspiring specialist had to pass muster with a committee comprised of a representative from the Fellah Department, a psychologist, and an educationalist, and then pass two exams: a written exam on a "social topic" and a "piece of translation from English to Arabic."[15] While the selection procedure guaranteed that candidates were well qualified to succeed in an academic environment, it also seemed to ensure that few if any of these specialists would have been familiar with village life before being thrust into a village setting. That is to say, the ministry seemed to be appealing for an increase in "self-help" activity from villagers, but very high standards and the general lack of social mobility in Egypt meant that exceedingly few people who had grown up in a village environment would ever be qualified to take on the role of an agricultural and cultural specialist in a similar community. The pattern of interaction was based more on a missionary model than on one of self-help. It was contact with civilized, educated persons that would uplift villagers. The program placed emphasis on paternalistically imposing modern standards on the villages rather than negotiating some sort of accommodation between the village and cosmopolitan society.

The ministry's attitude toward local governance also cast doubt on its commitment to self-help principles. On the one hand, the Social Welfare Center scheme entailed the establishment of a variety of committees and boards to administer the affairs of the community. Each center was to have a General Assembly, a Board of Directors, and committees for economics and agriculture; health and building; culture, sports, and entertainment; and charity and conciliation. Through such committees, "The public are taught not to rely on assistance from outside but to rely on themselves through the formation of committees."[16] However, the ministry did not provide local boards with the resources with which to carry out their responsibilities to their constituents. Yet, the villages' responsibility to meet the needs of the national government—collection of taxes, military recruitment, guarding state property, and so on—was clear and the government provided guards to meet those needs. Responsibilities like sanitary and health needs were not well provided for, and they often languished.[17] Thus, while the state supported local initiative in theory, in practice it often kept scarce resources under central government control.

Fryer's aide, Savilla Simons, appears to have been quite aware of the challenges facing the Rural Social Centers in Egypt. One of her suggestions was that the U.S. government work with the Egyptian government to revamp the four- to six-month course at the Cairo School of Social Work for Directors of Rural Social Centers "in order to provide training for village organizers and personnel for the rural social centers." The thrust of the training program, she argued, should not be toward fostering elite-level management, but rather toward developing a rural leadership that would be able to stimulate "interest in self-improvement, in organizing self-help projects and in ways of getting villager participation."[18] Overwhelmingly, the American interest was in building upon and improving the extant Egyptian rural program, with its emphasis on training and human betterment. Americans evinced far less enthusiasm for supporting mere land reclamation projects.

The Formation of EARIS

Fryer arrived in Egypt fully briefed on existing efforts toward rural social reform. While there, he was able to dissuade the Egyptian government from using all of the U.S. aid for land reclamation, and he was able to convince the Egyptian government to steer some of the money toward rural improvement along the lines Americans favored. The compromise he worked out took the form of EARIS. According to the agreement signed on March 19, 1953, the United States and Egypt would cooperate in a plan which combined land reclamation *and* an ambitious expansion of the Rural Social Center idea. The United States government would contribute $10 million in cash (with which Egypt could buy equipment and supplies on the world market), and the Egyptian government would provide the equivalent of an additional $15.7 million in Egyptian pounds for domestic expenses.[19] Much of the work would be done with American World War II surplus earthmoving equipment that remained in North Africa and was otherwise being unused.

On the reclamation side, the agreement envisioned converting 80,000 feddans from desert and swamp into arable land. As originally proposed, 60,000 feddans would be irrigated in two desert areas near the Fayyoum Oasis (about 100 km southwest of Cairo), and an additional 20,000 feddans would be drained from a brackish lake just south of Alexandria on the Mediterranean Coast. Both operations—desert reclamation and marshland reclamation—required leaching and drainage to lower the salt content in the soil so as to make it arable. Both also required the use of heavy equipment for leveling the earth and constructing canals, as well as the employment of pumps for moving water. The two regions, with their different kinds of reclamation challenges, were chosen in order to provide examples of cost-effective, technology-utilizing land reclamation methods in the two conditions prevalent on the 96 percent of Egyptian land that was not farmed: deserts in the interior of the country and swamplands along the northern coast.

The second component of EARIS was to be community development, which was essentially a continuation and expansion of the Rural Social Center idea. The innovation in the case of EARIS was that these social centers would be woven into the fabric of wholly new communities. Thus, the life peasants embarked upon in the newly reclaimed lands would be a departure from old customs and an embrace of new and productive methods. Together with the government, they would begin to eliminate the rural poverty that dominated the Egyptian countryside.

In the American mind, at least, community development seemed to be the more important of the program's two aspects. The stated objective of the Egyptian-American agreement (that was drafted by the Americans but agreed to by both parties) was:

> Cooperation between the two governments to improve the social and economic conditions throughout all Egypt, by carrying out a broad demonstrational program of development which attacks, through self-help, community participation and direct assistance, the basic problems of rural life for the people in the Provinces of Buheira and Fayyoum.[20]

In this formulation, the project objectives seem solely devoted to community development, while the notion of land reclamation is absent.

In the Egyptian domestic arena, the prospect of close and long-term cooperation with the U.S. government met with opposition in some corners. To some extent, the opposition was to cooperation with any foreign government. Egypt had generally westward-looking rulers since 1805, had been living under varying amounts of British control since 1882, and hosted a large expatriate community widely perceived to be profiteering from the labors of the Egyptian peasantry.[21] In the eyes of some, Egypt was poised to achieve greatness if only the meddling effects of foreigners could be minimized.[22] In addition, Egypt's small but vocal Communist movement had spoken out repeatedly against Anglo-American imperialism and perceived any move by the Americans in Egypt somehow to be part of an aggressive design on the region.[23] Many leftist activists had become part of the revolutionary leadership by 1953, however,[24] and tempered their public anti-Americanism, if not their private.

An additional source of opposition to the EARIS plan was operational rather than ideological. Government ministries were anxious not to lose control over development projects in Egypt, and the Permanent Council for the Development of National Production (which represented Egypt in the EARIS negotiations) feared that if ministry officials were involved in any way in EARIS planning, they would sabotage the efforts. Consequently, the PCDNP counseled the U.S. mission not even to discuss EARIS plans with the ministries in the early months.[25]

Moving Toward Implementation of EARIS

Conceptualization and implementation of the EARIS program was rocky in its early stages. Seven weeks after the project agreement was signed, the EARIS program had no budget, no project plan, a single map, and only two Egyptian counterparts to work with American technicians. A total of four Americans had seen the land to be reclaimed.[26] The delay was due in part to the fact that EARIS was being planned by an American committee of 15 technicians, many on urgent temporary assignment from their responsibilities at posts in Washington and around the world. Although they met daily, their energy could not always compensate for the fact that many were unfamiliar with Egypt and the American aid mission there. In their disarray, they had not been able to inform the government of Egypt in which precise fields counterparts were needed until late May. Further, the need to coordinate spending with Washington not only required time for cables to pass back and forth, but also a more thorough level of advance planning than teams unfamiliar with local conditions in Egypt could easily muster.[27] Further adding to confusion, the head of American technical assistance in Egypt, Dr. John Nichols, was informed in April that he was being relieved of his position after less than a year of service. His replacement would be Si Fryer, who had worked hard in February and March to complete the EARIS agreement.[28]

Fryer's selection to head the mission was an indication of how highly the Technical Cooperation Administration valued its program in Egypt. Fryer was the head of TCA in the entire Near East and Africa region, and his appointment to Egypt signaled admiration for his abilities rather than a desire by his superiors to laterally promote him out of Washington. Approximately two weeks before his expected departure date, however, Fryer was told he was not to go to Egypt after all. Harold Stassen,[29] the new Administrator of the Foreign Operations Administration (which combined the activities of the Technical Cooperation Administration, the Mutual Security Administration [MSA], and the Economic Cooperation Administration)[30] instead selected Admiral Harold Stevens for the Cairo posting.

Stevens had no background in development work. He had been a career Navy man who met Stassen when the latter was president of the University of Pennsylvania and the former was the head of the school's Navy ROTC program.[31] Thirty years later, EARIS technicians interviewed for an Agency for International Development evaluation of the program were almost uniformly critical of Stevens's tenure. They criticized his military bearing, his poor administrative skills, and his difficulty working productively with Egyptians.[32] A former Egyptian head of the project remembered that Stevens was "a nice guy" but one who didn't understand the technical aspects of EARIS and remained rather distant from the project.[33] Stevens may have been attractive to Stassen in part because the Mutual Security Act of 1952 reorganized foreign aid under an explicit security rubric. Stevens, as a military man, might better pursue the security-connected aspects of American aid policy than the educationalists, extension agents and visionaries who flocked to Point Four during the Truman Administration.

Stassen's remaking of the foreign aid bureaucracy in the autumn of 1953 was thorough; a deep-cutting "reduction in force" pared the Near East and Africa Development Service's Washington operations from 19 people to 4. More than 100 others lost their jobs in Point Four, leading to "wholesale demoralization"[34] among those who remained in Washington. As the fall wore on, one Point Four veteran complained, "Point 4 is slowly but surely losing its individuality. . . . If communications are slow in getting to you, please understand we are explaining and educating the MSA boys on how and why we did it certain ways when we were in TCA."[35]

It is hard to assess how much the absence of strong leadership in the Egyptian mission and general uncertainty about the direction of foreign assistance during the summer of 1953 affected EARIS's planning process. Planning proceeded quickly over the summer, especially after Ramadan ended June 15. Sixteen Egyptian participants joined the task force July 1, and the group split into six committees: Agricultural Services, Community Organization, Education, Housing and Planning, Public Health, and Reclamation. Each group circulated discussion papers and developed plans for marshland to be reclaimed by the Abis project; the two desert reclamation projects in Fayyoum (at Quta and Qom Oshim) took second seat, as they would do for much of the life of EARIS.

As envisioned by the planning committee in 1953, three criteria guided the EARIS project:

1. It would introduce something new to Egypt, including better methods of operation, better integration of related activities, and new "balanced" programs that introduce "facilities and services concurrently such as schools, community health centers, health clinics, etc."
2. It could be replicated if desired in other parts of Egypt.
3. It would produce early results, with three years as an outside target.[36]

Americans involved in planning EARIS placed considerable emphasis on the need for all phases of activity to be planned concurrently so that infrastructure could be built and settlers transported promptly upon the reclamation of the land, with the first group to arrive after one year.

Perhaps the easiest aspect of planning was the reclamation work, due to several factors. Technicians on both sides had significant prior land reclamation experience, and many of the Egyptian technicians had received their training in American universities and consequently "spoke the language" of their American counterparts.[37] In addition, the nature of the work allowed for rather precise delineation of the job to be done and the results to be obtained. Upon convening, the reclamation subcommittee rapidly scaled down plans for the project. It judged that the costs of desert reclamation in Fayyoum on the scale originally envisioned would far outstrip available monetary and water resources. The subcommittee thus reduced the original 62,000-feddan target 79 percent to 13,000 feddans.[38] Meanwhile, the subcommittee extended the schedule for completing reclamation work in Abis from the initial "three to four year" target[39] to six years, apparently because initial estimates included only the period required for washing and leaching the soil and not the time required to conduct preliminary studies and major works. As envisioned by the subcommittee, a comprehensive survey and soil study of the entire area needed to precede any reclamation. Following the conclusion of the survey work, the land would have to be turned and leveled, and irrigation canals and drainage ditches constructed. Only after that work was completed could the flooding and draining of the land begin. Flooding and draining to wash salt from the soil, which was coordinated with the annual flooding of the Nile from August to November, would take at least three years to make the land productive. The exception was some land in Abis that the State Domains Administration had begun reclaiming in 1948.[40] Prior work in Abis would allow settlement on 1,120 feddans by November 1954, and an additional 4,480 feddans three years later.[41] Work in Fayyoum mostly required the extension of extant irrigation canals (which had to be lined to prevent water seepage into sandy soil). Planners originally estimated that the Fayyoum areas would be ready for settlement in eighteen months, but upon study quickly revised their estimates and delayed planned settlement until 1957 at the earliest.

The fluidity of project parameters raised the ire of the housing and planning subcommittee, which felt that other groups' slow progress made any progress on their part impossible. In particular, their charge to draw up housing and village plans could not be executed without basic decisions as to where the villages would be located, how many people would live in each village, and how large the average family would be.[42] In addition, members of the planning subcommittee strongly objected to the presumption that all land in Abis would remain agricultural. They pointed out that some land in the northern and eastern areas of Abis abutted expanding areas of Alexandria and might serve greater economic use in the future as industrial rather than agricultural land. In addition, a contemplated rail line connecting Alexandria and Marsa Matruh (some 290 km to the west) would roughly bisect Abis, yet EARIS plans in no way incorporated such a possibility.[43]

The education subcommittee's deliberations appeared divorced from the workings of its counterparts. Its program was entirely oriented toward establishing an "Egyptian-American Audiovisual Education Center" in or near Alexandria that would perform work without charge for EARIS schools and projects and work for a fee for other organizations in Egypt. The committee members wrote, "Modern audiovisual methods of instructing school children and adults have proved highly successful in developing interest and motivation, in demonstrating ideas and applications, and in explaining the 'why' and 'how' of technical subjects."[44] Building up a library of photographs, films, posters, and more, the center would thus extend its influence far beyond the school classroom to include lessons in community organization, agricultural extension, public health education, and other subjects.

The public health subcommittee also extended its vision beyond the boundaries of Abis. It highlighted the fact that diseases like bilharzia, malaria, and trachoma were endemic to rural Egypt and caused disability and lowered productivity. The real killers, however, were diarrheal diseases, which accounted for one third of deaths in Egypt overall and over half of infant deaths. The charge for EARIS, then, was primarily to ensure safe drinking water and sanitation throughout the reclaimed land. EARIS's other needs were consonant with needs throughout the Buheira Province where Abis was located: the availability of primary medical care and midwifery services in the villages, and the regional eradication of the parasites that caused the debilitating diseases.[45]

Among all the groups, the community organization subcommittee had the most well-developed and ambitious plans. Led by a Lebanese-born rural sociologist named Afif Tannous in the employ of the U.S. Department of

Agriculture, the committee stressed the need for immediate action even though actual resettlement was years off. In general, the proposed program emphasized the need to exercise care in selecting and preparing settlers for resettlement. The subcommittee's discussion paper even suggested that the Village Council, which American planners envisioned as the most important democratizing feature of the EARIS plan, be organized and established in the year prior to resettlement, that is, while the new settlers were still in their old villages. Thus even before resettlement "the various officials working in the community should not supersede the Council in making decisions and taking action, but should act as helpers and guides."[46] In fact, Tannous suggested that the democratically selected council be empanelled before final selection of settlers in 1954. How one could select a democratic government without a clear electorate is a detail not clarified in the original document.

Another component to Tannous' plan of community organization was the selection and training of professionals who would work daily in the new EARIS settlements. Tannous suggested that these individuals each spend a month in the villages from which EARIS settlers would be selected before relocation took place. The training period would both serve to orient them to the problems of rural Egypt and utilize their services early in the resettlement process. Tannous suggested an additional month of training each year through 1958, and an additional six months of training in the United States for a select few in 1959.

A third component was the institution of a program in rural studies at al-Azhar University to train Islamic scholars for work in the rural areas of Egypt. The effect would be threefold: the scholars so trained could be more effective community leaders, help diminish pervasive superstition among villagers, and "collect, dramatize and publicize Koranic and traditional statements in support of various improvement projects . . . [since the tradition is] replete with positive statements regarding health, agriculture, cooperation, community consensus, learning, self-improvement, social justice, etc."[47] Tannous proposed that the rural education program begin immediately at al-Azhar.[48]

The EARIS agricultural committee proposed solutions that were national, not local. It recommended establishing a national apparatus that would both research issues of importance to the Egyptian farmer and pass that information on, "entirely free of any inspection, regulatory and law enforcement responsibilities." It further counseled that the efforts of various ministries involved in rural life had to be coordinated and integrated to minimize "duplication of services and expense."[49] Establishing a separate bureaucracy to carry out these functions in EARIS would merely represent a replication of already redundant efforts. Instead, the American mission sought to bring American methods of agricultural extension to Egypt, and based compliance on farmers' self interest rather than compulsion.

In at least some American quarters, the EARIS discussions raised qualms about the overall American program in Egypt. Working side by side with Egyptian professionals led at least one American to believe that the problem in Egypt wasn't the level of available technical knowledge—as the entire Point Four program assumed—but rather the methods of applying that knowledge. One American expert on the EARIS task force wrote in an informal letter to his superior in Washington

> We seem to be offering technical advice in fields in which Egypt has little need of technical advice, to people who are themselves highly competent. . . . The main thing we can offer is methodology—management, extension, a philosophy of service, application of ideas. We have land use specialists, drainage men, social workers, educationists, etc. trying to make themselves acceptable as technical advisers to men and Ministries who have devoted lifetimes to this work. You feel a sense of inadequacy as you stroll thru the Agricultural Museum and see how much knowledge they have accumulated, how many fields they have explored, how thoroughly they have researched, and then think of how two or three American agriculturalists can add something worthwhile to this attic-ful.[50]

By supplementing areas in which the Egyptians already had interest and expertise, the aide suggested, the American aid program diluted its efforts to create new fields of activity in Egypt. According to this aide's figuring, reclamation and construction costs in EARIS would exhaust the larger part of its funds. He suggested, even as planning was in its initial phases, "I think you are going to be surprised at the modest role of community services, health, agriculture and education when the first trial balances are struck."[51] Equally troubling was his assertion that the Egyptian government would carry out the reclamation aspects of EARIS "even without our money or advice."[52] These concerns would prove prescient as the EARIS program moved from planning to implementation.

The Worsening Context

After signing an initial agreement governing EARIS administration in April 1953 and completing initial planning in August of that year, the Egyptian and American governments quickly signed agreements for land classification in Buheira and Fayyoum, and major works and land reclamation in Buheira.[53] Through the fall, however, the tenor of the larger aid relationship changed for the worse, and this seems to have had at least some effect on the execution of the EARIS plan. Two events combined to complicate Egyptian-American relations at this time: the yet-unresolved dispute between Britain and Egypt over the British military base in the Suez Canal, and the need to finalize congressional appropriations for foreign aid to the Middle East. As mentioned in chapter 1, the British presence in the Canal Zone had long been an issue of contention for the Egyptians, who began negotiations to end the British presence there immediately following World War II. The British presence was guaranteed by a treaty in 1936, negotiated by a young Anthony Eden, and set to last 30 years. After the World War, many Egyptians believed that the continued British presence in Egypt infringed on Egyptian sovereignty, and the issue of forcing the British out of Egypt became the primary rallying cry of Egyptian politics.[54]

Interest in expelling British troops did not diminish when the Free Officers took over the government in the summer of 1952. When the former Minister of Social Affairs, Ahmed Hussein, was posted to Washington as the new Egyptian ambassador in the spring of 1953, Gamal Abdel Nasser told him his posting would likely last less than a year, and his primary mission was to gain American support in pressuring the British to leave the Canal Zone.[55] Throughout the Anglo-Egyptian negotiations, the United States— under the personal leadership of Ambassador Caffery—sought to mediate a solution which accommodated Egyptian desires for complete independence and preserved Britain's role as a partner in the Cold War and a long-standing ally of the United States.

In practice this balance proved hard to maintain, particularly as the Conservative government of Winston Churchill became less flexible in the face of opposition at home to the complete dissolution of the Empire, and the Egyptian government became impatient at the perceived British intransigence and the seemingly interminable delays in gaining additional American aid. Throughout 1953, the United States government was on the verge of granting military and economic aid to Egypt, but in each instance delayed the award of aid at the request of the British. In January Foreign Secretary Eden urged that the United States supply no arms until he had a chance to meet Dulles in London the next month. In February the British Embassy objected to virtually every item on the list of weapons the United States proposed to provide to the Egyptians. The problem became more urgent when Congress appropriated $135 million for aid to Middle Eastern countries for the 1954 fiscal year. In October the Department of State announced that $25 million of that amount would go to Israel but remained mum regarding aid to the Arab states. State Department officials working on the Middle East hoped very much that an announcement of significant aid to Egypt might help offset regional concern about aid to Israel, but the aid decisions were perpetually delayed. Caffery complained to Washington in early November:

> British will probably (as they did in case of military aid last year) make every effort to prevent US economic assistance to Egypt at this point. . . . If we fail

to do anything positive at this juncture (particularly since possibility of early economic aid has been mentioned to Badawi and Egyptian Ambassador) we will be a long time convincing Egyptians that US foreign policy is not (repeat not) "made in Downing Street."[56]

Alarm from the American embassy in London and the State Department's Bureau of European Affairs convinced Secretary Dulles that he needed to consult the British and not merely inform them about providing economic aid to Egypt.[57] But the secretary's patience was not limitless. He personally drafted a message to Eden on November 13 reading in part,

> We have been holding up assistance to Egypt in effort to help settlement Suez matter. However this settlement has dragged out to a point where we cannot continue much longer without very grave effect upon our Arab relationships. If you felt that it was likely there would soon be new moves in Suez matter which might produce agreement, we could still hold up briefly but our time is fast running out.[58]

Several days later Eden replied, "I must most urgently ask you to postpone a decision on proposed economic aid to Egypt at least until we have had a chance of discussing it at Bermuda." Eden judged that awarding the aid now "could not fail . . . to have a serious effect on Anglo-American relations."[59] Secretary Dulles told Minister Eden in Bermuda that the United States could not well delay aid past January 1, 1954, which drew a personal letter from Churchill to Eisenhower cautioning such aid "would, I am sure, have a grave effect in this country on Anglo-American relations." American aid to Egypt was yet again delayed.[60]

Egyptian government officials complained publicly and privately that the United States government was not neutral at all in the Anglo-Egyptian dispute, and the promise of American aid was being dangled as a carrot to win yet more concessions from an already flexible Egyptian negotiating position.[61] Meeting in Cairo on November 19, 1953, the chief of the political section of the Egyptian Foreign Ministry complained to Embassy economic counselor Robert Carr "that the prospects of American aid were being used to strengthen the British position in the Suez negotiations with Egypt."[62] The next day Gamal Abdel Nasser, at that time Vice Premier, said in a speech in Minya al-Qamh, "America is closely linked with Britain her ally. The two have a common enemy, Russia, and America will not please us to infuriate Britain. Do not believe for a moment that America will help us, as she and Britain, her ally, have one plan and one set policy. If we want to build a strong country and have our children free, we should have faith in ourselves and totally depend on ourselves."[63]

In its internal analysis, however, the Egyptian Foreign Ministry placed the issue of American aid to Egypt primarily in a global context rather than one involving Anglo-Egyptian relations. A widely circulated internal memorandum on American aid in early December quoted the exact passage from the Abdel Nasser speech cited above, but based most of its analysis on a speech Assistant Secretary of State for Near Eastern and African Affairs Henry Byroade delivered to the World Affairs Council of Northern California on November 1. That speech recognized that the Western powers' colonial histories raised suspicions in the newly independent countries as to their motives, and Byroade continued that, "In determining our own policies we must frankly recognize that suspicion of the West will probably endure for many years to come. We must do everything possible to prove that this suspicion has no basis. We must be willing to offer capital and technical assistance for economic development without seeking political advantage."[64] The internal ministry comment suggested that Byroade's view "is consonant with the general view of resisting communism. It is known that the weapon of communism is exploiting economic weakness in countries until they come to be forced into its grip. When the United States offers economic assistance it does not offer it innocently to these people but with an eye toward its vital interests in resisting communism."[65] Thus, while the Egyptian government's public statements emphasized Egypt's weakness in the face of an Anglo-American cabal, its internal statements suggested how Egypt might derive strength from its position in Western strategy. While the extent to which playing the "communist bogeyman" played a part in Egyptian negotiating strategy is unclear, the foreign ministry accurately perceived that its advantage lay in emphasizing global issues rather than regional ones.

Egyptians faced a further encumbrance as they sought aid from the United States government: appropriations required congressional approval, and congressional desires were often widely at variance with those of the administrative agencies in terms of the amount of aid, its content, and timing.[66] A significant problem from the Egyptian perspective was that unexpended balances of foreign aid resources gave the appearance that Egypt required no further assistance, when in fact the appropriated money had been obligated but simply not yet spent. EARIS was a large part of this problem—$10 million was allocated for the program in March, but spending could not begin until agreements were reached on plans, and the bulk could not be spent until heavy work began on the two areas to be reclaimed and resettled.

A further problem was that Congress appropriated money for regional programs, and the State Department was slow to program for individual countries out of that amount. Thus, although the State Department had "suggested" an appropriation of $20 million to Egypt in FY 1954 out of the regional allocation of $135 million, midway through the fiscal year there still had been no public indication of how much aid Egypt might receive.[67] Aid to Israel had been announced in October 1953 and was a source of displeasure among Arab leaders who remained unsure of their funding level and thus could not plan how to spend the money. In time, the cycle fed on itself: The difficulty of holding well-planned projects permanently in abeyance meant fewer such projects were planned. With fewer projects planned, the need for American aid declined. The problem became more complex when American staff appointments failed to keep pace with the envisioned aid program. In September 1953, for example, 101 positions were programmed for the Foreign Operations Mission in Egypt, but only 34 of those positions were filled.

As EARIS agreements were slowly signed through the autumn of 1953 amidst uncertainty over the general shape of American aid to Egypt, the U.S. Operations Mission attempted mightily to put a good face on Egyptian operations. In a regional aid conference in December in Istanbul, Cairo Mission director Harold Stevens laid out the conundrum well. On the one hand, he stated that "The [political] climate is now right [for large-scale American assistance] and the ever growing number of requests from the government of Egypt indicate the ground-work was well-laid."[68] On the other hand, he conceded, "[It] cannot be ignored in a discussion of possible economic aid . . . that the Government of Egypt has several times thought it was about to receive some such aid, which was not forthcoming. We are now in a position where we are almost certain to lose prestige if we do not provide some such assistance."[69]

EARIS itself progressed apparently uneventfully through 1954, the initial period of earth moving and major works. Settler selection began in February and village construction in May, again with little apparent discord. American records for this period are almost nonexistent, and technicians who worked on the project described it as a time of good cooperation between the Americans and their Egyptian counterparts. EARIS was virtually absent from the Egyptian press, in part because growing tensions with the U.S. government led Egyptians to downplay cooperative efforts, and in part because the army leadership which was running the country identified more closely with the competing army-run Tahrir Province.

Tahrir Province as an Alternative to EARIS

When the EARIS discussions came close to reaching an agreement in March 1953, sources close to the negotiations leaked the information to the press with the aim of provoking a public outcry. When this gambit failed, a group of army officers led by Major Magdi Hassanein approached the Cabinet two days after the EARIS agreement was signed to propose a reclamation and resettlement plan of their own. Four days later, their proposal to create Tahrir Province was approved.[70]

The proposal for Tahrir Province closely resembled the plan for EARIS with one exception: It was more ambitious. Whereas EARIS proposed to reclaim 80,000 feddans, Tahrir proposed to reclaim 600,000 feddans. Whereas EARIS called for developing the capacities of rural farmers, Tahrir called for "total human conditioning." Whereas EARIS's goals were relatively circumscribed, Tahrir's goals were deliberately broad. The director of the Tahrir project, reflecting back on his work, stated that there were no less than ten:

1. increase Egypt's arable land
2. derive benefit from Nile water just washing into the sea
3. alleviate unemployment
4. learn from successes Israelis had had in desert reclamation
5. modernize Egyptian agriculture
6. create a model society
7. apply the most modern scientific methods to Egyptian agriculture
8. change the shape of the map of Egypt from a Y-shaped arable area covering about 3 percent of the total land (the Nile Valley and the Delta), thus giving a victory to revolution
9. reclaim land to such an extent that it is a kind of revolution in itself
10. provide an opportunity to apply native Egyptian know-how to Egyptian problems[71]

Examining the list, three themes seem dominant. The first is an impatience bordering on urgency. Thus land reclamation is seen as a "revolutionary" rather than evolutionary process, and action is immediate rather than after a period of study and experimentation. The second is a certain amount of xenophobia, both in the employment of purely Egyptian expertise and in the urgent need to keep up with Israeli progress across the border. This xenophobia is implicit in the Tahrir plan itself, intended as it was as a "genuinely Egyptian" alternative to EARIS.[72] Finally, Tahrir was breathtakingly broad in scope. The problems it sought to address were not those of the land to be reclaimed, but of the nation. Tahrir would alleviate unemployment and begin to alter the map of Egypt; it would provide the first breath for a model society that would revolutionize the countryside. More than simply a plan, Tahrir represented the entire future of Egypt, or so its planners hoped.

More than anything, the planners of Tahrir seemed most concerned with the idea of modernity. In Hassanein's book, the Arabic word for "modern" (*hadith*) appears time and time again. Larger farms were necessary because they were more modern and allowed the use of modern machinery.[73] Science was "the connection to the modern world,"[74] and thus Tahrir Province needed to utilize scientific planning methods. Most striking was Tahrir's vision of the modern settler, "without endemic diseases, able to read and write, not wearing the traditional blue galabiyya."[75] To achieve this goal, male settlers were compelled to wear plaid work shirts and dark pants (color-coded to their job descriptions) while women were dressed in skirts and blouses. Settlers participated in daily compulsory physical exercise, as well as exercises to promote individual, family, and group responsibility.[76] Women attended daily and weekly lessons on the importance of family hygiene and regular housecleaning.[77] Settlers attended compulsory religious instruction to eradicate "superstition" and learn "true" Islam.[78] Education and activities were to eradicate the vestiges of pre-Tahrir life and introduce an entirely new, "modern," "scientific" mode of living.

The planners of Tahrir did not create their schemes in an intellectual wilderness, nor were they as far from mainstream Western academic thinking as they might appear today. A General Director of Tahrir Province, Dr. Aziz Sidky, joined the project two years after his graduation from Harvard with a Ph.D. in regional planning.[79] Many of the social scientists at work on the "human conditioning" aspects of the plan were trained in the United States,[80] despite Hassanein's protest that Tahrir was an "entirely Egyptian" enterprise. Finally, Hassanein's ideas embraced some of the economic ideas that were in the air at the time: In particular, that economic development can only follow from massive investments of economic and human capital. Hassanein's thinking was also clearly influenced by Marxist economics—his book is loaded with terms such as "feudalism" and "modes of production"—reflecting some of the admiration widespread in the developing countries of that era for the progress that the Soviet Union had made in the 35 years since its own revolution.

The rivalry between Tahrir Province and EARIS, while present, seems to have been controlled. Hassanein's book made several digs at the EARIS organization for being too timid in its design. At one point, he ridiculed one of the first EARIS brochures for proudly announcing the development of an improved oven for peasant homes. "One of the primary goals [of Tahrir] was to create a completely new society for the Egyptian peasant, and for EARIS, it was to make a new kind of oven."[81] With an almost millennial tone, Hassanein proclaimed that Tahrir "reclaimed the desert and the peasant and the village,"[82] all with the most scientific techniques and all without foreign assistance.

Tahrir appeared infrequently in the American records, and when it did it was generally regarded as a white elephant. Americans were especially skeptical of Tahrir's social component, which was thought both naive and sketchy in its early stages of planning. The first American official permitted to see Tahrir, in April 1954, wrote:

> It appears . . . that along with cooperative farming [the Tahrir planners] have accepted many communal ideas without realizing the great problems involved or the difficulty they will have in obtaining conformity from the villagers. The project officials would probably be better off if they had *no* notions, at the present, concerning the future social organization of the villages rather than the hazy poorly thought out ideas they are accepting.[83]

Most irksome to this official were the impotence of the village council in influencing decisions of the regional government and the role of a "social expert" for each cluster of six villages,[84] who would supervise villagers' adaptation to Tahrir, assisted by a "'socialist police,' completely divorced from the army and the regular Egyptian police force."[85] At least in its conception (for the first settlers had not yet arrived in Tahrir), Tahrir belied its roots as a project of the military regime, and was at its core paternalistic and anti-democratic. The Tahrir slogan of "work, knowledge and justice"[86] seemed to American eyes to reflect the planners' value of those principles in precisely that order. Such priorities lay a shaky foundation for Tahrir and for Egyptian society if Tahrir's principles were expanded to cover distribution of land made available by land reform.

The second American criticism of Tahrir was that it was not economically sustainable as a model for reclamation. Funds for Tahrir were in short supply for the first several months, and their sudden availability in November 1953 coincided with the confiscation of the property of the old royal family, an obviously non-recurrent source of financing.[87] The project cost more than $3,300 per family,[88] leading embassy officials to muse that "a great deal of money is being spent that would probably bring more benefit to Egypt if it were utilized for less dramatic but more productive schemes."[89]

Something to Show for EARIS

The EARIS organization published two brochures during its early months. The first appeared to have been published in the summer or fall of 1954, just prior to the scheduled arrival of the first settlers on the land.[90] Written mostly in Arabic, the first brochure contained a message by Hussein Fahmy, the head of the Permanent Council for the Development of National Production (and, by virtue of that post, co-director of EARIS). The message laid out the importance of eradicating poverty and pointed to EARIS's innovation in establishing a model farm—"not in order to maximize the fertility of the soil, but in spreading prosperity and health and education and raising the standard of living among the new workers and landowners."[91] EARIS had no settlers yet, however, and little to show for its efforts other than heavy machinery that had been moved in place. The narrative of the brochure concentrated almost entirely on plans, committees, and agreements, and, outside of Fahmy's introduction, mostly left the human element out.

EARIS published its second brochure in March 1955, the same month as the arrival of the first settlers. The second brochure drew heavily on the first, although the passage of time allowed the description of far more details and accomplishments. EARIS brought to Egypt 21 45-horsepower medium tractors for plowing, leveling, harvesting, and threshing, 10 large trucks, 26 trailers with multi-ton towing capacity, and 2 80-horsepower heavy tractors. EARIS built 262 red brick houses for settlers in the first village (all supplied with potable water), a mosque, a school, a public laundry, a social center, and more. EARIS prepared 1,120 feddans of land and was prepared to distribute much of it to 88 settler families. EARIS gave each settler a 5 £E grant to cover his family's living expenses during the first six months, and a 33-year balloon mortgage for the land and house under the terms of which payments were not to exceed 45 £E/year.[92]

The brochure faithfully communicated the same message in Arabic and English, and indeed lifts several sections from the earlier, primarily Arabic edition. A significant difference was that since work was slow to begin on the desert reclamation work in Fayyoum and this brochure was so results-oriented, the marsh reclamation projects in Abis overshadowed the desert-based Fayyoum projects even more than it had in previous reports. Given its role as promotional material for EARIS, the second brochure did not mention some of the early problems that the EARIS planners had not anticipated. For one, the planning committee had insisted that all settlers be landless farmers, and thus had not provided for a barber in the village. In addition, the first death in the village pointed up the absence of planning for a graveyard.[93] For the most part, however, EARIS's facilities were superior to those found elsewhere in rural Egypt and initial difficulties attracting settlers were quickly overcome.

It was not only because EARIS had accomplishments to tout that the second brochure had a different tone than the first. Although the English text of the brochure continued the past practice of referring to "settlers," the Arabic captions to pictures all referred to the settlers as "new landowners."[94] The change was almost certainly meant to have an effect on landless Egyptians who aspired to own land,[95] although whether the Egyptian or American staff of EARIS prompted this innovation is unclear.

Several other photograph captions seem to have been modified depending on whether they were directed toward English- or Arabic-speaking audiences. For example, one caption read in English, "The selected settlers, brought to the new village for orientation before they move their families in, inspect their social center. They will undertake new responsibilities for citizenship in the new community." The Arabic translation read "The new landowners upon their invitation to visit the village and see the social center which encourages their hopes for a happy future."[96] Another reads in English, "EARIS staff interview the settlers before they move to their new homes, acquaint them with the conditions of life in the new village," but in Arabic, "A visit of Service officials to the new landowners in their original villages to study their problems before taking them to the new village."[97]

The changes in language, while subtle, testify to the very different audiences for the brochure. The American audience was clearly one interested in community development and social change. The English-language captions tend to convey attitudes of responsibility and partnership, precisely the kinds of values that the American plans for EARIS sought to propagate. The Egyptian audience, by contrast, was more interested in improvements in material conditions. The term "new landowners" is only part of a larger effort throughout the brochure to portray EARIS as an opportunity for settlers to enjoy higher living standards—and by extension, a success of the new government. More immediately, the Arabic captions served to make EARIS more attractive to potential settlers who might be reluctant to leave their homes for an uncertain future.

Aside from the reference in an English-language caption to "new responsibilities for citizenship in the new community," the second brochure was sketchy about the vaunted community development aspects of the program (which had been all but omitted from the first brochure). Indeed, the words "community development" did not appear in the brochure at all. Instead, the brochure described "community services," and in this way: "EARIS experts in social welfare, health, education and agricultural extension promote social improvement in village communities. . . . The aim is to develop and create an improved rural community and to develop the new residents to the point where they can administer their own community. It is expected that the pattern developed by EARIS can be applied in other areas of Egypt."[98] The program was in no way elaborated, nor were the means for its implementation described. By the spring of 1955, community development had become a terse two paragraphs in a twenty-page document.

Among American government officials, the eclipse of community development at the time of settler arrival was ominous. A Washington official wrote Harold Stevens in April,

From a philosophic point of view our participation in EARIS involves, I am sure you agree, the extremely important democratic principle of self-determination, which is so inherently a part of our way of life; our joint responsibility for EARIS in this sense overrides in importance even the "self-help" aspects which are so essential if settlers are to benefit fully and thus contribute most effectively to the development of their own communities. The paternalistic attitude towards the fellahin so prevalent in Egyptian Government circles is a matter of serious concern to qualified observers, who, while they can and do applaud the government's declared policy of improving the living standards of the people, have grave apprehensions with regard to the manner in which the policies are being put into effect—fears for the government itself, which, while its intentions are not questioned, may not be aware of the inherent dangers involved, which might well result in the eventual negation of all their efforts. As far as EARIS is concerned, where the U.S. is a full partner in an understanding involving the destinies of human beings, we cannot afford to be put in the position of being a party to action diametrically in conflict with established democratic principles which are a very part of us.[99]

Another Egyptian Alternative

Egyptians' resistance to some of the "softer" aspects of EARIS in 1955 did not prove that they had turned away from ideas of local development—ideas that, as noted above, predated the American interest in Egypt by more than ten years. In particular, Egypt embarked on a massive program in 1955 to establish social centers throughout the countryside. The program was executed by the Permanent Council for Public Welfare Services, an organization founded in 1953 to distribute wealth obtained from the sale of the former royal family's confiscated holdings in Egypt. Aiming to eradicate rural poverty, the Egyptian program of "Combined Centers" sought to bring health, education and welfare services to the estimated 60 percent of the Egyptian rural population that was beyond the reach of any extant program.[100] Under the plan, each center would have a doctor, a census-taker, a health expert, a midwife, agricultural experts, and an assortment of assistants, bringing the total number of social welfare workers to approximately 25 to serve a population of 10,000.[101]

The scheme differed from EARIS in several respects. First of all, it was not a resettlement program, but rather one of extending services to existing villages. Second, the Combined Centers plan had as its primary aim to increase rural income directly by introducing new activities to the countryside. In pursuit of that, the plan foresaw initiating widespread programs of bee keeping, silk-worm raising, and simple processing of agricultural products in the rural areas themselves, in addition to more traditional activities of animal husbandry and livestock improvement.[102] EARIS was entirely agricultural in its conception. Most significantly, the Combined Centers program represented an Egyptian approach to decentralized power. Specifically, the plan called for substantial autonomy for each participating province, or *mudiriya*.[103] Under the plan, each ministry involved in social services would designate a chief for each province. These chiefs would then constitute a "Regional Services Council" responsible for social services in that province. The Combined Centers would interact with that council, and villages without centers would appoint local committees to interact with the council and utilize their schools as loci for the provision of services, under the direction of a local social affairs expert.[104]

Thus, the Egyptian plan for Combined Centers called for decentralization *from the top down.* The central government provided services, and the fundamental problem was how to distribute those services throughout rural Egypt. The EARIS plan, however, was exactly the reverse, at least as the Americans conceived it. EARIS sought to build social welfare institutions from the village level up. Under this scheme, the larger bureaucratic organs would serve the interests of the local communities, thereby creating the basis for more democratic governance. While the Combined Centers plan would allow for increased bureaucratic efficiency because it coordinated disparate social programs and monitored their application in the field, it did not transfer power from powerful ministries headquartered in Cairo to small village councils, and thus was unlikely to serve as a force for democratization in Egypt.

The reason Egyptian policymakers were especially loathe to decentralize power has something to do with the split in Egyptian society between educated, often Westernized elites and the rural peasantry. An Egyptian author writing on social programs in Egyptian villages commented that it was difficult to get educated Egyptians to work in villages, "especially at first when they have to overcome the villager's suspicious nature, convince him that they really mean to serve him and manage to win his confidence. . . . [But the] fellah is at heart an easy going fellow with a lot of patience, good humor and common sense."[105] Dr. Rizky Anwar, the American-educated Egyptian engineer who led EARIS in the late 1950s, recalled recently that "Most farmers are illiterate and vicious,"[106] and he barred the American community development specialist from living in an EARIS village with his wife out of fear for their safety.

Whereas Americans looked to the Egyptian countryside and saw yeoman farmers, many educated Egyptians looked and saw the poor and destitute who cried out for help and guidance. Turning over control of the governmental apparatus to the poor would be tantamount to allowing the inmates to take over the asylum; while many Egyptians favored administering assistance as effectively as possible, there seemed to be little call in the Egyptian government (or among the Egyptian public at large) for a radical democratic experiment.

Dr. Anwar explained the Egyptian attitude by saying, "To start with a landless farmer and transfer him from his original habitat and then teach him to participate in this new community takes time. The Americans wanted to do this very quickly."[107] Anwar pointed to cooperative societies as the appropriate vehicle for inculcating democracy rather than immediately through the governmental system. Cooperative societies, which had existed in Egypt since the early twentieth century, operated under the guidance of an agricultural engineer. The societies made agriculture-related decisions for groups of farmers. Composed of farmers and with leaderships elected by their members, cooperative societies made decisions within a restricted sphere.[108]

Lack of enthusiasm in Egypt for a radical decentralization of power had at least three other causes as well. The first was that Egypt was led by a military regime, and military officers stood at the helm of many government operations.[109] The majority of Free Officers were in a hurry to improve Egypt and did not wish to tarry while progress needed to be made. As mentioned above in chapter 3, the RCC eliminated opposition political parties in 1953, and tolerance for political dissent decreased as the new regime strengthened its grip on power. Such are not the dynamics of rural democratization. A second reason was that, at least in the initial phases, the rural centers relied almost wholly on the central government for their funds. With no independent source of money they could have no independent source of authority. One author wrote in 1958, "As the public authorities bear the brunt of almost all big projects, the regimentation which ensues is inevitable."[110] A third reason was that Egypt's geography has favored strong central governments from the pharaohs to the present day.[111] The vast bulk of the population is and has always been located along the mostly navigable Nile and in the flat Delta plains. As hills and mountains protected regional autonomy in areas as diverse as Lebanon, Italy and Yemen, so too did the absence of such protection strengthen efforts of those who sought to dominate the Egyptian population.[112] Egypt's capital since the Arab conquest in 639 C.E. has been located at the point where the Nile splits into two branches, allowing the government in power proximity to both the communities clustered along the shores of the river valley and those spread across the Nile Delta.

By the spring of 1955, members of the U.S. Operating Mission in Egypt feared that their hopes to play a constructive role in encouraging Egyptian democracy were doomed. The aid mission's community development officer wrote, after commenting favorably on the Egyptian government's Combined Centers program, and noting Egyptian officials' determination that the centers remain "purely Egyptian" wrote:

> There appears to be a definite attitude prevalent in the GOE that the necessary competence exists in the government to rehabilitate the rural areas of Egypt without outside assistance and there is therefore a reluctance to request or accept assistance of any kind.

> After having studied the present program of rural development . . . it appears that USOM/E could make appreciable contributions to the program in the fields of organization and training. However it would seem to be unwise to attempt to sell USOM/E assistance, therefore it would appear that the mission could make its most effective contribution through the EARIS project. However in the face of existing attitudes in the GOE, the EARIS project to have any appreciable impact on a nation wide development program would, no doubt, have to be an outstanding demonstration, particularly in the phases of settlement, community administration, organization and development. . . .
>
> Within the EARIS organization, at the present time, it appears that neither the environment, organization nor desire exists to accomplish a successful rural development demonstration. Within the Egyptian staff there is a basic lack of understanding of why community development, what it is, how it functions and possible accomplishments. The organization does not have anyone on the staff who is familiar with an overall development program and is seemingly reluctant to hire such personnel.[113]

His colleagues shared his dismay. In early June 1955 the American technicians working on EARIS revolted and sent a joint memorandum to Admiral Stevens complaining about EARIS' organization and execution.[114]

The American Staff Revolts

The staff memorandum had three main complaints. The first was that the "program has suffered from a deplorable lack of active co-direction." The original project agreement called for EARIS to be jointly administered by the head of the Permanent Council for the Development of National Production and the head of the American aid mission, but in practice the two men were "seemingly . . . unable to give an appreciable amount of their *individual* and even less of their *joint* time."[115] Consequently, there was no co-direction at all. The second complaint was that Egyptian administration was unacceptable. The technicians complained that the Egyptian administrator's position "has developed into a form of sole dictatorship, which resulted in a lack of morale in the entire American staff and has created an operation which is becoming the complete antithesis of a cooperative effort."[116] The American with operational responsibility for the U.S. mission's participation in the EARIS program, Roscoe Bell, enjoyed standing only in the American mission. EARIS's organizational chart contemplated no American counterpart for the Egyptian EARIS administrator in order to maintain clear lines of authority, but in so doing effectively ceded complete control of the program to the Egyptians. Bell bitterly protested his impotence to shape the organization, and twice in 1955 recommended to Admiral Stevens that his job be abolished and that the mission no longer entertain the notion that EARIS was anything other than an Egyptian operation.[117] Finally, the technicians complained that the Egyptian administration of EARIS did not effectively utilize the expertise of the Americans detailed to the project. This was in part because many Americans did not have Egyptian counterparts with whom they regularly collaborated, and in part because Egyptian technicians often resented American encroachments on the implementation of their plans. Given that EARIS had become an Egyptian organization, the Americans were uncertain how to ensure that they remained relevant to the operation of that organization aside from funding it.[118]

The technicians also included a curious paragraph in their memo that read, "The U.S. technician possesses a personal and professional dignity and integrity which are his by virtue of his American birthright, training and experience. It is the responsibility of the Mission and EARIS to assure that these attributes are not violated."[119] The statement is presumably a further attack on Dr. Azzouni, since the staff noted that "This situation has developed at a level above the individual technicians, who enjoy a satisfying personal and professional association."

While the technicians' document is damning, it shows little understanding of the predicament in which Dr. Azzouni found himself. While Azzouni did enjoy autonomy in day-to-day administration, he was clearly unable to gain approval from his superiors for major decisions, nor did he have the authority to make those decisions independently. His "dictatorship," then, may have been a response to his actual powerlessness to do the job that had to be done.[120]

The files do not contain a response by Stevens to the memorandum prepared by his technicians, and one may not have been prepared. By mid-1955, EARIS had by most descriptions become an entirely Egyptian program, albeit with the support of American funds and some American surplus land-moving equipment imported from Morocco. The only land ready for settlement had been substantially reclaimed by the Egyptian State Domains Department before the Americans expressed interest in Egyptian development, let alone a project like EARIS. EARIS operated out of the former Royal Palace in Abdin, several miles from both the Point Four headquarters and the American Embassy in Garden City. Egyptians in the Cairo office outnumbered Americans five to one, and no Americans worked permanently in the field alongside hundreds of Egyptian technicians.[121]

This is not to say that the American contribution was not critical to the shape that EARIS took. EARIS throughout its life enjoyed the services of a dedicated and skilled staff, and that staff was recruited and maintained by a system of premium pay and bonuses that the Americans' financial contribution to the program made possible. Egyptians working for the EARIS organization earned up to twice as much as their counterparts in the Egyptian government, and an incentive system provided for annual performance-based bonuses of up to two months' salary on top of that.[122] They also enjoyed better equipment and increased status over their counterparts in strict Egyptian government employ. For example, every engineer working on EARIS had his own jeep, which no doubt made the execution of his job far easier. The increased wages and benefits enjoyed by EARIS employees meant both that morale among Egyptians in the organization was high and that dismissal for failure to perform was a serious threat.[123]

The American financial contribution also created excesses, however. In particular, housing costs in the first village were far higher than could be sustained in any kind of large-scale development program. In the rush to build a model village with well-laid streets and sturdy red brick dwellings with indoor plumbing, housing costs for each unit ran an average 780 £E—450 £E over budget.[124] Although construction costs for the second village were some 30 percent lower than for the first, they were still far higher than had been anticipated, and, more importantly, far higher than could be sustained were the program to be widely imitated throughout Egypt.

In the summer of 1955, the International Cooperation Administration dispatched a team to evaluate the overall American aid program in Egypt. The American contribution of $40 million in Development Assistance funds in November 1954 (which followed the Egyptian government reaching an agreement with the British for the latter's withdrawal from the Suez Canal Zone), combined with the contribution of tens of millions of dollars worth of surplus American agricultural commodities under the newly enacted PL-480 program,[125] had radically changed the aid program in Egypt. The evaluation team arrived to find a mission unsure of itself and unclear how it might carry out its responsibilities effectively.

The evaluation team was led by a Philadelphia banker named R. Stewart Rauch, Jr., and included two ICA staff members. Before departing Washington the team spoke to a wide variety of officials about the Egypt program. The official word was remarkably positive, especially given rising tensions in the Egyptian-American relationship at the time. Two members of the ICA program staff, for instance, felt compelled to refer to the "conspicuously improved relationship between Egypt and the US" compared to earlier in the decade.[126]

The Washington officials involved in community development projects, however, were less sanguine. They had two objections to the mission's operations in Egypt. The first was that the mission's programs were overly tied to the Egyptian ministries, while the real policy decisions were made at a far higher level. In this view, the ministries were the locus of the permanent bureaucracy, which was neither dynamic nor trusted by the revolutionary regime. Action came from the RCC and from the army, and with these organizations the mission had few contacts and little influence.[127]

The second criticism was that the mission's whole approach to development was too command-oriented. Although reference was not made here to Admiral Stevens's military bearing and background,[128] recently resigned Community Development Specialist Carl Taylor complained that the optimal technique was "not to run the show" for the Egyptians, which too often the mission attempted to do. The chief of the Community Development Division in ICA, Louis Miniclier, complained that "there had been little understanding of the human element in the community development program, either by Admiral Stevens or by Mr. Azuni [sic]."[129] The sort of human development that Point Four had stressed in its early days—self-help with gentle guidance from outside—seems to have failed in these officials' estimation on two counts, then: in the execution of actual community development programs, and in the overall organization of the program so as to assist the Egyptians to assist themselves.

The evaluation team was also briefed at length on the shortcomings of the new Egyptian government. An Egyptologist with experience in the CIA and OSS opined that Abdel Nasser was "well intentioned and reasonably capable, within his limits. He does not know how to run a government. His advisers are totally incapable."[130] The Office of Trade, Investment and Monetary Affairs complained that the "Army people, in charge of RCC, are not politically and economically skillful," thereby drying up the supply of private investment capital.[131] The State Department group was perhaps the most positive about the Egyptian regime. They described the RCC as "relatively good, relatively liberal" but facing "serious if not insuperable economic problems."[132] Adopting the position of realists, one officer commented that "We regard the regime as the best in sight, want to maintain its stability, help it with its economic development problems."[133]

The evaluation team arrived in Egypt on June 19, 1955 and stayed for just over three weeks. The team maintained an active schedule of meetings and tours, and consulted with both U.S. government and Egyptian government officials. They reserved some of the harshest words in their final report for the EARIS program, writing that it had become "a travesty on its original concept."[134] Their criticism of EARIS fell into five areas. The first was that the Egyptian administrator (and, the team presumed, his government) believed in Egyptians' ability to carry out all operations unaided, and thus failed to capitalize on the American staff present. The second was that the organization's administrative structure meant that for a matter to get joint consideration it had to pass through the Egyptian administrator, whom Americans perceived to be hostile to them and their ideas. The third was an absence of Egyptian counterparts for American technicians, particularly in community development and education—precisely the areas in which American ideas were seeking to have the greatest impact. The fourth involved revising accounting methods that made it difficult to retain skilled and semi-skilled workers. Finally, attitudes in the EARIS program were at loggerheads: the Egyptian technicians often were loath to adopt new methods, and the American technicians often favored "telling people" how to do things better rather than "cultivating a receptive attitude."[135]

In practice, Egyptians reclaimed land in Buheira and Fayyoum with little input from American experts. The Egyptian administrator, Dr. Azzouni, often vetoed collaboratively arrived at suggestions from Egyptian and American staff, thereby discouraging effort and innovation at lower levels. The evaluation team complained that too many decisions had to reach the administrator at all, thereby both creating a bottleneck and nullifying the co-direction aspects of the program.[136] The team recommended establishing positions of "Deputy Co-Directors" of EARIS, in order to inject active American co-direction into the project. They also advocated accentuating the experimental philosophy of EARIS so as to encourage more flexibility from Egyptian technicians.[137]

Overall, the team expressed the belief that many of the problems in the Egyptian aid program were far bigger than the aid program itself. They wrote:

> It is obvious that no one in Egypt is responsible for the current indecision in the US cotton policy; the Israeli intransigence in Gaza; the decision to encourage signature of the Turkey-Iraq military pact; or Sudan's reluctance to sign an agreement with Egypt in connection with Nile water rights. . . . These four factors outweigh all others in determining Egypt's attitude toward the US and, indirectly, the extent to which Egypt is willing to accept US counsel and guidance in solving her economic problems.[138]

On particulars, however, the American program in Egypt was still seriously lacking.

The team assigned part of the blame for this to the lack of any planning body within the Egyptian government to coordinate ministerial requests for foreign aid, creating a situation in which no one in Egypt had a clear idea of how much aid was being received or from what source.[139] The observation is odd, because the task ought to have been subsumed in the charge of the PCDNP—the body whose wide-ranging development plans formed the basis of plans to utilize $40 million in American aid to Egypt nine months earlier. The observation on the part of the evaluation team suggests two things: first, that the ministries had successfully formed their own relationships with foreign organizations and agencies with little involvement of the central government, and second, that the PCDNP had by this time become marginalized.

Part of the blame, too, was shared by an administrative system in Egypt in which authority was delegated sparingly to lower echelons. As a consequence, "top officials, including Prime Minister Nasser, are burdened with countless minor decisions which make concentration on key issues virtually impossible."[140] U.S. government officials shared the blame for possibly having "oversold" the benefits of American cooperation in the early days of the Revolution, thereby giving the Egyptian government "exaggerated expectations of the physical benefits which would accrue to Egypt from the U.S. technical assistance program."[141] The team criticized American officials who signed agreements to "improve Egyptian agriculture," thereby setting the goals so grandly that the actuality could not fail to disappoint. Under fire as well were overly tedious and restrictive regulations emanating out of Washington. The team quoted at length a cable from Ambassador Byroade to Washington complaining that endless red tape drove the Egyptians to procure a large order of railroad engines from Hungary rather than from U.S. suppliers. Byroade termed the confusion Washington had created "scandalous," and said many in Egypt hereafter foreswore any interest in bidding on future contracts with the American aid program.

Looking forward, the report concluded that the mission should be looking to reduce its size, since many of the mission's labor-intensive cooperative technical projects would soon be ripe to be assumed entirely by the government of Egypt. Development assistance—the capital-intensive, labor-extensive projects that had come to dominate American overseas aid by that time—would continue in the future. The most important outstanding project was the High Dam at Aswan, and construction was unlikely to begin on the program during FY 1956.

The evaluation team's report appears never to have been shown to the government of Egypt, and in fact remained a classified document. Back in Washington, officials in the International Cooperation Administration commented favorably on most of the Rauch team's findings, although they defended their lack of coordination with overall U.S. foreign policy goals because so doing required a timeliness and clear direction from the State Department that they were unlikely to receive.[142]

EARIS continued to reclaim land through 1955 and 1956 until American cooperation terminated with the onset of the Suez Canal Crisis. Settlement in the second village began after the 1956 war, although Americans were not involved. When the American aid program to Egypt resumed in 1958, EARIS was among the first programs to be resumed, and it continued to operate as a joint program until 1963, three years after the original termination date.

Differing Assessments

While American technicians working on EARIS in the mid-1950s thought it to be a project beset by problems, many Egyptian and American technicians look back upon it as a success. Egyptians, in particular, regard EARIS as one of the most successful projects of its kind in the history of Egypt. Concentrating as they were on assessing the physical progress the organization achieved, Abis in particular became regarded as a thoroughly successful land reclamation project. Abis now supplies the city of Alexandria—only five kilometers away—with vegetables. Land values have multiplied more than one hundred-fold. It is now perhaps the richest land in the Buheira Province.[143] It stands in the estimation of some as "a spectacular success"[144] and "the most successful land reclamation project in Egypt."[145] Although Abis may not have succeeded in creating a politically active peasantry along the lines the Americans first envisioned, Egyptian engineers who worked in the EARIS organization recalled goal-directed work, a "spirit of learning," and a spirit of innovation.[146] EARIS certainly left a lasting impression on the engineers who worked on the project, although this appears to have been a remote goal in the planners' minds. The large number of settlers who have constructed second floors on their houses attests to the wealth of the Abis area, as do stories of sons able to pursue education because their families were able to survive economically without their labor.[147]

Current estimations of EARIS's success make it difficult to assess the program. An AID evaluation study in 1983 noted that "the impact of the project on the income and wealth of the beneficiaries has been enormous,"[148] but conceded in an appendix that "It is highly unlikely that the overall project is economic."[149] One consultant on the study estimated that the $1,400/feddan cost of EARIS (including infrastructure) was more than twice the amount acceptable to Egyptian planners in the early 1960s.[150]

Most striking, however, are Egyptians' and Americans' differing assessments of the project. Egyptians believed that they possessed the technical skills to reclaim vast areas of land in their country, and lacked only the capital and the heavy machinery to do so.[151] The EARIS program gave them both, in addition to the ability to work side-by-side with world-class reclamation experts. Egyptians who worked with Americans in EARIS were engineers and technicians, and they enjoyed the added benefit of working on a relatively small, elite project, mostly insulated from the political calculations suffusing ministerial projects. They were, in other words, allowed to exercise their full professional judgment, and the experience stood as a contrast to programs in which they worked previously and subsequently.

Americans, however, had very different goals for EARIS. Inspired at least initially by the belief that simple American know-how could make vast inroads against the scourge of poverty in the post-colonial world, Americans perceived the EARIS organization as a sort of hothouse for Egyptian-American collaboration on both the technical and sociological roots of rural Egyptian poverty. Much more than a reclamation project, Americans conceived

EARIS as a partnership that would lay the basis for radical change in the Egyptian countryside. As plans for the High Dam at Aswan progressed, the stakes for EARIS rose even higher. With the dam, Egypt would almost surely reclaim more than one million additional feddans of land and resettle more than one million Egyptian farmers and their families. Americans hoped that such a massive change in Egypt would be carried out along lines that the U.S. government believed to be consonant with America's long-term interests in Egypt and the region.

EARIS, it seems, was never able to establish a stable identity as a joint operation. From the opening days it seemed to have suffered from neglect from its co-directors. Indeed, true collaboration seems scarce even in the first stages of the project, when American officials outlined plans for various aspects of EARIS administration, and representatives from the cumbersome Egyptian ministries were somewhat belatedly included in meetings to draw up plans. Egyptians were able to establish control over the organization because of their superior numbers in EARIS and the fact that their operational responsibility meant that they were the ones who truly controlled what happened in the field. Language barriers played a role as well,[152] as did Egyptians' superior understanding of their domestic bureaucratic culture.

EARIS's greatest failure, however, may not have been its inability to make the "servicio" concept[153] work in Egypt, but rather its failure as an archetypal reclamation and resettlement project. Driven by the desire to make EARIS something different from and better than anything which had preceded it in Egypt, EARIS's reliance on premium salaries, premium facilities, and premium management helped ensure the success of the project itself, but not the success of the overall American development program in Egypt. To be fair, experiments and prototypes are rarely cost-effective taken by themselves, and they must rely on future imitations and iterations before their costs can be recouped. In this light, it is perhaps not surprising that the EARIS experiment proved more expensive than extant Egyptian methods of land reclamation.[154] But in point of fact EARIS spawned no imitations; its costs could not be spread among several projects that built on the EARIS model.[155]

The reasons for this may have something to do with the politics of the time. EARIS settlers arrived in March 1955. In the previous month Iraq had joined the Baghdad Pact, a pro-Western military alliance bitterly opposed by the government of Egypt but quietly supported by the United States. Also in the previous month, Israeli troops attacked an Egyptian base in the Gaza Strip, killing more than 30 Egyptian soldiers and civilians. Abdel Nasser took the raid as a sign of his pressing need for arms, and when the United States repeatedly rebuffed his efforts, he sought those arms from the Soviet Union, via Czechoslovakia. The Western press was beginning to sour to the revolutionary regime in Egypt, and the Egyptian press was beginning to sour to the West. Times were bad for promoting American yeoman democracy in the Egyptian countryside.

More important than the immediate political milieu, however, was the Egyptian domestic context. Egyptian officials appear never to have embraced fully the ideas about which Americans waxed lyrical: the landowning farmer, collaborative activities among neighbors, and grassroots democracy. Americans had to rely on graphs, charts, and a hard sell to convince their early Egyptian collaborators that community development planning had to begin at the same time as land reclamation and major works planning. Hindered by language barriers and an inability to casually visit projects in the field, Americans could not monitor the development of what they thought was the most important component of EARIS, that is, the development of American-style communities in rural areas.

In the years after 1956, Egyptian development followed a pattern unlike the two great social experiments of the earlier part of the decade: EARIS and Tahrir Province. The path taken was something of a combination of the two, with collective farming over a general framework of land ownership. The government abandoned Tahrir's brand of mandatory group activity even in Tahrir, but did mandate membership in agricultural cooperatives for the vast number of farmers.

Ultimately, the very different EARIS and Tahrir programs were both driven and foiled by the same need for quick, demonstrable results. Although American policymakers were seeking a long-term program of investment to promote change, their Egyptian counterparts did not feel they had the luxury to wait for long-term results. This is not to say that land reclamation in each locale did not represent an investment, for surely it did. Rather, the rapid rise and fall of the social aspects of both projects underlines the dramatic urgency that Egypt's leaders felt toward economic development in the early 1950s.

Chapter 5 ~

The Aswan High Dam

Few observers of the Egyptian economy in the early 1950s believed there was any hope of improving conditions in the countryside without an ambitious plan of land reclamation. The important raw material in land reclamation was water, both to wash salinity from the soil and to irrigate the soil once it had been cropped. Under extant irrigation practices, Egypt was using something on the order of 52 billion cubic meters (m^3) of water annually out of a river discharge at Aswan that averaged 93 billion m^3 annually in the years 1871 to 1945.[1] Using aggressive land reclamation practices, the Egyptian government hoped to utilize as much as 84 billion m^3 of the water, thereby increasing cultivated land by estimates that ranged from 25 to 50 percent. In order to gain complete control over the river flow, a high dam or series of dams would have to be built upstream to hold back floodwaters before they washed down the river and into the sea.

To those in the Egyptian government immediately following the revolution, the idea of a High Dam at Aswan held two other benefits. The first was the provision of cheap hydroelectric power that might be used to sustain energy-intensive industries such as fertilizer manufacturing and smelting, in addition to any number of smaller industrialization products in the country. The second was that a High Dam at Aswan could be a powerful symbol of the revolutionary government and its plans for the country. Seventeen times the size of the pyramids at Giza,[2] the Dam would be a project of the Ages.

From the project's inception in 1952, Egyptians contemplated American participation in constructing the High Dam. Americans, after all, led the world in dam engineering and irrigation projects. The American government had also indicated a keen interest in Egyptian economic development as part of its larger strategy of fighting Communism by fighting poverty. A drawn out effort to elicit American participation frustrated Egyptian officials in the early 1950s, however. Flood seasons came and went with the Americans asking for more studies and evaluations as conditions of participation. Egypt won preliminary approval of joint American, British, and World Bank financing in December 1955. But Egyptian officials did not fully realize the extent to which the highest levels of the American government would condition financing for the dam—an absolutely vital economic project in the Egyptian mind—on Egyptian cooperation in making peace with Israel. As financing unraveled through the spring of 1956, splits seemed to develop in American government policy toward Egypt. The American Ambassador in Cairo remained committed to the dam project, and he grew increasingly frustrated with foot-dragging in Washington. Meanwhile, the State Department implemented a joint U.S.-UK plan to isolate Egypt in the Middle East, a component of which was to allow dam financing to "wither on the vine." Finally, CIA briefings of Egyptian officials in Washington indicated a desire to lead the Egyptian government back toward cooperation with the Americans. Egyptian officials correctly read the conflicting American mood, and Abdel Nasser privately decided that he would nationalize the Suez Canal Company and use the revenues of the company to finance construction of the dam. It was clear Americans would no longer build the dam, a project that Americans and Egyptians agreed was the key to Egyptian economic development. If Egypt were to develop economically, it would do so without the participation of the U.S. government.

Egyptian Irrigation

Because Egypt receives negligible rainfall through the bulk of its growing area, Egyptian agriculture has always been dependent on irrigation. For much of history, Egyptians relied primarily on a method of basin irrigation connected to the annual flood of the Nile. Under that system, expanses of 1,000 to 40,000 feddans contiguous to the river were flooded when the Nile rose and remained flooded for 40 to 60 days. In the intervening period the ground absorbed water, and silt from the river settled, enriching the topsoil. After that period—by which time the river had fallen—the fields were drained using simple gravity, and seeds were planted in the rich, damp soil.[3] The basin system allowed a single crop per year, generally the winter crops of wheat, barley, berseem (clover), onions, beans, and lentils.

Muhammad Ali, who ruled Egypt from 1805 to 1848, made two great contributions to Egyptian agriculture: the spread of perennial irrigation methods and the introduction of long-staple cotton.[4] With regard to the former, in 1816 Muhammad Ali began improving the river banks and building a canal system under the supervision of his Minister of Public Works, a Belgian engineer named Linant de Bellefonds.[5] Canals enabled farmers to irrigate their fields at times other than when the flood was at its highest point, and thus allowed more than one crop per year. Thirty years later, plans were underway to build several barrages[6] in the Nile Delta, the effect of which was to raise the level of the river during its lowest point, generally in June and July. These months happen to coincide with the middle of the cotton-growing season, and the heightened water level permitted continuous watering of cotton and other crops through the heat of the Egyptian summer.

Interest in more ambitious irrigation projects began to grow in 1867 and continued through the end of the century, especially with the arrival of British irrigation engineers with Indian experience to supervise all manner of improving Egyptian agriculture.[7] These efforts culminated with the construction of the first Aswan Dam in 1902,[8] subsequently heightened during the period from 1907 to 1912 and again from 1929 to 1934.[9] The Aswan Dam had two principal effects. The first was to allow the storage of flood waters for their release during the low water season (thereby enabling widespread perennial irrigation), and the second was to afford some protection from uncontrolled flooding.

An Ambitious Plan

In 1946, three engineers working for the Egyptian Ministry of Public Works—Harold Hurst, R. P. Black, and Yusuf Simaika Bey—put forth an ambitious plan to even further expand the area of arable land in Egypt. The premise of their argument was that to maximize agricultural production, Egypt had to:

1. convert all of its agricultural land to perennial irrigation
2. maximize the amount of water reaching Egyptian agricultural lands
3. maintain the river at a constantly regulated level so as to ensure that the irrigation canals remained full.[10]

The elimination of basin irrigation would pose something of a hazard to Egyptian agriculture and to Egyptian cities in the Nile flood plain (which is to say, virtually all of them). Without basins in Upper Egypt to absorb excess water, a high flood might continue directly down the river and overrun the banks in Cairo and throughout the Nile Delta. At the same time, the expansion of agricultural land meant that if there were a year with a low flood, huge areas of Egyptian farmland might be drought-stricken.

The solution they suggested was a plan for over-year storage of water, or what they called "Century Storage."[11] They reasoned that a truly vast reservoir system could both absorb the highest of floods and build up a sufficient reserve of water to be used to eliminate the threat of several years of low floods. The most difficult part of their calculations was determining how large the reserves would need to be despite having less than 50 years of solid data on water discharge and an additional 30 years of less accurate data from which statistics could be computed. They knew that the flow of the river could vary markedly. Although the average of the years for which they had data was 93 billion m^3/year, actual totals were as low as 42 billion m^3 in 1913–14 and as high as 133 billion m^3 in 1894–95.[12] They also knew from the data they had that years of shortage and years of plenty tended to arrive in cycles, meaning that the storage capacity would have to be very large both to absorb several consecutive years of excess water and to supplement several consecutive years of shortage.[13] To arrive at their conclusions, Hurst, Black, and Simaika examined 75 different natural phenomena (including series of tree ring data and sedimentation data, some stretching back 4,000 years) to determine with reasonable confidence where the outer extremes of the variability of natural phenomena lay over a vast series of time.[14] Their conclusion was that such a project would require something on the order of 155 billion m^3 of total reservoir capacity.[15]

Hurst, Black and Simaika proposed that two extant central African lakes which feed the Nile—Lake Albert and Lake Victoria—be dammed and used as reservoirs for a Century Storage plan.[16] Because rainfall on both lakes was approximately equal to evaporation losses and because their steep sides meant capacity could be greatly increased without greatly increasing the lakes' surface area (thereby reducing evaporation losses), central African storage was thought superior to storage in the Sudan or Upper Egypt. Locating the reservoir in Egypt or the Sudan would mean that the reservoir would be a vast shallow pool in the middle of a desert and would lose huge amounts of water to evaporation.[17] The Century Storage proposal for the two lakes was part of a larger, more ambitious Nile control scheme they advanced incorporating additional dams, reservoirs, and canals in the Sudan and Egypt.

In 1948, an Egyptian agricultural engineer of Greek ancestry named Adrien Daninos conceived a proposal that combined the Century Storage idea of Hurst, Black, and Simaika with a proposal to site additional storage capacity at Aswan, rather than in the central African mountains. The next year he approached international experts connected to the United Nations and won preliminary endorsement. Daninos's plan held the promise of both storing some 150 billion m^3 of water mostly within Egypt's boundaries, and generating significant hydroelectric power which could be used to fuel Egypt's industrial development.

Whatever its merits, Daninos's plan was not warmly received. The Ministry of Public Works' experts judged it an impossible project, in part because the reservoir would extend over an expanse of water-permeable sandstone, resulting in severe water losses through seepage. In addition, high temperatures and low humidity in the region of Aswan would mean that billions of cubic meters of water would evaporate every year, undermining attempts to build up a reserve.[18]

A mere week after the revolution occurred in July 1952, Daninos set out again to sell his idea of a High Dam at Aswan. He was more successful appealing to generalists than specialists, and in October the Revolutionary Command Council requested that the Ministry of Public Works' in-house staff—Hurst, Black, and Simaika—examine Daninos's plan and put forth their opinion. In their report to the RCC, they conceded that the Daninos proposal for Century Storage at Aswan might possibly have an equivalent effect to their own Century Storage proposal for central Africa. In order to make a determination, however, extensive studies—partly to determine the precise contours of the proposed reservoir, and also to investigate the nature of the rock in the area—would be necessary. They further suggested that if their own scheme for storage in the African lakes were combined with Daninos's proposal, the total arable land in Egypt would increase from the 7.1 million feddans that either project could irrigate individually to 8 million feddans.[19]

The anonymous member of the RCC staff[20] who forwarded the experts' memo to the leadership had little interest in the African lakes scheme. In his cover memorandum, he compared the Daninos plan not to the Hurst, Black, and Simaika plan to utilize the African lakes—the official plan of the government since 1949—but rather to a series of smaller plans to be carried out in Egypt and the Sudan. In such light, the High Dam at Aswan plan proved far superior. This was especially true because of a high dam's capacity to generate vast amounts of electricity that could be "the basis for the anticipated industrialization of the country, which will rapidly raise the standard of living among the populace and solve the problem of the increase in population."[21] Urging the immediate commencement of further feasibility studies, the memorandum suggested that if the Egyptian governmental budget were insufficient, the government should approach the American Point Four administration for assistance. Thus, the Americans were linked to the High Dam project since its inception. The memo further suggested that the Egyptian government enlist an international team of hydrologists present in Egypt to investigate an irrigation scheme in Wadi Rayyan to explore the Aswan basin, establishing a pattern of cooperating with international experts which would also characterize the project.[22]

While the High Dam generated significant enthusiasm in government circles, Adrien Daninos did not. Daninos had a checkered history with the pre-revolutionary government. He brought suit against it in 1947 for its failure to award him a contract for land development before the war, and subsequently complained loudly and forcefully against the entire governmental apparatus, from the Prime Minister on down.[23] His estimates for the possible additional amounts of Egyptian land that could be reclaimed—ranging from 13 million feddans in 1945 to over 50 million feddans in 1951—were fanciful, and gave him something of the appearance of a quack.[24] Several months after the revolution, a World Bank officer wrote of Daninos in a memorandum to his files, "Whether a crackpot, I do not know, but investigation would tell whether his scheme had merit, irrespective of his personal idiosyncrasies."[25] Daninos' ignominy was sealed barely a year after the revolution, when a team of international consultants were deliberating on specific plans for the High Dam. According to a Point Four memorandum of conversation with one of the consulting engineers,

> Mr. Steele mentioned Mr. A. Daninos, an Egyptian resident, who claimed to be an engineer and originator of the High Dam proposal. He considered this person incompetent as a dams engineer and noted that Mr. Harza [another of the consultants] had to write a strongly worded letter to this gentleman requesting him to desist from interfering with the deliberations of the American members of the International Consulting Board.[26]

While Daninos enjoyed brief fame in Egypt after the revolution as the mastermind of the High Dam scheme,[27] the purpose of such accolades were more to demonstrate the wisdom of the Free Officers than their embrace of Daninos. Profiles of Daninos fell into a genre of reporting which emphasized that the Free Officers' plans for progress in the "New Era" endorsed ideas or persons present in Egypt before the revolution but ignored by the previous government. The purpose was to reinforce a sense of national pride by suggesting that Egypt's problems arose not from a paucity of resources but rather of governmental acumen.[28]

Although tentative approval for the High Dam plan came in the early fall of 1952, it wasn't until late November that the Minister of Public Works "declared [the] new Aswan Dam [a] top priority project" and dispatched a technical team south to begin testing the potential reservoir bed.[29] On November 10, Prime Minister Naguib sent a memo to the American Embassy asking for an immediate grant of wheat, and a long-term grant of $100 million for several economic development projects, chief among them the High Dam and the attached hydroelectric works. The American Ambassador was dismayed by the high dollar amount requested, as well as Egypt's seeming determination to proceed with the dam before the completion of the requisite feasibility studies. He complained to Washington, "Such projects as construction of [a] new Aswan Dam and [the] creation of [an] iron and steel industry are chimerical at [the] present juncture and would in *no* way meet [the] more urgent economic needs of Egypt." He went on to complain that members of the RCC were "economically illiterate" and expressed hope that the industrial survey[30] might present an opportunity to educate them on what Americans considered an appropriate development plan.[31]

The Aswan High Dam Moves Forward

Despite deeply held American reservations about the dam project, it continued to move forward. Plans for the dam received a boost when Germany announced it would pay "Israel and representatives of world Jewry" 3 billion marks as reparations for the Holocaust.[32] Hoping to quell charges of favoritism toward Israel, the West German government quickly approached the Egyptian government about assisting with the High Dam. On October 18, 1952, a consortium of two German companies "submitted proposals for the preparation of tenders for the design, execution and financing of the dam," and a month later the Egyptian government requested that they send technical experts to Aswan to begin designing the project itself.[33]

So began an interesting phenomenon in the historiography of the dam. Most of the scholarship on the dam completed in the 1960s and afterward have stressed the involvement of German engineers and consultants in the project.[34] American involvement, when it has been mentioned, has generally been limited to financing—a role which the American government rather publicly renounced in July 1956. Such accounts are influenced by the politics of the soured Egyptian-American relationship after 1956, but they poorly portray the hopes and plans of the period before then. In fact, American engineers were deeply involved from the start in planning the dam and in carrying out feasibility studies.[35] The government of Egypt repeatedly approached the United States for assistance—which was often granted—and as time passed many in the American Embassy came to identify the dam project as the linchpin of the future of Egypt, and of America's involvement in Egypt. A growing number of Egyptians doubted the wisdom of relying on the United States to construct the dam, but those involved in the engineering aspects of construction (rather than the political aspects) appear to have had an affinity for the United States and its store of the leading dam and land reclamation experts in the world. The Americans involved in preliminary studies considered German involvement a distraction from the eventual likelihood that the dam would be an American project. By the time that Western financing for the High Dam was withdrawn in 1956, the Germans had long been reduced to bit players.

Concurrent with the Egyptian government's approach to the Germans, the Egyptian government also formally requested American assistance for preliminary studies. They reached agreement that the United States would finance an American firm's execution of an aerial survey of the proposed dam basin for $300,000, and that the U.S. Army Map Service would process the photographs.[36] The FY 1954 foreign aid budget included an additional $150,000 to bring the survey to completion.[37] In January 1953, the Egyptian Finance Minister wrote to the World Bank (known officially as the International Bank for Reconstruction and Development, or IBRD) seeking financial support for the dam project. The Bank responded that it would first require a $200,000 site reconnaissance study (to be financed by the United States government), and then consider large-scale financing only upon completion of a study of the dam's possible impact on all the countries in the Nile Basin. The Bank estimated that it might take as long as three years until it was ready to go ahead with a decision on financing.[38]

Although the American commitment to the High Dam project was still small in absolute terms, it aroused alarm among some in Washington. In a bid to win support for the High Dam, the Director of the TCA program in Egypt penned a long letter to the agency's administrator in Washington in April 1953. He wrote, "*This water must be stored, this land developed, these millions fed and clothed,* by whatever means are necessary to the task. Not to do so has so obvious portent of intensified human misery, accelerated political corrosion and impending threat to world peace as to banish the alternative." He concluded by recommending that "a minimum of $20,000,000 per year for six years be considered as appropriate in aid of this project."[39] Such aid levels, however, far exceeded the levels considered appropriate for technical assistance at the time. A TCA economist in Washington scrawled on the top of the letter, "Still *very* vague—'big money minded'—and contemptuous of Pt IV. . . . The estimates of *aid* are utterly premature."[40]

In the spring of 1953, congressional support for aid to poor countries was maintained only by the fact that the dollar amounts were relatively low and the returns reported to be very high. The altruistic impulse was under attack from budget cutters alarmed by high levels of taxation after World War II, and the fear that foreign aid would be a steady drain on the U.S. Treasury motivated many. Coming at this time, then, proposals for multi-million dollar, multi-year American commitments to develop the Egyptian economy were received coolly in Washington, and no such commitment for Egyptian aid was forthcoming. In fact, the Cairo director of TCA was removed from his position within months, and the aide who was suspected of authoring the long memo left Cairo several months after that.[41]

With or without American acquiescence, the dam project gained momentum. In March 1953, the German consortium Hochteif and Dortmunder Union presented preliminary plans for a High Dam project to the government of Egypt based on their investigations of the Aswan area. The plans called for a hundred-meter high and five-kilometer long rock-filled dam, with electric works on the western bank. Submission of the plan was not reported in Cairo's main daily papers, perhaps suggesting some uncertainty on the part of the Egyptian government toward the viability of the project.[42] The government of Egypt then invited an international team of five consultants[43] to review the German plans, which they did the following month. The German plans flabbergasted them. The consultants stated that they had insufficient information to draw any firm conclusions, but added that the German plans were predicated on the false premise that the riverbed had a rock bottom at no more than 83 meters, when in fact the rock bottom was far below that. Consequently, they judged that the plans were "inappropriate" for the prevailing conditions at the site. They suggested that numerous additional studies were required before they could render a judgment on the feasibility of a High Dam at Aswan.[44]

In private, the American consultants were even less charitable. One, I. C. Steele, told an official of the Technical Cooperation Agency:

> The German Report proved to be a detailed technical presentation with recommendations for practically all elements of the structure. This reviewer was amazed to see such detailed recommendations based on such preliminary and incomplete data, and in some cases no data. It appeared to be prepared with the view to impress the casual reader with the volume of theoretical considerations involved in a large engineering project. . . . Mr. Steele refrained from direct criticism of the German efforts but it became rather plain during discussions that this report was of little technical value to the Government of Egypt in furthering its aim to realize a High Aswan Dam.[45]

The Embassy and Operations Mission sent a joint cable after the consultants' report was completed which echoed Steele's views. They wrote:

> German action to date has virtually been limited to the dispatching of a few engineers who have made some preliminary surveys. They have, however, produced some fine-looking designs for a huge earth rock-filled dam and the Egyptians have naively assumed that the much-vaunted technical genius of the Germans has thus easily settled the question of the project's feasibility, leaving only a small amount of additional field work to be done. Until the Egyptians disabuse themselves of this misconception, any overt American attempt to be of further assistance on the project will be regarded with suspicion if not hostility by the Egyptians.[46]

The Cairo press corps, however, reflected the jubilant optimism of revolutionary progress rather than the sober caution of the consultants. One magazine reported that Egyptian officials told the international panel, "'We don't want compliments. Tell us even your smallest doubts, and we will give them the greatest consideration.' The experts shook their heads and said admiringly, 'There is nothing more to add. Sound work speaks for itself.'"[47]

In this environment, members of the RCC decided to proceed on the dam on political rather than technical grounds and enlisted the press in their campaign. The Egyptian leadership appeared to equate caution with opposition, to the frustration of American Embassy officials who wished for the success of the regime but feared embarking on so grand a project with such faulty preparation. In an attempt to gain control over the situation, the U.S. State Department in the early autumn of 1953 contemplated assuming the cost and responsibility for completing all of the remaining field surveys "and any other studies or work" to determine the dam's feasibility, although it appears to have rejected this course of action.[48] Henry Byroade, then Assistant Secretary of State for Near Eastern, African and South Asian Affairs and the future American ambassador to Egypt (and future High Dam proponent), told Egyptian Finance Minister Abdel Galil el-Emary in mid-September, "We do not wish to leave half-finished structures as monuments to failure, and therefore we hesitate to commit funds for surveys lest they lead to a commitment which we cannot see through to a conclusion."[49]

Byroade's reluctance can be read in at least two ways. The first is in light of the problem of congressional appropriations for long-term, capital intensive aid projects. A ten-year project—which the High Dam was—would require the support of five successive Congresses, and if any of them rejected the High Dam project it would freeze construction in whatever status it was at the time. Another way to read Byroade's reluctance, however, is as an expression of caution over identifying the United States too closely with a project that might prove unfeasible or be executed poorly once construction began. Failure on the High Dam might be blamed on the United States, creating a huge downside risk for those who wished to promote American interests in the Middle East.

The Challenge of Financing

The International Bank for Reconstruction and Development, or World Bank, provided precisely the fig leaf that Byroade wanted to preserve. World Bank financing would not require the biennial approval of congressional authorization and appropriations committees. In addition, World Bank representatives could use their position as bankers protecting the safety of their capital and demand additional studies and assessments of the dam project without being seen as trying to undermine the government of Egypt. Finally, the Bank had close enough relations with the U.S. government that the latter could count on the Bank acting in a way consonant with American governmental interests.[50] In this way, coordinating American foreign aid policy with the World Bank (which had been independently considering the High Dam project since el-Emary wrote Bank President Eugene Black in January of that year) would allow Americans to take much of the credit for what went well while distancing the United States if conditions worsened.

Throughout 1953, the High Dam had far more support in the U.S. Operations Mission and U.S. Embassy in Cairo than in the Washington bureaucracies. In its preliminary budget request, the Embassy asked that $2 million be allocated in FY 1955 for engineering studies of the High Dam.[51] After the proposals made their way through the Eisenhower Administration, the Foreign Operations Administration (FOA) requested only $500,000 for an engineering study and a desk study of the Nile Valley.[52]

Part of the problem with initiating a large-scale American aid program at this time was the status of ongoing negotiations between the British and Egyptians. The issues in dispute were the continued British military presence in Egypt and the status of the Sudan, which had been ruled jointly under an Anglo-Egyptian condominium since 1899. Negotiations had begun before the revolution but remained stalemated, partly because the central dynamic of the pre-revolutionary political environment in Egypt centered on each party trying to be more anti-British than the next. The government of Great Britain was greatly concerned after the revolution that the United States apply pressure on the Egyptians to arrive at some acceptable settlement with the British. In 1953, Prime Minister Winston Churchill and Foreign Secretary Anthony Eden personally intervened repeatedly with President Eisenhower and Secretary Dulles to delay the award of significant aid to Egypt for fear of increasing Egyptian recalcitrance in the negotiations.[53] Although the State Department expressed frustration with the British—both because they clung to maximalist negotiating positions and because they hamstrung American policy toward Egypt—the American officials continued to honor the requests of their British allies. It was this intervention during the first months of 1953 that confounded the Egyptian Chief of Air Force Intelligence, Ali Sabri, who was in Washington trying to work out an arms deal. He left in February, bitter and convinced that the United States would never supply Egypt with arms.[54]

The perceived languor with which the rest of the world viewed aid to Egypt in general, and treated the RCC's Aswan project in particular, raised ire in Cairo. The pro-Western secretary of the National Production Council, Muhammad Selim, complained to the head of the American aid mission in November 1953 that "the IBRD had done nothing for the Middle East and did not appear to be interested." He added that "compared to other countries, Egypt had not been well treated in respect of U.S. economic aid."[55] Selim may have been thinking in particular of an article which appeared in the weekly news magazine *al-Musawwar* the previous June, which reported that Turkey enjoyed $70 million per year in economic aid and $150 million per year in military aid from the United States—six times what Egypt received.[56] In December

1953, still lacking what they believed was a firm commitment by Western powers to the dam project, Selim said that "Egypt would do it itself if necessary."[57] Three weeks later, an Embassy political officer with close ties to the RCC cabled Washington, "A usually well-informed Egyptian source has stated that . . . the RCC has taken a definite decision to proceed with construction of the High Aswan Dam. . . . Recent meetings of the RCC . . . had been devoted to the study of a specific plan for financing the construction of the dam without relying on foreign assistance." The cable concluded:

> The Egyptian government is aware of the financial strain which such a course of action will entail but simply cannot wait any longer for the Western powers to make up their minds whether or not to help Egypt in what is considered to be the one project which can bring about any significant increase in national production. He implied that Egypt would be glad to receive foreign assistance, notably from the IBRD, but would be prepared to carry through the project on its own resources if necessary.[58]

Although the U.S. government was able to forestall any effort to gain outside funding, relations between Egyptian and American government officials grew more tense through 1954. In a typical instance, news that topographical maps based on aerial photography the FOA had commissioned would not be ready until September 1954—a full year after the photography was completed, provoked dismay on the Egyptian side. Selim complained:

> This information might seriously affect the attitude of GOE top political circles toward the USAOM/E program as a whole. He stated that already this group is very dubious of the value of USAOM/E assistance, and that he thought the further disappointment of a major delay in delivery of the High Dam aerial maps would make the establishment of new assistance projects increasingly difficult.[59]

Amidst growing dissention over what Egyptians perceived to be tepid American support for the High Dam, on the political front the government of Egypt reached an agreement with the British government on July 27 over the Suez Canal Base. The agreement raised expectations in both Egypt and Washington that American aid to Egypt would increase, both as a reward for Egyptian behavior and because aid to Egypt could no longer be construed as working against British interests in the country.

The U.S. Embassy Gets on Board

Whether to preserve their position with the Egyptian government in Cairo or because of a true conversion to the merits of the High Dam plan, the U.S.

Operations Mission in Cairo and the Embassy became unabashed supporters of the High Dam plan in the autumn of 1954, when preparing their FY
1956 budget requests. An Operations Mission assessment in October 1954
judged that Egypt's highest economic priority was developing agriculture
and natural resources, and "within this field of activity emphasis must focus
on bringing additional desert land into cultivation through the Aswan Dam
project and through conserving and improving production on existing cultivated land areas."[60] Turning apocalyptic, the Mission identified the future
economic well being of Egypt with the construction of the High Dam, noting, "Unless the estimated 2 million additional feddans of cropped land to
be provided by the construction of the High Dam at Aswan are brought into
production, Egypt will be unable to supply food for its people and will enter
a period of progressive deterioration."[61]

Throughout October 1954, dire predictions of what would happen without the dam continued to flow from U.S. government officials in Cairo. One
cable to the State Department stated, "Without the High Aswan Dam, the
outlook for Egypt appears hopeless."[62] The American aid mission in Cairo
predicated its aid proposals on the proposition that "in the final analysis,
Egypt's only hope for 1) economic viability, [and] 2) ability to feed her population . . . lies in the construction of the High Dam at Aswan," and consequently recommended that U.S. aid funds for fiscal years 1956 to 1958—a
proposed grant of $40 million for each of the three years—be allocated *in
their entirety* to the High Dam project.[63] In an interesting twist, the Mission
proposed that Congress authorize all $120 million in FY 1956, so as to "lay
the economic base necessary to attract loan financing by the IBRD of part of
the remaining balance required to complete the [dam] structure."[64]

As suggested above, part of the Embassy's enthusiasm for the High Dam
project may have arisen from an expectation that they soon might have tens
of millions of dollars to spend. While Egyptians were thinking such aid
would total $100 million or more, even the lower $40 million figure finally
agreed to by the United States represented a significant sum of money. The
economic aid figure was higher than most Americans in Cairo expected in the
summer of 1954, since they thought any aid amount would have to be split
between military and economic assistance. In the late summer, however, it became apparent that the U.S. government would grant only economic aid to
Egypt because the conditions attached to American military aid were unacceptable to the Egyptians. The Mutual Security Act of 1954 stipulated that
countries receiving military assistance from the United States had to agree
that the American arms would only be used for legitimate defense and internal security, and that recipient countries had to accept a Military Assistance
Advisory Group to supervise implementation.[65] The government of Egypt,
still wary of foreign entanglements in domestic affairs, and having just gotten

an agreement to oust British "advisers," refused the conditions attached to American military aid.[66]

Although an agreement to award Egypt $40 million in American economic aid was signed on November 6, 1954, the U.S. government continued to explore avenues to provide Egypt with additional American military aid. Specifically, the CIA dispatched Colonel H. Alan Gerhardt and Colonel Wilbur C. Eveland to Cairo in late November to meet with Abdel Nasser and his aides to further explore a military aid agreement. The effort was ultimately unsuccessful, because the CIA could not circumvent the requirements of U.S. law, and Abdel Nasser felt that domestic politics precluded his signing a Mutual Defense Agreement. The CIA representatives did arrange, however, to give Abdel Nasser $3 million in cash, and to permit $5 million of the $40 million economic aid package to be used secretly for military purchases.[67]

Also in November 1954, an international panel of consulting engineers met for several weeks in Cairo and finally gave the go-ahead for construction on the dam. Of the five primary consultants, three were from the United States: I. C. Steele (who had objected to the German design in March 1953), Lorenz G. Straub and Karl Terzaghi. Andre Coyne of France also participated, and the German Max Pruess participated as an expert on the dam's ability to withstand bomb damage.[68] Although the local Egyptian press quietly noted their presence in Egypt, it did not report their deliberations. The consultants' report appears not to have been published, although engineering publications summarized its contents and noted how the four non-German consultants threw out the German plans and constructed one of their own, over the objections of Pruess.[69]

The imprimatur of the international engineers further piqued the interest of the World Bank. In November 1954 two Bank-sponsored engineers traveled to Cairo to study the engineering plans. In late January 1955, Bank economist John de Wilde went to Cairo and spent six weeks gathering information about the Egyptian economy and its capacity to service foreign currency loans for a project as vast as the High Dam.[70] Toward the end of his trip, de Wilde told an Assistant U.S. Treasury Representative in the Middle East that in his opinion:

> [D]uring the next decade and a half the problem will not be how to raise or maintain the standard of living but how to keep it from falling too fast. The High Aswan complex is the keystone in any development effort directed toward this end, inasmuch as it is the only project on the horizon capable of slowing down the rate of decline [of per capita income] sufficiently enough. In effect the High Dam postpones the disaster inherent in Egypt's population surge, gaining, one would hope, sufficient time for science, birth control, and

exploration for as yet undiscovered resources to combine in providing a solution to this Neo-Malthusian dilemma.[71]

Dire as the need for the dam was, however, the Bank was unwilling to shoulder the entire burden itself. In particular, estimates for the total foreign currency requirements of the project ran at approximately $300 million, and Bank economists assayed that Egypt did not represent a "good bankable risk" for a loan of that size. Consequently, funding for construction would have to come from a number of sources, with a U.S. grant in aid representing a significant component of total financing.[72]

Foreign aid for the dam was contingent on political factors as well as economic ones. Concurrent with the signing of an American assistance agreement in November, British Foreign Secretary Eden began floating ideas of a joint U.S.-UK effort to promote a peace plan in the Middle East. Code-named Alpha and only getting underway in January 1955, the plan sought to use a method patterned on the successfully completed negotiations over control of Trieste in October 1954. In that case, a joint U.S.-UK proposal for settlement—including territorial compromise and financial inducements for each side—solved a dispute between Italy and Yugoslavia that had been smoldering since the end of World War II. In the case of Trieste, the keys to settlement were limiting the amount of negotiating that would take place, and winning approval for the settlement from each country's leaders before the terms of the plan became public.

In the exploratory period of Alpha discussions, American and British authorities agreed that the Egyptians should be approached before any other party, in part because their agreement would have made it difficult for Israel to continue arguing that the Arabs did not desire peace.[73] Throughout these discussions, too, officials in Washington and London mentioned funding for the Aswan Dam as the chief inducement to the Egyptians. Several times in the early months of 1955, high-level officials in the State Department attempted to gain approval from Secretary Dulles and President Eisenhower to mention specific funding figures for American support for the High Dam—generally an initial grant of $20 million for early work and another $100 million over five years for construction—when the time came to raise Alpha with Abdel Nasser.[74] Eisenhower and Dulles were extremely wary of promising large-scale multi-year aid to the Egyptians at so early a stage in the process, and there is no evidence that such aid levels were discussed.

Whether by coincidence, intuition, or intelligence, in late March 1955 Abdel Nasser and his foreign minister, Mahmoud Fawzi, approached American officials and broached the issue of exploring a peace agreement with Israel.[75] At the time, Ambassador Byroade had been waiting for an opportune moment to raise the issue with Abdel Nasser. The Egyptians' seizing the initiative, however, raised hopes of Alpha's success. Immediately following the discussions, Fawzi and Abdel Nasser departed for the conference of nonaligned nations at Bandung. Although Washington-based officials were clamoring for Byroade to again raise Alpha with Abdel Nasser upon his return from Bandung, Byroade continued to report back that the time was not ripe, either because of Abdel Nasser's dark mood or escalating tension on the Egyptian-Israeli border. Abdel Nasser again raised the issue of obtaining American arms that spring, which the Department of Defense undertook to study.[76]

With the matter of American financing for the High Dam still unresolved by the summer of 1955, lower-level American officials working on aid to Egypt found themselves having to fight for the program anew. The Foreign Operations Administration dissolved itself July 1 and the International Cooperation Administration assumed its responsibilities in the foreign aid arena. Unaware of the Alpha plan and perhaps sensing that a proposal as large as the High Dam would meet a cool reception from the conservative Republican political appointee who led the ICA, a staff agricultural economist in the Cairo mission explained, "If the U.S. is to be interested in anything in Egypt we must be interested in this; we have so much technical experience in huge project developments that we can be of enormous assistance to Egypt in all phases of the project."[77]

Continued haggling over arms sales to Egypt in the summer of 1955 culminated with the Egyptian purchase of tens of millions of dollars worth of Soviet-bloc arms from Czechoslovakia.[78] Rather than poison the atmosphere of Egyptian-American relations, however, the deal had the effect in at least some arenas of making significant U.S. aid seem a more urgent priority. Weeks after news of the arms deal broke, Cairo papers ran lead stories citing nonexistent American reports that the Soviet Union had offered to finance the High Dam.[79] It marked the first time that news of the High Dam appeared on the front page of the Egyptian daily *al-Ahram,* perhaps indicating that Egypt's leaders finally believed that the dam would be built, with or without American financing. The Operations Mission in Egypt continued to hope that it would be built *with* its participation. In its funding proposal for FY 1957, the mission wrote in mid-October 1955:

> The only means available to the United States for combating or neutralizing this Soviet offensive in Egypt is to concentrate on assistance to the Government of Egypt in its economic development plans, which center around the construction of the High Aswan Dam and its related projects.
>
> The Communists have offered assistance in this program also, and if the United States is to counter their efforts the only course of action open is to endeavor to assist the Government of Egypt to reach agreement with the Sudan on the division of the Nile waters and then to help the Government of Egypt work out a financing scheme for the Dam.[80]

Signs began to abound, however, that the bloom was off American aid. The Operations Mission cautioned Washington that there was "increasing suspicion of, and growing indifference toward, US technical assistance. . . . [I]f FY 56 development aid is withheld for long or, if when offered, the amount should be deeply disappointing, [the Government of Egypt] may well decide to reject all US aid, including [Technical Assistance]."[81] Concurrently, negotiations among Western powers over proposals for financing the dam began to take their final shape. Undersecretary of State Herbert Hoover Jr. cabled Secretary Dulles in Paris that he had met with World Bank Chief Eugene Black and Secretary of the Treasury George Humphrey, and that they had agreed that Egypt required $400 million of foreign exchange over 15 years to finance the dam. They agreed that the IBRD could contribute $200 million, the U.S. $134 million, and the UK $66 million.[82]

The nascent IBRD offer, however, was competing not only with a Soviet offer but also with one from an Anglo-French-German consortium. Under that arrangement, individual governments would underwrite the work of their own countries' firms on the dam. The consortium offer had the distinct advantage for the Egyptians of not requiring that a comprehensive agreement with the Sudan be reached regarding compensation for flooding and division of the Nile waters prior to the beginning of any construction—negotiations that could possibly take years to complete. American officials in Cairo were stung by British participation in the consortium, since it was their understanding that the British shared the American commitment to financing through the IBRD. Americans also saw British perfidy in their apparent disinterest in pressing the Sudan to reach an agreement on sharing Nile waters despite Britain's perceived ability to do so.[83]

What transpired in the late autumn of 1955 was a poker game between British and American officials over dam financing. The British government continued to explore the possibility of executing the project without U.S. involvement, while the Americans were adamant that lack of American participation would mean the lack of U.S. funding. In the event, Whitehall gave in to the pleadings of the British ambassador in Washington, and agreed to the logic that any Western proposal to finance and build the High Dam should be the product of joint consultation between the U.S. government, the British government, and the World Bank.[84]

The Egyptian Mission to Washington

Despite a strong willingness by American government officials to freeze out other financing options, a firm American offer was still delayed. The Egyptian Minister of Finance, Abdel Moneim al-Kaissouni, led an Egyptian delegation to Washington in late November to try to conclude an agreement with the United States and the World Bank. A briefing paper preparing the U.S. Undersecretary of State for a meeting with the Egyptian Minister of Finance in November averred, "We are not now in a position to give assurances regarding what the U.S. may contribute financially other than to say that we strongly favor the project and its early commencement."[85]

While the delegation was in Washington, a rumor began to circulate there that Abdel Nasser had threatened to accept the Soviet aid offer if an IBRD proposal was not received by January 1. The Cairo Embassy denied hearing reports of any specific threat, but reminded Washington that it had reported in October that Egyptian officers working on the dam project told the IBRD representative that the government of Egypt would be "free to act" by January 1956. The Embassy assured Washington that the Egyptian regime "unquestionably prefers Western assistance to Soviet aid regarding which performance is unknown and untested."[86]

The Embassy seized the opportunity to remind the Department of State of its strong support for the dam project and the risks of not coming forth promptly with American financing. In a long cable on November 28, the Embassy again reiterated the importance of the project to Egyptian economic development, and the "mass starvation and consequently growing social and political discontent" that would likely arise if the dam were not built. The High Dam, the Embassy wrote,

> is thus a "must" for Egypt. . . . If Kaissouni can not obtain before [his] departure from Washington satisfactory assurance [of] Western assistance for [the] High Dam, [it is] not unlikely [that the Government of Egypt] will, out of desperation and with little delay, accept [the] Soviet offer [of] High Dam aid. This would, of course, be [a] major setback for [the] U.S., the effects of which would be far-reaching and probably irreparable.[87]

The Embassy's urgent support for the project, however, appears to have increased its isolation from Washington. Just two days later, in a thinly veiled plea to the Department of State, Ambassador Byroade complained that the Egyptians and British appeared well-informed about negotiations in Washington, yet the American Embassy in Cairo had to rely on the British Embassy for information. The American Embassy was thus prevented from playing any constructive role in the ongoing diplomacy.[88]

As negotiations in Washington drew to a close, the Soviet bogey again grew large. The aid mission in Cairo justified its request for increased American aid to Egypt over the next eleven years by stating that were the Western powers not to invest in Egypt now, it "would intensify internal pressures to accept Soviet bloc offers [of] financing, which are now pyramiding." The aid mission repeated its belief that members of the Egyptian cabinet "do not want Soviet bloc aid but are forced to it unless [the] West provides it. They much prefer United States aid, technical and financial."[89]

Supporting Egypt only in the face of Soviet offers for aid, however, created the possible appearance that Egypt might be drawing some reward from its policy of nonalignment with the Western powers. The State Department in particular found this appearance troubling, not only because allies like Turkey and Pakistan might feel that they had derived less than they might have from their support of American foreign policy, but also because of the threat that other nations in Asia might feel that their best hopes lay in neutralism rather than alignment. Consequently, the State Department distributed talking points to its Middle Eastern embassies that emphasized that American interest in the High Dam long predated the Czech arms deal, was a characteristically altruistic endeavor by the American government, and represented only a small amount of money compared to the billions that the United States had granted to allied countries in the region. In addition, the cable tried to portray the project as a Western project financed by the IBRD rather than a tool of American foreign policy.[90]

The Egyptian negotiating team left Washington December 18 carrying with it three interconnected offers to finance construction of the High Dam: a draft letter of intent from the IBRD to loan Egypt $200 million, and *aides mémoire* from the American and British governments to provide initial grants of $54.6 million and £5.5 million, respectively. The financing would be sufficient to cover the first phase of construction of the dam—construction of a coffer dam—estimated to take some four years. After the coffer dam was built, additional American and British financing would be forthcoming to bring the project to completion. In order to preserve its freedom of action, the Bank delivered its letter of intent unsigned and informed the Egyptians that once all of the terms of the IBRD, American and British offers had been accepted, Bank President Eugene Black would approach the executive directors of the Bank and ask that the final commitment be approved.[91]

While American negotiators believed at the time that the negotiations had been successful, the response of many Egyptians was disappointment. In a searing interview between American officials in Cairo and the custodians of the High Dam program for the RCC, the latter lashed out at the IBRD for what they believed was a demeaning and paternalistic attitude toward Egypt. They complained that the Bank officials passing judgment on the Egyptian plans were entirely ignorant of conditions in Egypt and the problems of constructing a vast project in a remote area hundreds of miles away from a major city. They further complained that the Bank's insistence on competitive bidding for all aspects of the project would delay construction even further, and for no perceptible benefit. They also protested Eugene

Black's implication that the American and British offers of preliminary financing were insufficient guarantees of the additional aid required by the Bank's letter of intent. Finally, the Bank had reserved to itself various powers to "intervene . . . in the internal and external affairs of Egypt" without a clear delineation of when such powers might be asserted. "On the other hand . . . the Bank has committed itself to very little," they complained, while "what little it has committed itself to is subject to review in the event that 'exceptional circumstances' should intervene. What were 'exceptional circumstances'? They might be anything."[92]

The Egyptian interlocutors explained the opinion of many in Cairo that the negotiators had left Washington without sufficient assurances of financing to begin the project. The Embassy's reporting cable on this discussion and another one like it expressed alarm that the United States seemed to be alienating Muhammad Selim, the American-educated Secretary of the National Production Council. The Embassy protested that Selim was "enthusiastically pro-West and has proved on every occasion [to be a] valuable friend. . . . We were shocked to find Selim . . . greatly disappointed and even resentful of treatment received from World Bank."[93]

The Embassy proposed that the Bank could meet most of the objections of the Egyptians by being more explicit about their future actions. There was no simple solution, however, to Abdel Nasser's fear that an agreement with the West on High Dam financing would give the West a "virtual veto" over Egyptian national security expenditures. The Cairo Embassy proposed that the United States government demonstrate maximum flexibility on "technical, administrative and engineering grounds" so as to overcome Egyptian reservations in other areas.[94]

Salvaging Alpha

Concurrent with the negotiations in Washington, planning was underway to make a last-ditch effort to save Alpha. Alpha had lain dormant for months, and the shipment of Soviet-bloc arms raised the fear that the Israelis might launch a preemptive military strike against Egypt before the assimilation of those arms gave the Egyptians military superiority. Once war broke out it would be difficult to contain and the resultant instability would not only provoke a regional war but also make Soviet entry into the dispute all but inevitable. Fear of a preemptive strike meant that negotiations had to be successfully concluded in an exceedingly short time frame, probably less than three months and certainly less than six.[95] Washington's plan was to send a special presidential emissary to conduct highly secret discussions with Gamal Abdel Nasser and Israeli Prime Minister David Ben Gurion. Encouraging the process were indications that Abdel Nasser would be willing to make peace with Israel, his secret approach to the Americans shortly before leaving for the Bandung Conference (noted above) and an agreement with the CIA in December 1955—still classified to this day—to make peace with Egypt's northeastern neighbor. Under the terms of that agreement, the peace process would be carried out in three phases: a narrowing of Arab-Israeli differences via an intermediary, a period in which Abdel Nasser would build Arab support, and finally face-to-face negotiations between Abdel Nasser and Ben Gurion.[96]

Eisenhower chose for the mission Robert Anderson, a close personal friend with no particular experience in the region.[97] His status as a neutral party in the Arab-Israeli dispute, as well as his friendship with the president, were hoped to be conducive to productive diplomacy. In addition, his lack of present government office gave him some anonymity and allowed his highly sensitive negotiations to remain secret. In a private meeting with the President and Secretary of State before his departure, Dulles told Anderson that the United States held four bargaining chips to use with Egypt, paraphrased as:

1. Concentrating the Baghdad Pact on a Northern tier defense and not soliciting additional members from the Arab states, essentially ceding leadership in that sphere to Egypt,
2. Helping (or hurting) Egypt's cotton market, which provided 80 percent of its foreign currency earnings,
3. Providing financing for the High Dam,
4. Possibly constructing a second canal over the Sinai Peninsula, financed by the oil companies and adding to Egypt's revenues.[98]

Although it was clearly discussed, there is no indication whatsoever that U.S. representatives—presidential, diplomatic, or intelligence—ever made a clear link between High Dam funding and the Anderson mission in discussions with the Egyptians. The American bargaining position vis-à-vis Israel was left more vague. Essentially, Dulles sought to convince the Israelis that they were in their strongest bargaining position now, before Soviet-bloc arms gave the Arab side military superiority over the Israelis.[99]

Knowledge of Anderson's visits to Cairo was held extremely closely in the Egyptian government. Only Interior Minister Zakaria Mohieddin[100] and the Director of the Prime Minister's Office for Political Affairs, Ali Sabri, were aware of and participated in the discussions.[101] The U.S. Embassy staff in Cairo—initially including the ambassador—also appeared to be left in the dark, as was the U.S. Embassy in Tel Aviv.[102] The Anderson missions appeared to have been run in close cooperation with the CIA station in Cairo, utilizing the CIA's extant relationships with the Egyptian government's leadership, the analysis of Cairo-based CIA operatives, and the CIA station's separate transmission channels for coded messages.[103] Although the precise details of the CIA's involvement with the Anderson mission remain classified, many years later CIA regional chief Kermit Roosevelt admitted to playing a leading role as an intermediary between Anderson and the Egyptians. The grammar surrounding the excised matter in declassified U.S. documents indicates that at least one Cairo-based CIA officer was involved in the series of meetings with Egyptian government officials.[104]

Anderson, accompanied by his CIA retinue, first met with Abdel Nasser and Zakaria Mohieddin on January 17, 1956. Over the course of an informal four-hour dinner at the latter's residence, Abdel Nasser posited that Arab attitudes toward cooperation with the West had hardened since the formation of the Baghdad Pact and the Gaza raid in the early part of 1955. Over the long term, however, he was "relatively confident of his ability to dispose of a settlement between Egypt and Israel and still maintain a strong position in the Arab world." Indeed, Anderson concluded that Abdel Nasser was far more captivated by the idea of assuming the leadership of the region than the idea of sealing a regional peace, and Abdel Nasser hoped that the Western powers could use their influence to build up his leadership.[105]

Over the course of the next several days, the Egyptian leadership continued to meet with Anderson and the CIA. Abdel Nasser made clear his belief that steps had to be taken on the Arab side to "establish an atmosphere" in which the Arab states would accept a settlement, and such steps would take time. He also firmly refused the face-to-face negotiations desired by Ben Gurion. After Anderson shuttled to Israel, CIA representatives remaining behind drafted a letter to President Eisenhower for Abdel Nasser's signature. The letter, which Abdel Nasser agreed represented his views, pledged not to attack Israel, accepted the UN resolution on Palestine, and promised an end to blockades and secondary boycotts of Israel upon conclusion of a settlement. In exchange, the letter expressed the need for a "continuous and substantial" land link between Egypt and her Arab neighbors to the East, repatriation and compensation of Palestinian refugees, and the right of Jordan to decide on the final status of Jerusalem. While Abdel Nasser authorized the letter's authors to state to Eisenhower that the letter represented his views, he refused to sign it until the Israelis signed a similar letter.[106]

Anderson returned to Cairo at the end of January. He briefed Abdel Nasser and Zakaria Mohieddin on his talks with the Israelis and established a mechanism whereby Zakaria Mohieddin and Ali Sabri would meet at regular intervals with CIA representatives to both work toward proposals to solve the Arab-Israeli conflict and monitor efforts to build support for such proposals in the Arab world.[107] He then retreated to Athens to allow time for such work to take place.

Approximately upon Anderson's departure from Egypt, IBRD President Eugene Black arrived in Cairo to discuss financing for the High Dam. The visit was wholly unrelated to Anderson's trip, and negotiations were rocky as Abdel Nasser and his subordinates continued to complain that the Bank committed itself to very little while reserving for itself the prerogative to intervene in vast areas of the Egyptian domestic economy. Black remained uninformed about the Anderson mission, although Undersecretary of State Hoover urged Black four days after his arrival in Cairo not to present Abdel Nasser "with a take or leave it proposition," for reasons which were unspecified but which Black was assured involved "vitally important considerations of [the] highest interest to [the] entire Western world."[108]

Through February, calls grew in the United States to supply Israel with American weapons to defend itself against the growing military might of the Arab armies.[109] The announcement of a shipment of tanks to Saudi Arabia on February 16 created an even greater clamor in Washington. Queries from Washington for advice on how the damage from an arms sale to Israel might be minimized among Arab countries drew panicked responses from Ambassador Byroade and Kermit Roosevelt to the effect that not only could such a response not be minimized in any way, but that any arms deal with the Israelis at the current time would end any possibility for Arab-Israeli rapprochement.[110]

Lower levels of the Embassy, entirely uninformed about the Anderson mission, were growing frustrated at apparent difficulties in the Egyptian-American relationship. The Embassy and the Operations Mission sent a joint message to the Department of State and the ICA in late February. They wrote:

> The United States has not fully realized the beneficial effects on its relations with Egypt which might reasonably be expected from its Egyptian aid program. This has been due in part to the fact that the requirements, conditions and procedures involved in the giving of aid have been such as to create frustrating delays, have not always taken due account of Egyptian sensibilities, and have caused tension between American officials, on the one hand, and Egyptian officials, on the other, including those most friendly toward the United States.[111]

Aid to Egypt, however, had by this time risen far above the ability of the Egypt desk officers in Washington to affect. Congressional appropriations for the initial tranche of American aid for the High Dam were unlikely to be obligated before June 30, the end of the fiscal year, in which case they would revert to the Treasury. Because of hostility in Congress toward the High Dam proposal, and Government Accounting Office regulations that restricted fiscal sleight of hand, it was unclear how the U.S. government might be able to remain involved in the Aswan project.[112] While the Anderson mission held out the prospect of succeeding, as yet it had yielded no fruit.

Anderson quietly and on short notice returned to Cairo March 3, only to discover en route that Abdel Nasser expected to be fully occupied with several days of meetings with the leaders of Jordan, Syria, and Saudi Arabia. Anderson insisted that he could not wait until those meetings concluded, and Abdel Nasser, Ali Sabri, and Zakaria Mohieddin met with Anderson and at least one CIA representative for three-and-a-half hours the night of March 4, and again the evening of March 5. Perhaps chastened by his discussions with other Arab leaders during the day, Abdel Nasser expressed extreme caution toward moving toward peace with the Israelis. In particular, he insisted that Egypt negotiate a settlement through a third party and not with any Israeli or American Jewish negotiators. He further asserted that Egypt would not advance peace proposals on its own, but rather would lead an Arab response to proposals advanced by the United States or some other third party. At the same time, he countered Americans' urgency over the possibility of war by suggesting that war could be averted in Sinai if Israeli and Egyptian troops each withdrew one kilometer from the border, separated by a strengthened UN peacekeeping contingent.[113]

The American interlocutors were stung by Abdel Nasser's positions, which seemed both firmer and more pessimistic then those he had expressed in previous discussions. Gone was any promise to "deliver" Arab support for a peace treaty; Egypt now refused even to bind itself to supporting American proposals which it would have had a hand in drafting. Anderson wrote angrily that Abdel Nasser's position was "inconsistent with the idea that we have continuously discussed that Egypt assume the position of leadership in the Arab world and of having the national prestige and courage to make proposals which the other Arab States could be induced to adhere to."[114] He concluded, "What we can most realistically hope and work for is not the settlement of the dispute but the avoidance of war."[115]

Later the next day a new cable analyzing the discussion was drafted; the language and argument are sufficiently different from the first cable reporting on the meeting to suggest that it had a different author, although it also went out with Anderson's approval. The second cable was more understanding of Abdel Nasser's predicament. It did not accuse him of perfidy, and it appeared sympathetic to the challenge Abdel Nasser faced building and preserving a position as an opinion leader in the region. Whereas the cable written immediately after the meeting expressed some disgust with Abdel Nasser, the cable written the next day mused that the most immediate problem was tempering the reaction of the Israeli leadership when it discovered that a settlement was not imminent.[116] Writing a day later from Athens, Anderson was even more temperate. He expressed Ambassador Byroade's view that Abdel Nasser's positions must have reflected his discussions with other Arab leaders that weekend and the CIA station's view that "growing restiveness" among Palestinian refugees in Jordan and Syria made peace with Israel more difficult.[117] Glosses on the situation failed to assuage a travelling Secretary Dulles, however, who in a "speculative exercise" on March 8 suggested a major shift in American policy toward Egypt, isolating Egypt in the region, supporting Egypt's foes, and selling defensive arms to the Israelis.[118] Four days later, when Anderson briefed President Eisenhower and Acting Secretary of State Hoover on his trip, Eisenhower decided that Abdel Nasser had "proved to be a complete stumbling block" to the Anderson mission, because he was "apparently seeking to be acknowledged as the political leader of the Arab world." Eisenhower decided that the best course to take would be to undermine precisely the kind of Arab solidarity Abdel Nasser was seeking to build in the region. Such action would at the same time reduce Abdel Nasser's influence and make more unlikely the outbreak of a coordinated Arab attack on Israel.[119]

Omega

Immediately thereafter, Fraser Wilkins, the Director of the State Department's Office of Near Eastern Affairs, drafted a Top Secret memorandum that posited that "there seems little likelihood the US will be able to work with Nasser in the foreseeable future." Wilkins advised that dramatic public actions would provoke a dramatic public response by Abdel Nasser, and consequently advised a quieter course of action. In particular, he recommended that over the next month the United States delay the conclusion of several pending agreements with Egypt. These agreements covered not only U.S. financing for the High Dam, but also export licenses for military goods and PL-480 food aid. Wilkins expressed the hope that such actions would lead Abdel Nasser to "soon conclude that relations with the US were not proceeding smoothly and would raise the question with American officials. The response might be that friendly relations between countries are reciprocal." Concurrently, Wilkins suggested a series of moves to counter Egyptian influence in the region and step up American ties with surrounding states, and that these activities be coordinated with Great Britain.[120]

A week later, the British Ambassador in Washington delivered a long memorandum to Secretary of State Dulles explaining the British government's appraisal of the situation. Although it was not clearly a response to Wilkins' memorandum, it was similar in approach and tone. It observed that Abdel Nasser had gained great popularity in the Arab world because he stood up to the West and acquired Soviet-bloc arms, and that consequently,

"Whatever policy we pursue, we must expect increasing hostility from Colonel Nasser."[121] Perhaps not surprisingly, the primary difference between the American and British memoranda is that the former concentrated on isolating Egypt and Abdel Nasser, and the latter concentrated on aiding Egypt's opponents in the region like Iraq, Jordan, and Saudi Arabia, all of which had close ties to the British.

These machinations appear not to have been lost on the Egyptians. Between the time that Wilkins drafted his memorandum and the British sent theirs, an Egyptian diplomat in Washington, Anwar Niazi, perceived a definite chill in Egyptian-American relations. In an internal memorandum he wrote that the American press had

> recently begun to attack the Egyptian government and say that the American government is reconsidering its policy toward Egypt. While some attacks seem Zionist-inspired, the news of reconsidering policy toward Egypt seems inspired by the Department of State. This may be because the Department had faith in its policy toward Egypt but is disturbed to think that Egypt hasn't acted accordingly.[122]

Niazi went on to outline several points on which the U.S. government had supported Egypt, including not bowing to Israel despite pressure from its supporters in the U.S., refraining from joining the Baghdad Pact, and earmarking for the High Dam nearly twice what Israel would get in aid for the current year. He continued that a Republican victory in the 1956 elections would benefit Egypt because Zionists had less influence among Republicans than Democrats. Egypt could help promote that outcome, he argued, by toning down its anti-Western and anti-American propaganda in the Middle East. In return, Egypt could expect to receive American funds for the High Dam, American PL-480 aid, and an assurance that the United States would not wage a trade war on Egyptian cotton nor place a strict quota on the American importation of that cotton.[123]

A March 28 version of the Wilkins memo became the basis for a presidentially sanctioned plan to put the Egyptian government on notice that its policies must change. Wilkins's new memo differed from the March 14 version primarily in that it portrayed Egypt as being more threatening to Israel, and it spelled out extensive coordinated Anglo-American regional activities to isolate Abdel Nasser. The policy was carefully tailored not to provoke a split with Abdel Nasser and the Egyptian government, but rather to arouse concern in Cairo and invite the question of how Egyptians might improve their relationship with the United States.

Pursuant to the new policy, a representative of the U.S. government—described in the Egyptian documents only as "a high ranking official known to us and known to be friendly to Egypt and the Arabs," and possibly Kermit Roosevelt—met with Egyptian Ambassador Ahmed Hussein the next day in Washington. The purpose of the visit seemed to be twofold: to send a message that Egypt faced threats from many quarters, and to assure Egypt that American friendship could be won if Egypt adopted a more friendly posture toward the West. On the former, the American official said he "would not dismiss the idea that the Israelis would try to assassinate Abdel Nasser," and blamed negative articles appearing in the press on Egypt's British and Zionist opponents. On the latter, Ambassador Hussein's interlocutor warned that

Cairo must take a position since its current position cannot be maintained. While Egypt is saying it is a friend to Western countries and requests various kinds of assistance from those countries, we find that Egypt is actually following a hostile policy toward those countries and does not refrain from attacking them and provoking people against them. Egypt must choose one of these two policies, and if it chooses hostility against the West, the West will have to decide its stance on that basis.[124]

The message appears to have gotten through to Cairo. A U.S. operative there reported that during the course of a meeting April 1, Ali Sabri "said he and Nasr [were] extremely upset by fears that [the] US Government and [the] UK Government have taken some secret policy decision to destroy Nasr and [the] position [of] his Govt in [the] area."[125]

Exactly what decisions the American and British governments took remains unclear to this day. Following President Eisenhower's decision March 28 to isolate Egypt, the U.S. government established an interdepartmental Middle East Planning Group under the leadership of Douglas MacArthur II.[126] In an operation code-named "Omega," the group set out to implement the policy directives already approved by President Eisenhower and to pursue other options. The records of Omega remain largely classified because they constitute the details of an intelligence operation. However, the recent availability of the memoirs of the former British Ambassador to Washington Sir Roger Makins tell us more about Omega than we have ever known. According to those memoirs, the American proposal for Omega:

Envisaged withholding aid to Egypt, giving the Iraqis a powerful transmitter to counter Egyptian propaganda, bolstering the Western position in the Middle East and the Baghdad Pact . . . and encouraging France and Canada to send arms to Israel. The Americans wanted . . . to win the Saudis over from the Egyptians by persuading the British to make large concessions over Buraimi. This would allow the United States, so Eisenhower thought, to consolidate its position in Saudi Arabia and to build up King Saud as an alternative leader to Nasser in the Arab world.[127]

Extent American records suggest a three-phase process: a month-long "freeze" in aid agreements, followed by a three-month period of canceling remaining aid programs and building up regional rivals. The details of phase three remain classified, but likely involved efforts to promote domestic political challenges to the regime.[128]

Although among the goals of Omega were ostensibly to "bring around" Abdel Nasser and leave him "a bridge back to good relations with the West if he so desires,"[129] the records thus far declassified contain exceedingly little discussion of how such a result might be achieved or how a change in Egyptian policy might be determined. The records also show no evidence that the Omega group was closely monitoring the actions of the Egyptian government.

One party definitively left out of the intrigue in the spring of 1956 was the American Embassy in Cairo. Ambassador Byroade pleaded with Secretary Dulles for guidance on Aswan Dam financing, noting that he sent a proposal more than a month before and followed up two weeks later, all with no response.[130] He concluded that the "fact I am not informed [with] reference [to the] Department's thinking notwithstanding my recent trip to Washington will be increasingly apparent to top levels here." The Department declined to provide guidance, although it replied it was "mindful . . . [of the] difficulties which this silence causes you."[131] A week later, in an "eyes only" cable to the Ambassador, the Department alerted him in general terms to Operation Omega and enlisted his help monitoring any perceived softening in the Egyptian position towards the West.[132]

In early April, the head of the Egyptian Foreign Ministry's American Division, Samih Anwar,[133] suggested that the Egyptian government moderate its anti-American propaganda in the interest of maintaining cordial relations.[134] The archives contain no response to his suggestion, nor an indication of to whom, if anyone, in the Egyptian government his suggestion was referred. Later in April, Egyptian documents reported a discussion between the head of the Voice of America's Middle East Service, Garland Dooher, and the press attaché in the Egyptian Embassy in Washington. Dooher said that Americans in Saudi Arabia were trying to open a rift between the Saudi monarchy and the Egyptian regime by telling the former that Abdel Nasser was plotting a coup to overthrow the Saudi royal family. Dooher left intentionally unclear whether such actions were "at the behest of the American government or Zionist efforts," but he hinted that the British Foreign Ministry knew of them. At the same time, Dooher stated that Secretary of State Dulles was a true friend of the Arabs and by opposing the Zionists so strongly he was even risking a Republican defeat in November in the name of principle.[135]

In all of this, Samih Anwar began to perceive a pattern. The American approaches in the last month had common themes:

1. That America's policy had been in Egypt's interest and had been intended to win Egyptian friendship, then changed to a different policy when it became clear that Egypt did not appreciate what the American government has done for it.
2. That Egyptian propaganda has been and still is intense against the West, and the United States is hoping Egypt will temper its campaigns.
3. Appearances of a change in American policy toward Egypt are based on newspaper accounts and attacks on Egypt which are Zionist-based.

Anwar surmised that because all of these reports came simultaneously, they may have represented an indirect invitation by the United States for Egypt to meet it "in the middle of the road."[136]

There appeared, however, to be two separate American campaigns. The internal records of the U.S. government suggest that Secretary Dulles, President Eisenhower, and other Washington-based policy makers held out little hope of Abdel Nasser's return to the good graces of the United States, and remained unclear on precisely what steps they would demand be taken to effect a rapprochement. At issue was a complaint that since early 1955, "the United States has, in general, looked to Egypt under Prime Minister Nasser to take leadership in meeting the major problems in the Near East."[137] Abdel Nasser had not toed the American line, however, and in particular refused to bow to American appeals for him to take public steps toward peace with Israel. In Eisenhower's words, his "growing ambition . . . a sense of power . . . [and a] belief that he can emerge as a true leader of the entire Arab world" made him a menace to American interests in the region.[138]

In this, the highest levels of the American government reflected the thinking of the British government. Relying at least in part on the reporting of a source with purportedly high contacts in the Egyptian government, officials at the top of the British government concluded that Abdel Nasser's involvement with the Soviet Union posed a serious threat to British foreign policy. According to one author, the British foreign minister decided two months after news of the Czech arms deal broke that "we believe it would be advantageous, in any event, to overthrow [Abdel Nasser] if possible."[139] When King Hussein dismissed General John Glubb from his position as the commander of the Arab Legion in Jordan on March 1, 1956, Prime Minister Eden saw Egyptian fingerprints on the affair.[140] According to some accounts the incident made him irrational on the subject of Abdel Nasser. In a widely quoted passage from Anthony Nutting's book on the period, Eden railed to Nutting, "But what's all this nonsense about isolating Nasser or 'neutralising' him, as you call it? I want him destroyed, can you understand?"[141]

In what appear to be CIA approaches to the Egyptian Embassy in Washington, however, a rather different strategy seemed to be at work. In these approaches, the prevailing negative atmosphere was ascribed to the efforts of Zionist and British enemies of Egypt but not reflecting internal U.S. government policy at all. The CIA approaches to the Egyptians appeared very much to hold open the door to rapprochement with the U.S. government, and may have represented a degree of "freelancing" by CIA officials.

The first pieces of evidence in this regard are the memoirs of former CIA operatives Wilbur Crane Eveland and Miles Copeland. Eveland asserts that the Cairo CIA station, whose most prominent members were James Eichelberger and Miles Copeland, were dismayed by British plans toward Abdel Nasser.[142] Further, Eveland quotes former Embassy Counselor G. Lewis Jones as saying in September 1955—only six months after Ambassador Byroade arrived in Cairo—that Byroade had two big problems on his hands. The first was that he was annoying Secretary Dulles by too actively commenting on proposed U.S. policies toward Egypt, and the second was that he felt he had lost control of the CIA station, whose "large . . . contingent now was dealing with the Egyptian government at almost every level, as well as with the influential Egyptian press."[143] Shortly thereafter, Kermit Roosevelt began spreading the word that "Byroade had lost all rapport with Nasser,"[144] perhaps intended at least in part to boost Roosevelt's stature as the interlocutor with the Egyptians at the expense of the Ambassador.

For his own part, Copeland bitterly attacked Secretary of State Dulles in his memoirs, writing, "He had a mind that, once made up, couldn't be opened with a crowbar."[145] He added,

> Never having actually lived and worked among his Third World clients, [Secretary Dulles] had no "feel" for them. Having no feel, he was blindly convinced that he possessed a Machiavellian understanding of the world's regional problems, while to us field operatives, both CIA and State, his view of the world was no less primitive than the nonsense clouding the minds of most Middle Eastern politicos.[146]

Copeland argued further that much of the anti-American propaganda that so infuriated Secretary of State Dulles was in fact authored by the CIA, intended to bolster Abdel Nasser's regional position while not seriously affecting American interests.[147]

A further clue of possible policy confusion lies in Egyptian Foreign Ministry documents from the spring of 1956. In contacts throughout March, April, and May, American officials—whose CIA connection is presumed because they remained unnamed even in top secret Egyptian dispatches—stressed that the apparent change in U.S. policy toward Egypt was in fact the product of British and Zionist propaganda attacks. Long after the State Department documents indicate that all hope of rapprochement with Egypt had been abandoned, CIA officials urged the Egyptians to moderate their behavior to put relations with the United States back on track. Conversations with covert American contacts differed in at least two other significant ways from the plans conceived by the Omega group: these contacts seemed to hold the British in contempt while Omega was predicated on Anglo-American cooperation, and these contacts ascribed a huge role to the effects of Zionist agitation against Egypt whereas the Omega documents suggest no such strategy.

Byroade's Swan Song

It was in this maelstrom of cross-purposes and hidden agendas that Omega was implemented. In the early summer of 1956 Ambassador Byroade engaged in a long and ultimately futile colloquy with the department, arguing that the scheming, intrigue, and delay which characterized American thinking about the High Dam and the Egyptian relationship in general could only serve to drive the Egyptians into the arms of the Soviets.[148] Dulles had little patience for Byroade's lectures, and personally drafted a cable in late June informing Byroade that he would soon leave Egypt for a new post as Ambassador to South Africa, where he would "have somewhat less strain."[149] The Department also dispatched a long cable on July 9 cataloguing Egyptian perfidy in the face of "clearly demonstrated US desire to cooperate with [the] present regime . . . [and to] provide Egypt arms in legitimate quantity." It concluded,

> Further moves in [the] direction [of] appeasement with nothing more than [the] vague hope of still eliciting [a] positive Egyptian response would involve [the] abandonment [of] soundly conceived positions, with [the] possibility [of] far reaching repercussions and [would] result in further strengthening [a] regime [the] extent [of] whose activities against US and West [are] becoming steadily more apparent.[150]

The Embassy's response was rapid and cutting. Acknowledging that the Department's message was "some 90 percent accurate" in terms of the factual record, the Embassy pointed out that the Department seemed to have no understanding whatsoever of Egyptian motivations. The Embassy wrote,

> Department knows that while economic assistance provides a very useful lubricator for foreign policy operations which become closely intermeshed with those of other countries as a result of joint approaches to common objectives, economic assistance does not in itself establish basic common bonds between [the] US and recipients and does not buy repudiation of national objectives

which may not coincide with our programs and policies for containing [the] Soviet threat.

In a swipe at Secretary Dulles, the cable continued,

> Neutralism exists over a large portion of this part of the world. If we fail to develop means of fruitful cooperation with this large body of people and continue to consider them as being either in [the] enemy camp or as "fellow travellers" I fear that before too long we will begin to appear in [the] eyes [of] these people as being the unreasonable member of [the] East-West struggle.[151]

The Embassy's bitter message was sent the day after Byroade informed the Egyptian government that he would soon be leaving Egypt,[152] and seems for all intents and purposes to have been his "swan song." It drew no response from the Department.

By late May, it was apparent to most involved—on both the Egyptian and American sides—that there was little chance that the United States would in any way participate in funding the High Dam. All that remained was the end game. The State Department was most concerned by the possibility that an abrupt refusal to move forward might provoke an Egyptian backlash, and probably an immediate turn to the Soviets for financing. The department, therefore, continued a policy of delay, and in early June drafted a statement for emergency use suggesting that Egypt's economy could not support dam construction without undue dependence on foreign powers. The criticism of the Egyptian economy was personally suggested by Secretary Dulles, who believed that it would make it "embarrassing for the Egyptians to seek assistance from the Soviet Union."[153]

On the Egyptian side, Ambassador Hussein traveled to Cairo from May 18 to July 13 for consultations, and saw Abdel Nasser on July 8.[154] The previous day, *al-Ahram* had reported a State Department spokesman's claim that the United States stood ready to participate in funding the High Dam, despite the fact that the money which had been appropriated for the project in FY 1956 had been reallocated to other programs because they remained unspent at the end of the fiscal year.[155] According to Abdel Nasser's confidant, Muhammad Hassanein Heikal, Ambassador Hussein told Abdel Nasser that such a reallocation of funds was "purely routine," and in no way jeopardized long-term American funding for the project.[156] Heikal reported that Abdel Nasser understood that, in fact, American funding had become an impossibility, and to prove it advised Hussein to accept all of the remaining American conditions for High Dam financing.[157]

When Hussein met with Secretary Dulles in Washington on July 19, Dulles told him that the United States would not fund the project. His reasoning was twofold: First, the austerity such a large project would demand from the Egyptian populace would arouse resentment toward the United States, and second, that the American public would oppose aid to a country which seemed to be working against the interests of the United States. A week later, President Abdel Nasser announced the nationalization of the Suez Canal Company, the foreign currency from which he pledged to use to fund construction of the High Dam. In so doing, he set off the chain of events that would culminate in a coordinated Israeli, British, and French attack against Egypt, and vigorous American efforts in the United Nations to turn back its allies.

In the end, Egyptians built the High Dam with Soviet assistance, on plans very closely resembling those approved by the international consultants in 1955. The High Dam was completed in 1970, and in 1972 President Sadat asked Soviet advisers to leave the country. In the wake of the American-brokered treaty ending the 1973 Arab-Israeli war and the subsequent Camp David agreement making peace between Egypt and Israel, American aid and advisers flocked back to Egypt. The American aid mission in Cairo is now the largest in the world.

Throughout the 1950s, the High Dam project never really ceased to be an economic project for the Egyptians. However, in high-level discussions in the U.S. Department of State and among the National Security Council, it was never anything but political. While Egypt's leaders continued to view the High Dam as a key to the economic future of Egypt, Secretary of State Dulles and his subordinates in the Department of State regarded it as a mere bargaining chip in a bid for regional peace. Although the Egyptian government record is significantly less clear than the American one, Egyptian officials appear not to have grasped entirely the disinterest that high levels of the American government directed toward internal conditions in Egypt.

Conclusion

Viewed from Washington, the world of the early 1950s was an extraordinarily dangerous place. Communist expansion coincided with the collapse of colonial empires. The Soviet Union exploded a nuclear device in August 1949, and a Communist government assumed power in China, the most populous country in the world, less than two months later. After leading an allied response to the North Korean invasion of the South in 1950, the United States government adopted a defense posture based on unspeakable horror. "Brinkmanship," as the policy propounded by Secretary of State Dulles would be popularly known, meant convincing the enemy that any false move could result in a massive nuclear retaliation. The deterrent effect of such a policy came from the fact that precisely how much provocation would elicit a nuclear barrage was left unclear. In the mortal battle for the future of the Free World, United States government was like a physician tending to a critically ill patient. New symptoms could represent a serious advance for the disease, or be benign or unrelated. Constant decisions had to be made how and when to intervene. It was an awesome responsibility, and the stakes were incredibly high.

Viewed from Cairo, however, the early 1950s were mostly a time of hope and promise. Although the threat of Egypt's population overtaking its resources loomed in the background, optimism ran higher than it had in three-quarters of a century. The new military regime predicated its rule on results, and almost immediately upon taking power swept away the cobwebs of corruption that had accumulated over the years. Equally importantly, the young officers who now controlled Egypt succeeded where their predecessors had failed. They won agreement for the withdrawal of British soldiers from the Canal Zone. For the first time since 1882, foreign troops would leave Egyptian soil; for the first time since the Persian conquest in 525 BCE, Egypt was ruled entirely by Egyptians and not by conquerors or their descendents who remained aloof from the general population.

Previous accounts of the Egyptian-American relationship have emphasized that Egypt's leaders showed their true colors as the new government consolidated power in the years following the revolution. Once power on the home front was secure, they suggest, the Egyptian government became entrepreneurial as it sought to become the dominant regional power. In pursuit of such a policy, Egypt tried to engage the United States and the Soviet Union in a bidding war for Egypt's affections. The gambit failed, and the United States moved against Abdel Nasser and his government by withdrawing funding for the High Dam at Aswan.

The foregoing account casts that perspective into question. What is impressive when one considers the Egyptian-American relationship from the Egyptian perspective is the consistency of Egyptian policy. Egypt's leaders were preoccupied with the prospect of a looming Malthusian disaster resulting from its rapid population growth even before the revolution, and that preoccupation did not temper over time. Egyptian politicians were extraordinarily impatient for rapid and fundamental improvements in the economy, and that impatience was a constant throughout the period as well. Finally, Egyptians remained ambivalent about the role foreigners and foreign investment would play in the country's economic renaissance. Foreigners had benefited disproportionately from economic changes in the past, and the new government hoped to steer benefits to its citizens.

In contrast to the relative stability of the Egyptian side, American policy appears to have been in flux for much of the period under study. The amount of American aid to the Middle East increased dramatically in the mid-1950s. The goals of that aid changed as well, from an almost pure focus on technical assistance in 1952 to significant capital assistance under an explicit security rubric in 1956. From 1952 to 1956 the United States had no fewer than three different bureaucracies responsible for foreign assistance to Egypt: the Technical Cooperation Administration, the Foreign Operations Administration, and the International Cooperation Administration. Finally, the stated goal of American aid in 1952 was aiding and stabilizing the new government of Egypt, but in subsequent years the United States three times used aid as a carrot to modify Egyptian policy toward a third country: in 1953 and 1954 to promote an Anglo-Egyptian agreement over the Suez Canal base, and in 1956 to promote direct peace negotiations with Israel.

The point of this exercise is not to assign blame, but rather to understand the dynamic that led to the breakdown in the Egyptian-American relationship. The most important conclusion is that the fault lay not with one party or the other, but with the relationship itself. Americans and Egyptians were unable to build a partnership strong enough to withstand the stresses to which the relationship was subjected. This failure was surely due in part to the actions of each government that antagonized the other, but it had significant roots in the global environment as well. Several times Britain pressed the U.S. government to sacrifice its program in Egypt in the interests of the Anglo-American alliance. The Israeli government had a strong interest in preventing Egypt from growing too close to the United States, and almost certainly had a coordinated policy to try to disrupt Egyptian-American relations. The Soviet Union shared the Israelis' interest and found that it could make mischief for American plans in the Middle East at relatively little cost.

Efforts to build a mutually beneficial relationship in the face of these challenges, while initially promising, often ended disappointingly. Public and private American investment in Egypt's economic renaissance never reached the levels Egyptians hoped for, and EARIS never became the sort of cooperative, grassroots political experiment that the Americans hoped it would be. Egyptians wanted American involvement in the High Dam at Aswan from the start, but Americans never quite grasped the urgency which Egyptians felt about the project, and Egyptians chafed at the years of thorough investigations and negotiations which necessarily precede a project of that size. While none of these three projects was an abject failure, none achieved the success for which either side had hoped. When the relationship entered a subsequent period of stress, there was an insufficient reservoir of good will in the two governments to overcome it. This failure was not entirely one of governments. Each of the three areas described above—discrete projects to boost GNP, EARIS, and the High Dam—sought to enlist non-governmental persons and organizations in their execution.

One of the striking characteristics of the period under study was that Americans and Egyptians who worked in daily contact most often had excellent relationships with their foreign counterparts. I met many people who, forty years after the fact, asked after old friends in the other country. People who worked in daily contact over a period of years understood and trusted their co-workers. Those who had less daily contact with those from the other side—be they officials in the Egyptian government or congressional and administration officials in Washington—had no common experience on which to rely. This led to repeated conflict within the American government, as is clearly attested to by the increasingly distraught communications between the State Department and the Cairo Embassy in 1955–56. Despite excellent reporting, diplomats in Cairo and Washington could not win over their superiors at home to seeing things from the perspective of the country in which they were posted.

More troubling are the indications that, during the spring of 1956, CIA officers were more sympathetic to the Egyptian position than their State Department counterparts, and they briefed the Egyptian Embassy in Washington along more permissive lines than their colleagues in Foggy Bottom. During that period the U.S. government surely spoke with more than one voice, making it difficult for the strained relationship to improve.

The overriding problem in this period, however, was that the projects analyzed here—industrialization and investment, EARIS, and the High Dam—had not yielded enough benefit by 1955 to induce the two governments to put aside their differences. When tensions rose, the projects had not yet developed sufficient constituencies in either government to sustain the relationship. The troubles implementing the joint projects did not fail because the relationship was troubled; rather, the difficulties in starting these projects and operating them successfully constituted much of the difficulty in the relationship. The programs were intended to establish a pattern of cooperation, but in fact proved how difficult cooperation could be.

Previous accounts of Egyptian-American relations during the early 1950s have concentrated on the period after September 1955, when Egypt became a preoccupation for the highest levels of the American government. Such a concentration misses much of the game. As has been suggested above, by the fall of 1955 the dynamics of the Egyptian-American relationship had already been set. The actions of the government of Egypt during this period were not merely a Cold-War gambit as they have been described heretofore. There is ample evidence for an alternative explanation: that they were appropriate and justifiable responses to the problems facing Egypt in the mid-1950s.

The curious thing about examining the Egyptian-American relationship from both sides is that each side felt weaker than the other side perceived it to be. Officials in each government recognized the constraints that they faced, but often only dimly understood the constraints of their counterparts in other capitals. While diplomats and intelligence officials struggled mightily to bridge the gap, in the end it was not a problem that understanding could resolve. Egyptian interests were guided largely by the need for economic development, and American interests were guided largely by the Cold War. While these interests could coincide for a time, they could not unify.

Ultimately, the Egyptian-American relationship broke down because it was unable to transcend the narrow basis on which it was formed. Maintaining and improving the Egyptian-American relationship never became a central concern of either government. While the relationship sometimes provided benefits to each government in terms of its larger goals, it was also a source of disappointment. Absent the creation of an alliance that could withstand the strains of a changing world, those strains split the relationship apart.

Notes

Introduction

1. RG 469, USOM/Egypt/C Subj Files, 1955–56, Box 6, Brooks McClure to W. H. Weathersby, "Obliteration of Point Four Insignia by Egypt," 16 April 1956.
2. RG 469, USOM/Egypt/C Subj Files, Box 9, Charles Jackson to Adm. Harold Stevens, "ICA Emblems on GM Locomotives," 29 August 1956.
3. For example, see Gail E. Meyer, *Egypt and the United States: The Formative Years* (Cranbury, NJ: Associated University Presses, 1980); William J. Burns, *Economic Aid and American Policy Toward Egypt, 1955–1981* (Albany: State University of New York Press, 1985); Peter L. Hahn, *The United States, Great Britain and Egypt, 1945–1956: Strategy and Diplomacy in the Early Cold War* (Chapel Hill: University of North Carolina Press, 1991); Geoffrey Aronson, *From Sideshow to Center Stage: U.S. Policy toward Egypt, 1946–56* (Boulder, CO: Lynne Rienner, 1986); and Muhammad Abd el-Wahab Sayed-Ahmed, *Nasser and American Foreign Policy, 1952–56* (London: LAAM, 1989).
4. For example, Ray Takeyh, *The Origins of the Eisenhower Doctrine: The US, Britain and Nasser's Egypt, 1953–1957* (New York: St. Martin's Press, 2000).
5. Burns's work explicitly studies how effective American aid was in shaping Egyptian behavior.
6. The obvious exceptions to this are cases in which the U.S. government was seeking to mislead the government of another country. Since the creation of the CIA, however, such actions have generally fallen to that agency and have thus far remained classified.
7. See Abdel Latif al-Baghdadi, *Memoirs, pt. 1* (Cairo: al-Maktab al-Misri al-Hadith, 1977, Ar.), Anwar al-Sadat, *My Son, This is Your Uncle Gamal: Memoirs of Anwar Sadat* (Cairo: Dar al-Hilal, 1958, Ar.); Rashed Barawy, *Economic Development in the United Arab Republic* (Cairo: Anglo-Egyptian Bookshop, 1970); and Abdul Ra'uf Ahmad Amr, *The History of Egyptian-American Relations, 1939–1957* (Cairo: al-Haya al-Misriya al-Ama lil-Kitab, 1991, Ar.).
8. See Raymond William Baker, *Egypt's Uncertain Revolution under Nasser and Sadat* (Cambridge: Harvard University Press, 1979) and Kirk J. Beattie,

Egypt During the Nasser Years: Ideology, Politics and Civil Society (Boulder, CO: Westview Press, 1994).

9. Miles Copeland, *Game of Nations: The Amorality of Power Politics* (London: Weidenfeld and Nicholson, 1969); Miles Copeland, *The Game Player: Confessions of the CIA's Original Political Operative* (London: Aurum Press, 1989); and Wilbur Crane Eveland, *Ropes of Sand: America's Failure in the Middle East* (New York: W. W. Norton, 1980).

Chapter 1

1. Afaf Lutfi al-Sayyid Marsot, *Egypt's Liberal Experiment: 1922–1936* (Berkeley: University of California Press, 1977), p. 206. On the epidemic, see Nancy Gallagher, *Egypt's Other Wars: Epidemics and the Politics of Public Health* (Syracuse, NY: Syracuse University Press, 1990).

2. Tariq al-Bishri, *The Political Movement in Egypt, 1945–1952,* 2nd Printing (Cairo: Dar al-Shuruq, 1983, Ar.) pp. 182–183.

3. Mohammed Neguib, *Egypt's Destiny* (London: Victor Gollancz, 1955), p. 101. P. J. Vatikiotis estimates the destruction of 750 establishments but does not give a source. See P. J. Vatikiotis, *History of Egypt from Muhammad Ali to Mubarak,* 3d ed. (Baltimore: Johns Hopkins University Press, 1985), p. 307.

4. Neguib, *Egypt's Destiny,* p. 102.

5. More than a month after the coup, *Newsweek* reported that membership in the ruling junta "was variously estimated at nine, twelve and eighteen younger officers." "Key to Middle East's Future: What Happens Next in Egypt," *Newsweek,* 25 August 1952, p. 32.

6. Mustafa Amin, "The Secret of the Free Officers," *Akhbar al-Yawm* (Ar.), 12 October 1952.

7. In fact, Caffery was posted to Egypt because he was not ready to retire. His experience, steady hand, and influence within the State Department (Acheson personally read his cables regularly) proved to be a great asset in the instability that arose after his arrival. Telephone interview with William Lakeland, 13 September 1994.

8. Khaled Mohieddin, who played a leading role in the coup, told an interviewer in 1980 that it was his understanding that a coup was checked in general with U.S. Air Force Attaché David Evans beforehand. Tarek Ismail and Rifa'at Said, *The Communist Movement in Egypt* (Syracuse: Syracuse University Press, 1993).

9. Telephone interview with William Lakeland, 13 September 1994.

10. Farouk left on his 420-foot, 4,561-ton yacht, the Mahroussa—"The Protected"—that held a 164-man crew. *Life,* 24 November 1952, p. 94.

11. See, for example, Anwar al-Sadat, *My Son, This Is Your Uncle Gamal* (Cairo, Dar al-Hilal, 1958, Ar.), p. 109.

12. Neguib, *Egypt's Destiny,* p. 118.

13. Lakeland interview.

14. "We have returned your land to you," *al-Tahrir* (Ar.), 17 September 1952, p. 7.

15. Per capita consumption of foodstuffs declined from 393 kg in 1929 to 345 kg in 1951–52. Abdel Razzaq Sidky, *The Agricultural Policy in the New Era* (Cairo: Government Press, 1953), p. 6. Consumption of nutritious staples at the time of the revolution were generally below pre-war levels. In particular, consumption of cereals and meat were down almost 10 percent, while consumption of sugar, tea, and tobacco were all sharply up. International Bank for Reconstruction and Development Archives, *The Economic Development of Egypt* (World Bank Report # A.S. 40-a), 25 August 1955, p. 47.

16. One author suggests that real national income was likely stable in the interwar period and fell during World War II, combining with population growth to produce a sharp decline in per-capita incomes and standards of living. Another notes that "between 1913 and 1937, the general index of agricultural production increased by 8% only as compared with a 40% increase in population." Charles Issawi, *Egypt in Revolution: An Economic Analysis* (Oxford: Oxford University Press, 1963), p. 32, and A. A. I. El-Gritly, "The Structure of Modern Industry in Egypt" (Cairo: Government Press, 1948), p. 575.

17. Wendell Cleland, *The Population Problem in Egypt: A Study of Population Trends and Conditions in Modern Egypt* (Lancaster, PA: Science Press Printing Co., 1936), pp. 34–35.

18. *Economic Development of Egypt*, p. 2 and American Embassy, "Agriculture in Egypt," 19 July 1952, p. 6.

19. Sidky, *The Agricultural Policy*, p. 1. *The Economic Development of Egypt*, p. 4, estimated that agricultural goods represented 90 percent of exports.

20. *Agriculture in Egypt*, p. 6 and *Economic Development of Egypt*, p. 1.

21. *Economic Development of Egypt*, p. 18. El-Gritly suggests a similar point when he argues that Egypt should seek to become a regional exporter of simple manufactured goods. El-Gritly, *Structure of Modern Industry*, p. 578.

22. *National Bank of Egypt Economic Bulletin*, vol. V (1952), p. 168. In the event, much of the capital freed by land reform went into urban construction rather than into industrial development.

23. Such projects were carried out by the Ministry of Agriculture and the extra-ministerial Permanent Council for the Development of National Production, and are described in chapter 3, below.

24. Ministry of Agriculture, "Estimates for Agricultural Features," 1955.

25. *Agriculture in Egypt*, p. 11. It is worth remembering that before land reform, 95 percent of landowners were peasants owning less than 5 feddans of land, and fully 53 percent of landowners owned less than 1/2 feddan of land. At the same time, .08 percent of landowners owned something over 20 percent of the entire cultivated area of the country. *Economic Development of Egypt*, p. 5.

26. William Roger Louis, *The British Empire in the Middle East, 1945–1951: Arab Nationalism, the United States, and Postwar Imperialism* (Oxford: Clarendon Press, 1984), p. 743. This is a characterization of the view of Sir John Troutbeck, who headed the British Middle East Office in Cairo.

27. Succinct accounts of the Middle East Command proposal can be found in John C. Campbell, *Defense of the Middle East: Problems of American Policy* (New York: Council on Foreign Relations [by] Harper & Brothers, 1960), pp. 40–46, and J. C. Hurewitz, *Middle East Dilemmas: The Background of United States Policy* (New York: Council on Foreign Relations [by] Harper & Brothers, 1953), pp. 92–97.

28. See, for example, "Key to Egypt: Farouk and the Pashas," *Newsweek,* 31 March 1952, p. 33, which credits the king with "decision and courage . . . handling some of the wiliest politicians in the world—the pashas, the rich educated class which controls Egypt."

29. Philip Toynbee, "Behind the Violence in Egypt," *New York Times Magazine,* 4 November 1951, pp. 13+. Toynbee contrasted Egyptians with Iranians, writing "The Iranians are a proud and indrawn people with an instinctive mistrust of the West; the Egyptians are a humiliated, violently emotional people who wish to play a grandiose role in the Middle Eastern world."

30. William H. Attwood, "The Problem King of Egypt: Farouk Is a Bewildered, Moody Monarch Who Vacilates between Self-Indulgence and a Sincere Desire to Help His People," *Life,* 10 April 1950, p. 102.

31. Ibid., p. 111.

32. Ibid., p. 116.

33. Ibid., p. 111.

34. Ibid., p. 116.

35. "Egypt for the Egyptians?" *New Republic,* 4 February 1952, p. 6.

36. See Manfred Halpern, *The Politics of Social Change in the Middle East and North Africa* (Princeton, NJ: Princeton University Press, 1963) for a substantially similar argument. Halpern worked in the State Department's Bureau of Intelligence and Research on Middle Eastern affairs in the early 1950s.

37. See, for example, Alfred Lilienthal, "Revolt Along the Nile," *American Mercury,* February 1952, p. 8.

38. The reference, of course, is to Atatürk, who transformed the rump of the Ottoman Empire into the modern state of Turkey. See "The Atlantic Report on the World Today: Middle East," *Atlantic,* December 1952, p. 17. After Gamal Abdel Nasser took power from Naguib, John Gunther compared *him* to Atatürk. John Gunther, "Inside Egypt," *Reader's Digest,* April 1955, p. 85.

39. Leigh White, "Egypt's 'Blessed' Revolution," *Harpers Magazine,* January 1953, p. 89.

40. Mark Alexander, "Egypt's Middle Class Revolution," *American Mercury,* November 1952, p. 24.

41. White "Egypt's 'Blessed' Revolution," p. 85.

42. Interview with Ahmed Hamrouche, Cairo Egypt, 15 April 1993; see also Khaled Mohi El Din, *Memories of a Revolution: Egypt 1952* (Cairo: AUC Press, 1995), p. 60.

43. White, "Egypt's 'Blessed' Revolution," p. 89.

44. Atlantic, "The Report," p. 17.

45. White, "Egypt's 'Blessed' Revolution," p. 90. White went on to assist Naguib in writing his first memoirs in 1955.

46. One of these mentioned the sudden availability of Coke and Pepsi in Cairo since the War, and touched upon modern politics by quoting a local guide as having said, "Mohammed Naguib, him liking tourists very much." Charles J. Rolo, "Colas on the Nile," *Atlantic,* December 1953, p. 109.

47. See, for example, "Naguib to Nasser to Chance," *Nation,* 27 November 1954, p. 453.

48. The Israeli-sponsored attacks on U.S. and British targets in Egypt in July 1954 (code-named "Operation Susanna" and more widely known in U.S. and Israeli circles as "The Lavon Affair") had the same goal. In the event, the United States refused to sell arms to the Egyptians without Egypt entering into a mutual cooperation agreement, which the Egyptians were unwilling to do. See below.

49. "As Middle East Crisis Worries the World, New Egypt Displays Its Power," *Life,* 16 April 1956, p. 29.

50. In 1950, the total circulation of daily newspapers in Egypt was a mere 18 per thousand of population, and there were 11 radio sets in use per thousand of population. Newspaper readership and radio use were both concentrated in the cities, leaving the countryside virtually bereft of such news outlets. Charles Issawi, "A Note on the Conditions of Economic Progress in the Middle East," *Economic Development and Cultural Change,* I:4 (December 1952), pp. 290–91.

51. Fuad Mattar, *Frankly about Abdel Nasser* (Beirut: Dar al-Qadaya, 1975, Ar.), p. 77.

52. Ibid., p. 78.

53. Sadat went on to become the President of Egypt. Shortly after the Revolution he played the role of red-hot propagandist and ardent nationalist, as evidenced by his many columns in the newspapers and magazines of the regime. Some associated with those publications, however, suggest that his views were not taken seriously within the RCC and that Abdel Nasser thought him "unsuitable for anything"; and, further, that the responsibility for his monthly stipend of £E2,400 was split evenly between Abdel Nasser and the CIA so that each could silence him at will. Interview with Hussein Fahmy, 28 November 1994.

54. Anwar al-Sadat, "Listen, America," *al-Tahrir* (Ar.), 24 November 1953, p. 3 [punctuation as in original].

55. This description of the book relies on the 14-page summary contained in Abdel Azim Ramadan, *Revolutionary Thought in Egypt before the July Revolution* (Cairo: Maktabat Madbuli, 1981, Ar.), pp. 188–203.

56. Ibid., p. 194.

57. Ibid., p. 195.

58. Ibid., p. 195.

59. Ibid., p. 196.

Chapter 2

1. P. J. Vatikiotis, *The History of Egypt from Muhammad Ali to Mubarak*, 3d ed. (Baltimore: Johns Hopkins University Press, 1985), p. 392.

2. John Waterbury, *The Egypt of Nasser and Sadat: The Political Economy of Two Regimes* (Princeton, NJ: Princeton University Press, 1983), p. 57.

3. Ahmed Hamrouche, *The Story of the July Revolution* (Cairo: Maktabat Madbuli, var. dates, Ar.).

4. The Permanent Council for the Development of National Production (PCDNP), constituted in December 1952, featured three Ph.D. economists among its eleven members, and five members with extensive corporate experience.

5. *The Economic Development of Egypt*, World Bank Report Report #A.S. 40-a, 25 August 1955.

6. Konrad Bekker in Berthold Frank Hoselitz, ed., *The Progress of Underdeveloped Areas* (Chicago: University of Chicago Press, 1952), p. 240.

7. United Nations, Department of Economic Affairs, *Measures for the Economic Development of Under-developed Nations* (New York: United Nations, 1951), paragraph 3.

8. McKim Marriott, "Technological Change in Overdeveloped Rural Areas," *Economic Development and Cultural Change*, I:4 (December 1952), p. 261.

9. The psychologists were to arrive somewhat later on the scene, but make their presence felt at the end of the 1950s and in the early 1960s. S. N. Eisenstadt and Daniel Lerner, for example, argued for the *mentalité* approach to development, implicitly suggesting that psychological issues had to be addressed in development plans as much as economic ones.

10. Simon S. Kuznets, "Quantitative Aspects of the Growth of Nations," *Economic Development and Cultural Change*, vol. V (1956), p. 9.

11. Some economists, like P. T. Bauer, suggested that most economic analysis of poor countries understated their incomes because of the relatively less-important role of cash in these societies.

12. P. N. Rosenstein-Rodan, "Problems of Industrialization of Eastern and South-Eastern Europe," reprinted in A. A. Agarwala and S. P. Singh, *The Economics of Underdevelopment* (Bombay and New York: Oxford University Press, 1958), p. 249. Soviet development, which sought self-sufficiency by building heavy and light industry without foreign capital, is the alternative model of industrialization Rosenstein-Rodan considered.

13. Albert O. Hirshman made the opposite argument. Writing later in the decade, Hirshman suggested that "uneven" growth was the most efficient avenue to progress, since development projects themselves create an urgent demand for inputs. The effect of the projects, then, is multiplied because of all the secondary investment that they induce.

14. Rosenstein-Rodan suggested the following classifications of per capita expenditures: light industries, £100-£400; medium industries, £400-£800;

heavy industries, £800-£1500. Rosenstein-Rodan, "Problems of Industrialization," p. 255.

15. Ibid., p. 250.

16. Ibid., pp. 248, 251.

17. He makes this argument in an article entitled "On the Political Economy of Backwardness," *The Manchester School of Economic and Social Studies,* 20 January 1952. Baran expanded his argument in later book, *The Political Economy of Growth* (New York: Monthly Review Press, 1957).

18. As suggested above, the United States was sympathetic to the idea of an alliance between the United States and progressive, proletarian forces, especially in the Truman Administration.

19. The economists were Alberto Baltra Cortez, National University of Chile; D. R. Gadgil, Gokhale Institute of Politics and Economics, Poona, India; George Hakim, Legation of Lebanon, Washington, DC; W. Arthur Lewis, University of Manchester, UK; and Theodore W. Schultz, University of Chicago. On the charge, see Resolution 290 (XI) of the Economic and Social Council of the United Nations, quoted in *Measures for the Economic Development of Under-developed Countries* (New York: United Nations, 1951), p. 3.

20. The authors wrote that in many poor countries, "the cultivators of the soil are exploited mercilessly by a landlord class which performs no useful social function. This class contrives to secure to itself the major part of any increase in agricultural yields, and is thus a millstone around the necks of the peasants. . . . In such countries land reform, abolishing this landlord class, is an urgent pre-requisite of agricultural progress." Ibid., paragraph 56. Subsequent paragraph references are taken from this work.

21. Ibid. An obstacle to the creation of this class, the authors note, may be a "lack of interest in material things . . . due to the prevalence of an otherworldly philosophy which discourages material wants." The authors do not have a solution to this problem.

22. Paragraph 84.

23. Taxation would in effect force saving, because the government could employ the capital in productive enterprises. Paragraph 246.

24. Paragraph 254. The report estimates that approximately 70 percent of total foreign investment was in the petroleum industry.

25. Ibid. Recommendation 13.

26. Paragraphs 97, 98. Hoarding in this case also refers to land speculation. Land values in Egypt climbed rapidly in the early twentieth century, and far exceeded values determined by the annual production of the land. By favoring land investments over industrial investments, Egyptian capitalists impeded the growth of Egyptian industry and created opportunities for foreign capital in Egypt. They also contributed to the continued immiseration of the peasants, for whom ownership of land grew increasingly out of reach. See chapter 3, below.

27. Paragraph 80.

28. Paragraph 163. In Egypt, such a survey was undertaken by Arthur D. Little consultants, under the aegis of the Permanent Council for the Development of National Production.

29. Better management practices were also expected to increase unemployment as workforces were trimmed to more efficient sizes. Paragraph 15.

30. The population growth rate in Egypt after the war was between 2 and 2.5 percent. International Bank for Reconstruction and Development Archives, *The Economic Development of Egypt* (World Bank Report # A.S. 40-a), 25 August 1955, p. 2.

31. Harvey Leibenstein, *Economic Backwardness and Economic Growth: Studies in the Theory of Economic Development* (New York: Wiley, 1957), chapter 8.

32. Merle Eugene Curti and Kendall Birr, *Prelude to Point Four: American Technical Missions Overseas, 1838–1938* (Madison: University of Wisconsin Press, 1954), pp. 53, 28.

33. Ibid., p. 55.

34. Kemmerer's overseas career began in the Philippines at the turn of the century, and his work "embraced countries in five continents" over the next 25 years. Ibid., p. 182.

35. Jean and Simonne Lacouture, trans. By Francis Scarfe, *Egypt in Transition* (New York: Criterion Books, 1958) p.49.

36. William R. Hutchison, *Errand to the World: American Protestant Thought and Foreign Missions* (Chicago: University of Chicago Press, 1987), p. 103.

37. AUB was founded as the Syrian Protestant College in 1866. George Sarton, quoted in John A. DeNovo, *American Interests and Policies in the Middle East, 1900–1939* (Minneapolis: University of Minnesota Press, 1963).

38. Ibid., pp. 10, 372.

39. Ibid., p. 373.

40. The Coptic Church is an Orthodox monophysite church that has its own pope.

41. Rockefeller Foundation, *Annual Report 1913–14* (New York: Rockefeller Foundation, n.d.), p. 11.

42. Kenneth Iverson, "The 'Servicio' in Theory and Practice," *Public Administration Review,* Autumn 1951, p. 226.

43. Ibid., p. 225.

44. Jonathan Bingham, *Shirt-sleeve Diplomacy: Point 4 in Action* (New York: John Day, 1954), p. 20. See also Walter R. Sharp, *International Technical Assistance: Programs and Organization* (Chicago: Public Administration Service, 1952), p. 5.

45. Iverson, "Servicio," p. 227.

46. Sharp, "International Technical Assistance," p. 5.

47. Iverson, "Servicio," p. 228.

48. Bingham, *Shirt-sleeve Diplomacy,* p. 10

49. Of course, Truman's domestic economic plan was called The Fair Deal, and he was a Democrat. The difference lies in the capitalization. Harry S. Truman, "Inaugural Address," *Public Papers of the Presidents of the United States: Harry S. Truman, 1949* (Washington: Government Printing Office, 1964), pp. 114, 115.

50. U.S. Congress. Senate. Committee on Foreign Relations, Subcommittee on Technical Assistance Programs. 83d Congress, 2nd Session. "Development of Technical Assistance Programs," 22 November 1954, p. 1.

51. W. Arthur Lewis, "Point Four—After Four Years: The land-poor farmer," *The Nation*, 31 January 1953, p. 98. Lewis's broader analysis of development, described above, paints a much less rosy picture.

52. The classic study on the subject is Alfred Charles True, *A History of Agricultural Extension in the United States, 1785–1923* (Washington: Government Printing Office, 1928). See also Gladys Baker, *The County Agent* (Chicago: University of Chicago Press, 1939).

53. Bingham, *Shirt-sleeve Diplomacy*, p. 16.

54. William J. Lederer and Eugene Burdick, *The Ugly American* (New York: W. W. Norton, 1958).

55. Ibid., pp. 207–208.

56. Ibid., p. 220.

57. Ibid., p. 47.

58. Eric Johnston, *We're All In It* (New York: E. P. Dutton, 1948), pp. 12–13.

59. William O. Douglas, *Strange Lands and Friendly People* (New York: Harpers, 1951), p. 5.

60. William O. Douglas, "The Power of Righteousness," *New Republic*, 28 April 1952, p. 13.

61. Truman, "Inaugural Address," p. 115.

62. "Aiding Underdeveloped Areas Abroad," *Annals of the American Academy of Political and Social Science*, volume 268, April 1950, p. vii.

63. Willard L. Thorp, "Land and the Future," in Kenneth H. Parsons et al. (eds), *Land Tenure: Proceedings of the International Conference on Land Tenure and Related Problems in World Agriculture Held at Madison, Wisconsin, 1951* (Madison: University of Wisconsin Press, 1956), p. 26.

64. Wolf I. Ladejinsky, "Land Reform in Japan: A Comment," in Parsons et al. (eds)., *Land Tenure*, p. 228. A circular airgram distributed by the Department of State in April 1951 set the primary objective of land reform to be "to improve agricultural economic institutions in order to lessen the causes of agrarian unrest and political instability," with a secondary goal "to discharge 'land reform' from the complex of ideas exploited by Soviet Communism." RG 469 Egypt Branch, Subject Files 1951–54, TCA/NEADS, Box 9, 17 April 1951.

65. The most famous of these was the program in Etawah, India, led by a former agricultural extension agent named Horace Holmes. The Etawah program was begun by American philanthropic organizations in the 1940s and then taken as a model for Point Four activities. The Etawah program drew on pre-existing programs in India for rural development through self-help, which in turn drew on the cooperative movement popular throughout the colonial world at the turn of the century. Such a movement was active in Egypt as well.

66. Discussions of community development in the early 1950s closely mirror discussions of civil society in current political discourse. The goal in both

cases is to create mediating institutions between the individual and the state which serve to make the state more responsive to popular direction. According to one account, the phrase "was first used officially at a Conference on the Development of African Initiative" in England in 1948. Irwin T. Sanders, *Community Development and National Change* [Summary of a conference sponsored by Center for International Studies (MIT) held at Endicott House] (Washington?: International Cooperation Administration, 1958) p. 3.

67. Writing in 1953, one academic suggested that "'Community development' has not yet been given content as a specially designated field of study except in the United States, where the term and its equivalents are well-established and increasingly explored and explained. Consequently, little has been written on community development in underdeveloped areas; less that is worth reading." Phillips Ruopp, *Approaches to Community Development: A Symposium Introductory to Problems and Methods of Village Welfare in Underdeveloped Areas* (The Hague: W. Van Hoeve Ltd., 1953), p. 345.

68. Sidney Dillick, *Community Organization for Neighborhood Development: Past and Present* (New York: William Morrow, 1953), p. 18.

69. Quoted in David E. Lilienthal, *TVA: Democracy on the March* (New York: Harper & Brothers, 1944), p. 36.

70. Carl C. Taylor, "Community Development in Economically Underdeveloped Areas," RG 479, USOM/E CSF (CGF) Box 1. Taylor, a Ph.D. sociologist, had been head of the U.S. Department of Agriculture's Division of Farm Population and Rural Life at the end of World War II. He spent much of his subsequent career in international work. He left FOA in 1955 to join the Ford Foundation as a consultant on Community Development.

71. Writing about the United States, TVA Administrator David Lilienthal wrote, "Centralization in administration promotes remote and absentee control, and thereby increasingly denies to the individual the opportunity to make decisions and to carry those responsibilities by which human personality is nourished and developed." Lilienthal, *TVA*, p. 139. Several Egyptians who worked with EARIS raised the TVA as an example of the kind of integrated development they were hoping to promote in Egypt. American EARIS documents did not mention this analogy, however, perhaps because of sensitivity to political opposition to TVA-type projects in America. When Si Fryer described EARIS to a press briefing as an "area development project" and was asked point blank if it were "Like TVA," he responded warily, "It has some of that element in it." See RG 469 TCA/NEADS/Egypt Branch/Gen Recs 1950–53, Box 4, "Press Conference Held by E. Reeseman Fryer," 3 April 1953, p. 17.

72. Conference on Community Development, p. 21.

73. Carl C. Taylor, *A Critical Analysis of India's Community Development Programme* (Community Projects Administration, Government of India, 1956), p. 58.

74. Tannous to Hannum, 28 July 1953, RG 469 Egypt Branch, Subject Files, 1951–54, TCA/NEADS, Box 6.

75. Lucian W. Pye, "Community Development as a Part of Political Development," Background Paper, Conference on Community Development Sponsored by Center for International Studies (MIT), 1957, p. 26.

76. David C. McClelland, "Community Development and the Nature of Human Motivation: Some Implications of Recent Research," Background Paper, Conference on Community Development Sponsored by Center for International Studies (MIT), 1957, p. 1.

77. RG 469, ECA, Assistant Administrator for Programs, Subject Files 1948–50, "Communism vs. Democracy in the East," 14 February 1950.

78. Opening Statement by Hon. Loy W. Henderson, in Foreign Operations Administration, *Report of Regional Conference on Community Development,* Tehran, Iran, 27–30 November 1954, p. 5.

79. Harry S. Truman Presidential Library, Official File 192 A, March-June 1949. Press release dated 24 June 1949.

80. H.R. 5615, 81st Congress, 1st session.

81. Sec. 2. The administration introduced a separate bill to provide for loan guarantees to American investors overseas (H.R. 5594). This bill passed the House but died in the Senate.

82. Secs. 10 and 9, respectively.

83. Hearings before the Committee on Foreign Affairs, 81st Congress, 1st session, on H.R. 5615. p. 25.

84. Chamber of Commerce of the United States, Report of Special Committee on Point Four program (approved by board of directors), hearing record, pp. 155–6.

85. *Congressional Quarterly Weekly Report,* XII:27 (2 July 1954), p. 825.

86. For example, while the House included a provision in the Mutual Security Authorization Act of 1954 extending overseas investment guarantees to cover losses from war or revolution, the provision was rejected in conference.

87. In 1956, for example, President Eisenhower requested $4.772 billion in foreign economic and military aid, and the House Foreign Affairs Committee reduced that amount by $1.1 billion. Eisenhower then met with the Speaker of the House and Minority Leader urging restoration of $600 million. He was unsuccessful, although the Senate passed the bill with only $361 million less than the president's request.

88. H.R. 6026, 81st Congress, 1st session.

89. Ibid., Sec. 2.

90. The new bill specified that the representatives be broadly representative of groups interested in the program including business, labor, agriculture, and education.

91. P.L. 535, 81st Congress.

92. H.R. 5615, Sec. 4(a).

93. The Partners in Progress Report, submitted in November 1951 by a committee chaired by Nelson Rockefeller, advocated a single agency to administer U.S. foreign aid. The Administrator of the TCA argued successfully at the time for TCA independence from better-capitalized economic and military programs.

94. The figure for TCA is the initial appropriation to the new organization. The figure for ECA is expenditures and loans; the appropriation in FY 1951 was only $2.11 billion, but the ECA carried over $2.14 billion in unexpended balances from FY 1950 to 1951. Hearings before the Committee on Armed Services, U.S. Senate, 82nd Congress, 2d session, on S. 3086, p. 38.

95. TCA was transferred to the MSA on June 1, 1953; MSA was abolished two months later and its remaining functions were transferred to a new organization, the Foreign Operations Administration (FOA).

96. Sharp, *International Technical Assistance*, p. 58. Emphasis in original.

97. The start date of new fiscal years shifted from July 1 to October 1 in the Ford Administration.

98. Quoted in *Congressional Quarterly Weekly Report*, XI:2 (9 January 1953), p. 56.

99. Message of 5 May 1953.

100. This was in part due to a limited pool of qualified technicians who were interested in working overseas, and in part to the difficulties and delays in gaining security clearances for overseas personnel. In many cases, by time a candidate's clearance had come through, he had found another job. Interview with Harry Hemmerich, 25 July, 1994.

101. The Chairman of the House Ways and Means Committee, Daniel A. Reed, said on May 28, 1953, "The time has come for curtailment [of foreign aid] . . . in order that we may follow the action already taken in Canada and England in providing tax relief." Quoted in *Congressional Quarterly Weekly Report*, XII:13 (26 March 1954), p. 376. For his part, the chairman of the House subcommittee responsible for foreign aid appropriations did not vote "for a dollar of aid since 1947, when he approved Greek-Turkish arms." *Congressional Quarterly Weekly Report*, XIII:13 (1 April 1954), p. ii.

102. Officially, the Commission on Foreign Economic Policy. Their final report is dated 23 January 1954.

103. Commission on Foreign Economic Policy, Report to the President and to Congress, Washington, DC, 1954, p. 12.

104. Ibid.

105. "President Awaits Aid Chief's Views," *New York Times*, 5 May 1955, p. 14.

Chapter 3

1. See, for example, Patrick O'Brien and The Royal Institute of International Affairs, *The Revolution in Egypt's Economic System: From Private Enterprise to Socialism, 1952–1965* (London, New York: Royal Institute of International Affairs [by] Oxford University Press, 1966), and Robert Vitalis, *When Capitalists Collide: Business Conflict and the End of Empire in Egypt* (Berkeley: University of California Press, 1995).

2. This view is expressed, for example, by Raymond Baker, *Egypt's Uncertain Revolution Under Nasser and Sadat* (Cambridge: Harvard University Press, 1978), pp. 60–69. Most of Baker's proof is gathered from speeches delivered some 12 or more years after the revolution.

3. Robert L. Tignor, *State, Private Enterprise and Economic Change in Egypt, 1918–1952* (Princeton, NJ: Princeton University Press, 1984), p. 15.

4. Kulliya al-Tijara, *al-Yubil al-Fiddi,* pp. 181–221, quoted in ibid., p. 208.

5. Ibid., p. 180.

6. Vitalis, *When Capitalists Collide,* p. 197.

7. John Waterbury writes, for example, "Beyond a vague aspiration toward industrialization and modernity, policy formulation tended to be dictated by real and perceived threats to the regime as not as part of a coherent economic strategy." *The Egypt of Nasser and Sadat: The Political Economy of Two Regimes* (Princeton, NJ: Princeton University Press, 1983), p. 49. See also O'Brien, *Revolution,* p. 68; Charles Issawi, *Egypt in Revolution* (London: Oxford University Press, 1963) p. 51; Baker, *Egypt's Uncertain Revolution,* p. 43. Robert Mabro disagrees, stating that "the first years of the Revolution in fact constitute a turning point" in Egypt's economic history. *The Egyptian Economy, 1952–72* (Oxford: Clarendon Press, 1974), p. 5. The same view is adhered to in Ali al-Gritly, *The Economic History of the Revolution, 1952–1966* (Cairo: Dar al-Ma'araf bi-Misr, 1974, Ar.) ch. 3–4, and, not surprisingly, in Rashed al-Barrawi, *The Economic Philosophy of the Revolution* (Cairo: Maktabat al-Nahda al-Misriya, 1955, Ar.), passim. The author of the latter volume was the chief economic adviser to the Free Officers. Barrawi's influence derived not from his stancing in the economics profession in Egypt, but rather from his position as the former economics instructor of many of the Free Officers from their time in the Army Staff College. Interview with Ahmed Hamrouche, Cairo, Egypt, 15 April 1993.

8. See Kirk J. Beattie, *Egypt During the Nasser Years: Ideology, Politics and Civil Society* (Boulder, CO: Westview Press, 1994), pp. 44–50.

9. "The Goal of the Revolution Is to Change the Corrupt System," reprinted in *Speeches and Statements of President Gamal Abdel Nasser, 1952–1956* (n.p.: n.d., Ar.), p. 44.

10. "Capitalism Will Not Control the Regime," (speech delivered to a celebration of the Liberation Rally in Shubra al-Khayma, 20 December 1953), reprinted in ibid., p. 218.

11. Ibid., p. 219.

12. It is often mentioned that only Khaled Mohieddin and Yusuf Siddiq among the 14-member RCC were Marxists.

13. Joel Gordon, *Nasser's Blessed Movement: Egypt's Free Officers and the July Revolution* (New York: Oxford University Press, 1992), p. 121.

14. Saad Eddin Ibrahim, "The Social Project of the July Revolution," *The Revolution of the 23rd of July* (Cairo: Dar al-Mustaqbal al-Arabi, 1987, Ar.) p. 362.

15. For a description of the land reform debate in the mid-1940s, see Tariq al-Bishri, *The Political Movement in Egypt, 1945–1952, 2nd printing* (Cairo: Dar al-Shuruq, 1983, Ar.), pp. 193–197.

16. National Bank of Egypt, "Notes and Comments," *Bulletin* V (1952), p. 167.

17. Ibid., p. 168. It is worth recalling in this regard that only a small fraction of the total land in the country is arable. More than 95 percent of the land in

Egypt was uninhabited and uninhabitable desert. This land was generally not owned and not worth owning.

18. Ibid.

19. A list of landholders who received some of the largest royal land grants can be found in Barrawi, *Economic Philosophy,* pp. 4–8.

20. RG 469, USOM/Egypt/CSF (CCF), 1951–54, Box 3. "Economic Report for Week Ending August 26," 28 August 1956.

21. These were enumerated by the TCA mission in Egypt as: channeling compensation for expropriated land to industry, distributing land over a five-year period, providing for the consolidation of land holdings, a graduated land tax, and standards for selecting those to whom land would be distributed. RG 469, USOM/E/CSF (CGF), 1951–56, Box 4. Harold Jorgenson to Byron Denny (Bureau of Land Management), "Monthly Report for August 1952," 5 September 1952.

22. Ibid.

23. According to one contemporaneous account, the reduction in rents was the most important consequence of the law. See "The Economic Effects of Agricultural Reform," *Al-Ahram al-Iqtisadi* (Ar.), October 1954, p. 1.

24. An English-language text of the law can be found in U.A.R. Ministry of Agrarian Reform and Land Reclamation, *Agrarian Reform and Land Reclamation in Eleven Years* (Cairo: General Organization for Government Printing Offices, 1963), pp. 223–247. The terms were tilted in favor of small landholders in 1958, when the mortgages became 40 years at 1.5 percent interest with only a 10 percent premium.

25. For example, Doreen Warriner, *Land Reform and Development in the Middle East* (London: Royal Institute for International Affairs, 1957), p. 32, cited in Keith Wheelock, *Nasser's New Egypt: A Critical Analysis* (New York: Praeger, 1960), p. 86.

26. Charles Issawi, *Egypt in Revolution: An Economic Analysis* (London: Oxford University Press, 1963), p. 161. One commentator went so far as to estimate that spiraling land prices allowed the average landholder had completely amortize his investment within 14 years, and that "indemnification under these conditions constituted a real gesture of political appeasement to the powerful of the old system by the state and a solemn rejection of the very principle of revolutionary expropriation." Anouar Abdel-Malek, *Egypt: Military Society,* trans. by Charles Lam Markmann (New York: Vintage Books, 1968), p. 73. Most observers agree that bonds were not honored in many cases and in practice landowners did not receive all of their promised compensation.

27. "Our Need to Increase Investment and Credit," *al-Ahram al-Iqtisadi* (Ar.), November 1952, p. 11.

28. "Three Solutions to Treat the Economic Problem in Egypt," *al-Ahram al-Iqtisadi* (Ar.), December 1952, p. 14. A report by A. D. Little estimated that personal savings in Egypt averaged 50 million £E/year, of which 1/3 was hoarded in gold or currency holdings, and 1/2 was invested in land. The remainder was only 8.3 million £E/year, or less than $1 per person per year.

See Republic of Egypt, Ministry of Commerce and Industry, *Opportunities for Industrial Development in Egypt* [Report to U.S. Government Foreign Operations Administration Under Contract SCC-21504 C-58780] (Cairo: Government Press, 1955), p. 39.

29. "Reaction Cannot Triumph," *Collection of Speeches, Statements and Declarations of President Gamal Abdel Nasser* (Cairo: Maslahat al-Isti'lamat, n.d., Ar.), part 1, p. 108.

30. Abdel Azim Ramadan, *The Social and Political Conflict in Egypt: From the 23 July Revolution to the March Crisis of 1954* (Cairo: Maktabat Madbuli, 1989, Ar.), p. 99.

31. A *Rose al-Yusef* interview with the Minister of Social Affairs carried the headline, "We are not bound by the thinking of a particular country . . . Egypt borrows from the American system and the Russian system . . . We need to use Egyptian capital first." 19 January 1953, p. 4.

32. RG 469. TCA/NEADS/Egypt Branch/Subject Files, 1951–54, Box 9. "Contributions which the Technical Cooperation Administration can make in assisting in the solution of Egypt's economic and social problems," attached to letter from Jefferson Caffery to Ali Maher, 20 August 1952.

33. The need for coordinated planning bodies was a recurrent theme among donor nations of the period. Britain insisted on the creation of such boards as part of its aid programs to Iraq and Jordan in the same period. See Paul W. T. Kingston, *Britain and the Politics of Modernization in the Middle East, 1945–1958* (Cambridge: Cambridge University Press, 1996), pp. 104–109, 127–135.

34. RG 84 Cairo Embassy/General Records 1950–52, Box 238. Cairo to Washington, 27 December 1952. "Appointments to National Production Council." The members were Abdel Razak el-Sanhouri, Hussein Fahmy, Ibrahim Bayumi Madkur, Muhammad Ahmed Selim, Rashed al-Barawy, Mohammed Mahmud Ibrahim, Abdel Rahman Hamada, Mohammad Aly Hussein, Aly el-Gritly, Yehia al-Alaily, and Shalabi Sarofeem. By 1955 the PCDNP had 22 members, including six ministers and six full-time employees. Hussein Fahmy, "Projects of Construction and Development in the Egyptian Republic," *al-Abhath* (Ar.), March 1955, p. 14.

35. Rashed al-Barawy, *Economic Development in the United Arab Republic (Egypt)* (Cairo: Anglo-American Bookshop, 1970), p. 51.

36. al-Barrawi, *Economic Philosophy*, p. 49.

37. Ibid., p. 49.

38. "Activities of the National Production Council," *al-Ahram al-Iqtisadi* (Ar.), November/December 1953, p. 16.

39. "The National Economy in the New Era," *al-Ahram al-Iqtisadi* (Ar.), September 1952, p. 1.

40. "President of the Production Council Speaks Frankly: White Is White . . . And Black Is Black!" *Akher Sa'a* (Ar.), 28 January 1953, p. 7.

41. "The Experts Only Have the Right to Advise," *Rose al-Yusef* (Ar.), 9 March 1953, p. 14.

42. "White is White," *Akher Sa'a*, p. 7.

43. Muhammad Wagdi, "New Contours," *al-Ahram* (Ar.) 2 January 1954, p. 7, reports on Minister of National Guidance Salah Salem's rejection of American economic and military aid as an attempt to buy Egyptian friendship.

44. National Bank of Egypt, *Bulletin* VII (1954), p. 157.

45. In January 1953 the Egyptian Foreign Ministry requested its embassies in countries "most similar to Egypt" in terms of their strategic, social and economic conditions to submit reports on the amount and effect of U.S. aid in those countries. According to the reports, aid to Greece in the preceding four years totaled almost $1.5 billion; Yugoslavia had received almost a half billion dollars in economic aid since 1945, and its 1951 aid package of $120 combined contributions of the United States, Britain, and France. Egyptian National Archives, Foreign Ministry Archives, Box 1550. Cairo to Ankara, Athens and Belgrade, 12 January 1953. Athens to Cairo, 1 February 1953. Belgrade to Cairo, 22 February 1953. For an interesting account of Egyptian hopes for significant American aid in the 1940s, see al-Bishri, *Political Movement*, p. 188.

46. Egyptian budgetary practice was to add unexpended appropriations from one year to the amount for the subsequent year. It is thus quite difficult to ascertain how much the Egyptian government spent on production projects since annual budgets of 10 million £E for four years might reflect either a 40 million £E expenditure or a one-time appropriation of 10 million £E which was never spent. See National Bank of Egypt *Bulletin* VII (1954), p. 160.

47. "Our Production," *al-Ahram al-Iqtisadi* (Ar.), November/December 1953, p. 1.

48. National Bank of Egypt, *Bulletin* VI (1953), p. 189.

49. National Bank of Egypt, *Bulletin* VII (1954), p. 261.

50. *Principal Production Projects* (Cairo: Majlis al-Da'im li-Tanmiyat al-Intaj al-Qawmi, 1954, Ar.).

51. The American involvement is described in RG 469 USOM/Egypt/CSF (CGF) 1951–56, Box 1. Statement of Harold R. Stevens, Istanbul, Turkey. 11 December 1953.

52. RG 469 TCA/NEADS/Egypt Branch/Subject Files, 1951–54, Box 10. Cairo to State, 22 August 1952.

53. RG 469 USOM/Egypt/CSF (CGF), 1951–56, Box 3. Nichols to Sacksteder, 2 September 1952. The other high-priority project was a desert range project to develop grasses that could survive in the Egyptian deserts.

54. In the event, Cabot left Egypt thinking that "no great relief" could come to Egypt from industrialization since it was a largely agricultural country and would likely remain so for the foreseeable future. Interestingly, he was one of the earliest boosters of the Aswan High Dam project. See Thomas D. Cabot, "Let's Do Business with Egypt!" *Christian Science Monitor*, 15 April 1953, p. 13.

55. Interview with George Sweeny, Cambridge, MA, 17 March 1993.

56. See Egypt, Ministry of Commerce and Industry, *Opportunities for Industrial Development in Egypt,* pp. 2–5.
57. Ibid., p. 6.
58. Ibid.
59. RG 469 USOM/Egypt/CSF (CGF) 1951–56, Box 3. "Long Term Functional Program Poultry."
60. Ibid.
61. RG 469 NEA Ops/NE Div/Egy Branch/Subj Files 1954–57, Box 3. Comptroller General of the United States, *Audit Report to Congress of the United States: U.S. Assistance Program for Egypt.* 30 June 1955.
62. "45,470 £E to Implement the Chicken Agreement," *al-Ahram* (Ar.), 2 September 1954, p. 9. See also "71,826 £E for Point 4 Agreements," *al-Ahram* (Ar.), 8 September 1954, which describes the independent auditing the PCDNP demanded of the Agriculture Ministry in return for the grant, as well as a warning that future livestock improvement programs would have to come out of the ministry's regular budget.
63. The United States concurrently carried out similar livestock improvement projects throughout the world. In Iran, for example, the projects involved 75,000 chickens in addition to goats, sheep, Brown Swiss bulls, and Cyprus jackasses. See Bingham, *Short-sleeve Diplomacy,* p. 53.
64. "Mass Chicklift: Churches Send Easter Gift to Egypt," *Life,* 29 March 1954, p. 101.
65. RG 469 TCA/NEADS/Egypt Branch/General Records 1950–53, Box 4. Harry Carr to E. Reeseman Fryer, 7 May 1953.
66. "At the Chicken Exhibition," *al-Ahram* (Ar.), 25 March 1952, p. 12.
67. "30,000 Chicks . . . Arrive in Egypt . . .By Plane!" *al-Musawwar* (Ar.), 13 March 1953, p. 40.
68. "Blessings to the Chickens this Week," *Akher Sa'a* (Ar.), 25 March 1953. In its articles about the importation and distribution of American chicks, *al-Ahram* made no mention at all of the United States, referring to the chickens only as "foreign" or "brought in from overseas." See "Immunization of a Quarter of a Million Chickens in the First Day," 25 March 1953, p. 5 and "Distribution of Superior Chickens," 29 April 1953, p. 9. *Akher Sa'a* ran an article several months after distribution of the chicks had taken place that concluded with the paragraph, "The experiment has prospered, and Bahtim is recorded as a success story, but there are thousands of villages in Egypt which still need such experiments, and such successes!" "Egyptian Animal Wealth on the Path of Recording a Record," *Akher Sa'a* (Ar.), 15 June 1953, p. 57.
69. The biggest concern for export stock was levels of pullorum, a bacterial disease caused by salmonella bacteria that lowers egg production. It is passed on in the eggs from a hen to her progeny. The imported American chicks received the highest certification for freedom from the disease. Once in Egypt, the American chicks were immunized for a number of disorders: Newcastle disease, fowl plague, and pox.

70. RG 469 DD Ops/NEA Ops/Office of the Chief/Subj Files re: Egypt 1953–63, Box 3. "Second Yearly Report of the Poultry Project in Egypt," 1 July 1954. One of the appeals of Rhode Island Red chickens was that their eggs were brown and thus easily identifiable. See Bingham, p. 55.

71. "Project to Improve Chickens in Egypt," *al-Ahram* (Ar.) 6 April 1954, p. 9.

72. "Point IV Chicks," *Akher Saʻa* (Ar.), 16 April 1954, p. 52.

73. "Interview with Egypt's Prime Minister Lieut. Col. Gamal Abdel Nasser," *U.S. News and World Report,* 3 September 1954, p. 29.

74. RG 469 DD Ops/NEA Ops/Office of the Chief/Subj Files re: Egypt 1953–61, Box 3. Cairo to State, 1 September 1954.

75. RG 469 DD Ops/NEA Ops/Office of the Chief/Subj Files re: Egypt 1953–61, Box 3. "Second Yearly Report of Poultry Project in Egypt," July 1, 1954.

76. RG 469 DD Ops/NEA Ops/Office of the Chief/Subj Files re: Egypt 1953–61, Box 3. Cairo to Washington, 18 November 1954. "Preliminary Note on Coryza of Fowls in Birds Imported into Egypt."

77. United Arab Republic, Ministry of Agrarian Reform and Land Reclamation, *Agrarian Reform and Land Reclamation in Eleven Years* (Cairo: General Organization for Government Printing Offices, 1963), p. 118.

78. Among the changes introduced by the Companies Law of 1954, directors faced mandatory retirement at sixty, could serve on no more than six corporate boards, could not be managing director of more than two companies, and each had to assume responsibility for some specific aspect of company policy. O'Brien, *Revolution,* p. 74.

79. The best summary of the broad variety of laws meant to encourage investment can be found in al-Barrawi, *Economic Philosophy,* chapter 5. See also O'Brien, *Revolution,* p. 71.

80. National Bank of Egypt, *Bulletin* VII (1954), "Economic Review: Egypt," p. 37.

81. "N.B.E. Report Stresses Need to Reassure Capital, Savings" [transcript of address of Mr. Aly Shamsy to the 54th annual ordinary meeting of the National Bank of Egypt], *The Egyptian Gazette,* 25 March 1954, p. 2.

82. RG 469 USOM/Egypt/CSF (CGF) 1951–54, Box 3. "Economic Report for Week Ending October 29," 29 October 1952.

83. World Bank, *The Economic Development of Egypt* (Report #A.S. 40-a), 25 August 1955, p. 17.

84. "Talk of the People," *Rose al-Yusef* (Ar.), 8 June 1953, p. 9.

85. "Egypt Itself Decides Whether to Join the Defense Organization," *Rose al-Yusef* (Ar.), 16 February 1953, p. 4.

86. The Egyptian government did not take steps to sharply curtail investment in business until September 1956, when it required approval for most new construction of significant value and took steps to limit the demolition of sound buildings. See National Bank of Egypt, *Bulletin,* IX (1956), p. 314.

87. National Bank of Egypt, *Bulletin* IX (1956), p. 109.

88. Federation of Egyptian Industries, *L'Egypte Industrielle,* no. 32/6 (June 1956), pp. 5–7, cited in National Bank of Egypt, *Bulletin* IX (1956), "Capital Formation and Capital/Output Ratio in Egypt," p. 310.

89. In terms of net capital formation, building represented 74 percent in 1954 and 62 percent in 1955.
90. 1954/55 Year Book, p. 136, cited in National Bank of Egypt, *Bulletin* IX (1956), "Gross Rate of Capital Formation in Egypt," pp. 19–20.
91. Ibid., p. 20.
92. National Bank of Egypt, *Bulletin* IX (1956), p. 152.
93. That is to say, the units of capital needed to be invested to increase income by a single unit.
94. National Bank of Egypt, *Bulletin* IX (1956), p. 314.
95. See O'Brien, *Revolution,* p. 71.
96. "Capital Formation and Capital/Output Ratio in Egypt," p. 310.
97. Adel Hamuda, *The Crisis of the Intellectuals and the July Revolution* (Cairo: Maktabat Madbuli, 1985, Ar.), p. 174.
98. Joel Gordon, *Nasser's Blessed Movement* (New York: Oxford University Press, 1992), pp. 76, 83.
99. Israeli agents attacked American and British targets in Egypt to try to head off Egyptian rapprochement with the Western powers.
100. "Production Council Accounts for Its Activities," *Rose al-Yusef* (Ar.), 8 March 1954, p. 10.
101. "Rebuilding Our National Economy," *al-Ahram al-Iqtisadi* (English supplement), April 1955, p. 4.
102. "The Road to Strength and Decent Living," ibid., p. 6.
103. National Bank of Egypt, *Bulletin* VII (1954), "National Production Council," p. 258.
104. "High Dam Project," *al-Ahram al-Iqtisadi* [English supplement], April 1955, pp. 16–17.
105. Nor did he mention Adrien Daninos, the Egyptian engineer of Greek ancestry who originally sold the idea of a larger dam at Aswan to the Free Officers. Daninos' and Hurst's roles are described in chapter 5.
106. "The High Dam Project," *al-Ahram al-Iqtisadi* (Ar.), April 1955, p. 16.
107. *Rose al-Yusef* (Ar.), 9 May 1955, p. 9.
108. This differs from the view of some. Raymond Baker, for example, asserts that the military leadership's minimal interest in capitalist development has "been enriched with a generous amount of deliberate mythology" intended to cast Egyptian capitalists in a bad light. *Egypt's Uncertain Revolution,* p. 62. It is the present author's contention that such a conclusion is harder to reach when reading only among documentation from before 1956.
109. O'Brien, *Revolution,* p. 83.

Chapter 4

1. RG 59, Top Secret, Cairo to Washington, 10 January 1953.
2. RG 84, Cairo, Box 252, State to Cairo, 13 January 1953.
3. RG 469, HQ Off/DD Ops/Economic Aid to Egypt, 1952–1955, Box 2, USOM/E to FOA, 15 March 1954, "Origin and Development of the Egyptian-American Rural Improvement Service (EARIS)."

4. Interview with Harry Hemmerich, Washington DC, 25 July 1994. One of Fryer's colleagues wrote him calling him a man "of heart, courage, idealism, sincerity and integrity." See RG 469, TCA/NEADS/Egypt Branch, General Records 1950–53, Box 4, Harry Carr to Si Fryer, 1 June 1953.

5. "*Fellah*" (pl. "*fellahin*") means "peasant" in Egyptian colloquial Arabic, and the Fellah Department sought to improve their lot.

6. See, generally, Ahmed Hussein, *Rural Social Welfare Centers in Egypt* (Washington: Embassy of Egypt, 1954), pp. 4–6. Hussein went on to become the Egyptian Ambassador to Washington in April 1953. There is no direct evidence that he became involved in steering American aid toward the Egyptian countryside, although he had good contacts throughout the American government predating his posting in Washington.

7. RG 469, NEA Operations, Near East Division, Egypt Branch, Subject Files 1954–1957, Box 3, Savilla Simons to Si Fryer, 5 February 1953.

8. Royal Government of Egypt, Ministry of Social Affairs, *Social Welfare in Egypt* (Cairo, 1950), p. 33.

9. Ibid., p. 12.

10. Ibid., p. 11.

11. Dr. Mohd. Munir al-Zalaky, "The Functional Relationship between Low Agricultural Incomes and the Low Agricultural Standard of Living in Egypt," commentary contributed to *Second Social Welfare Seminar for Arab States of the Middle East* (Cairo: Ministry of Social Affairs, 1950) p. 424. Hereafter referred to as SWSASME.

12. Halim Najjar, "Cooperation and Rural Society," SWSASME, p. 365. In this regard, Arab social thought resembled American social thought with regard to industrial education for the African-American population in the late nineteenth century. The establishment of technical institutes throughout the American South to teach trades and self-discipline to black Americans after the Civil War in many ways reflected the same focus on improving the self-image of the poor as a means of alleviating their poverty.

13. Committee I, "Report on Basic Rural Education," SWSASME, p. 27.

14. Royal Government of Egypt, *Social Welfare in Egypt*, p. 13. Such positions would always be filled by men, since the job entailed dealing with men in the village. Women were appointed to the home visiting and some of the health care positions that entailed contact with village women.

15. Mahmoud Fahmy, "How Should the Leaders Be Found and Trained, and How Should They Be Co-Ordinated in Policy and Program?" SWSASME, p. 192. Fahmy was Deputy Director General of the Fellah Department at the time, and its director during the discussions over EARIS in the spring and summer of 1953.

16. Royal Government of Egypt, *Social Welfare in Egypt*, p. 31.

17. See Abdullah el Araby Bey, "How Far Should Decentralization Be Practiced in Rural Social Organization?" SWSASME, pp. 185–186.

18. RG 469, NEA Ops/NED/Egypt Branch/Subject Files 1954–1957, Box 3, Savilla Simons to Si Fryer, 5 February 1953. Simons's ideas may have been

based, at least on part, on the industrial education movement in the American South. Beginning in Reconstruction and extending into the 1940s, the industrial education movement sought to bring rural Southern blacks together for an educational program which was partly training in technical skills, partly training to be educators, and partly rigorous manual labor so as to inculcate the work ethic among poor rural blacks. An overwhelming majority of the graduates of such programs went on to teach in rural schools, thereby spreading the programs' philosophy. Industrial education differed in a fundamental way from the American program in Egypt, however: whereas industrial education sought to promote political passivity among Southern blacks, the Egyptian program sought to promote a fundamentally new kind of political activity.

19. For the text of the agreement, see U.S. Department of State, RG 59, 874.00 TA/3–2153. Interestingly, initial negotiations targeted only desert reclamation in the Fayyoum Oasis, and not the marsh land reclamation just outside of Alexandria which came to receive primary attention as EARIS planning progressed over the summer (discussed below). See U.S. Department of State, RG 59, 874.00 TA/2–1853, Cairo to Washington, 18 February 1953.

20. U.S. Department of State, RG 59, 1950–54, 874.00 TA/3–2153, "Agreement for a Cooperative Program of Community Development and Rural Rehabilitation in the Egyptian Provinces of Buheira and Fayyoum between the Government of the United States of America and the Government of Egypt."

21. The expatriate community included both Europeans and individuals from other parts of the Ottoman Empire who drifted to Egypt in search of opportunity. Many such persons remained in Egypt for several generations without acquiring Egyptian citizenship.

22. Similar sentiments dominated the "Islamic Reform" movement of the late nineteenth century. The central idea of that movement was that the Arab world was backward because the true Islam had been buried under the accretions of centuries of misguided rule. Islam was not incompatible with modernity but rather the key to a superior civilization, if only it were properly applied. The resurgence of the importance of the Pharaonic past, both in the 1920s and after the revolution, is tied to similar ideas of the inherent greatness of the Egyptian people. For Islamic reform, see Albert Hourani, *Arabic Thought in the Liberal Age, 1798–1939* (Cambridge: Cambridge University Press, 1962). For Pharaonicism, see James Gershoni and James Jankowski, *Egypt, Islam and the Arabs: The Search for Egyptian Nationhood, 1900–1930* (New York: Oxford University Press, 1986).

23. The first issue of the Communist paper, *The Opposition*, featured a lead story entitled "The New Satan" warning that American imperialism was on the verge of replacing British imperialism in the region. An additional article provided "Dangerous information published for the first time on American imperialism and how it advances in Egypt." Quoted in Rifa'at al-Sa'id, *History of the Egyptian Communist Movement, vol. 2: The Public Press* (Cairo:

Sharikat al-Amal lil-Tabaʻa wal-Nashr wal-Tawziʻ, 1987, Ar.), p. 323. The connection of the Egyptian Communist movement to the Soviet Union is indirect. For the most part the party was led by members of Egypt's minority communities, especially Jews, and while the party's efforts had the effect of furthering Soviet foreign policy, there appears to be little evidence that the Soviet Union directed the party's activities. In any event, the party was exceedingly small and mostly elite in membership.

24. The most prominent Marxist in the Revolutionary Command Council was Khaled Mohieddin; other leftists from the Democratic Movement for National Liberation (known by its Arabic acronym, HADETO) such as Ahmed Hamrouche also played leading roles in the revolution. Descriptions of the roles of Marxists in the revolution can be found in Mohieddin's memoirs (published originally in Arabic as *And Now I Speak* (Cairo: Markaz al-Ahram lil-Tarjama wal-Nashr, 1992) and in English as *Memories of a Revolution: Egypt 1952,* trans. by TRIACC Translation Services (Cairo: American University in Cairo Press, 1995) and Selma Botman's *The Rise of Egyptian Communism* (Syracuse: Syracuse University Press, 1986), ch. 5.

25. RG 469, TCA/NEADS/Egypt Branch, General Records 1950–53, Box 4, "Report on TCA-Task Force Activities," September 1953. The impugned ministries include Irrigation, Social Affairs, Education, and the State Domains Department, which all played roles in implementation of EARIS.

26. RG 469, TCA/NEADS/Egypt Branch, General Records 1950–53, Box 4, Harry Carr to Si Fryer, 7 May 1953.

27. See especially, RG 469, TCA/NEADS/Egypt Branch, General Records 1950–53, Box 4, Fryer to A. B. Bonds, 8 April 1953 and Carr to Fryer, 7 May 1953.

28. RG 469 TCA/NEADS/Egypt Branch, General Records 1950–53, Box 4, Stanley Andrews to John Nichols, 4 May 1953. Andrews told Nichols that "a change in the Directorship of the Egyptian Mission would have been made" regardless of whether or not the program had expanded in March as a result of Fryer's efforts.

29. President Eisenhower appointed Stassen head of FOA after the first of what would be nine unsuccessful attempts by Stassen to gain the Republican nomination for President.

30. See chapter 2.

31. Richard Dekmejian interview with Erwin Hannum, 6 February 1981. The AID report states that Stevens went on to be head of Buildings and Grounds at Penn after his tour in Egypt. According to Dekmejian's interviews, Stevens assumed that position at Baldwin-Wallace College in Ohio when the head of the Egypt mission's education program became the school's president. Richard Dekmejian interview with A. B. Bonds, no date (1981).

32. The criticisms are summarized in Pamela R. Johnson et al., *Egypt: The Egyptian-American Rural Improvement Service, a Point Four Project, 1952–63* (Washington: Agency for International Development, 1983), p. D-14. They are drawn from Dekmejian's interviews with John Russell, Albert Farwell,

Erwin Hannum, Kenneth Platt, and Roscoe Bell. For a contrasting view of Stevens, see Dekmejian's interview with A. B. Bonds.

33. Interview with Dr. Rifky Anwar, Cairo, Egypt, 24 October 1994.

34. RG 469 TCA/NEADS/Egypt Branch, General Records, 1950–53, Box 3, Harry Hemmerich to Rocker Ackley, 14 September 1953.

35. RG 469, TCA/NEADS/Egypt Branch, General Records 1950–53, Box 3, Harry Hemmerich to Roger Ackley, 18 November 1953.

36. Ibid.

37. This is true both literally and figuratively. The language of science and engineering in Egypt was English (although French maintained its position during this time as the language of culture), so most Egyptian engineers could communicate to some degree with their American colleagues. Also, engineers who received some training in the United States often had a sympathy for and understanding of American culture that no Americans could match in terms of Egyptian culture.

38. RG 469, TCA/NEADS/Egypt Branch, General Records 1950–53, Box 4, Report of TCA-Task Force Activities, p. 10.

39. RG 469 TCA/NEADS/Egypt Branch, General Records 1950–53, Box 4, Press conference by E. Reeseman Fryer, 3 April 1953.

40. Hamdy El Shazly, "Abis as a Pilot Project in Settlement" (lecture, no date), United Nations Development Programme, Integrated Development and Settlement of New Lands Irrigated by High Dam Waters, UNDP/UNOTC/ARE-71, p. 1.

41. Ibid. The total area of land which could be reclaimed in the first two phases, 5,600 feddans, is presumably the same 5,600 feddans of land in the area already undergoing reclamation work by the State Domains Department at the time the EARIS agreement was made. The targets for 1957 and 1959 are a full year later than the projections made in the preliminary project draft submitted by American technician E. L. Armstrong in July 1953. See RG 469 HQ Off/DD Ops/NEA Ops/NED Egypt Branch, Records re: EARIS, Box 1, "Construction of Major Works and Land Development," 3 July 1953.

42. RG 469, HQ Off/DD Ops/NEA Ops/NED Egypt Branch, Records re: EARIS, Box 1. Report of EARIS Housing and Planning Subcommittee, 20 July 1953.

43. Ibid.

44. RG 469 HQ Off/DD Ops/NEA Ops/NED Egypt Branch, Records re: EARIS, Box 1. "A Proposed Educational Program for the EARIS Project," 23 July 1953.

45. RG 469 HQ Off/DD Ops/NEA Ops/NED Egypt Branch, Records re: EARIS, Box 1. "Proposed Health and Sanitation Program for EARIS," 8 July 1953.

46. RG 469 HQ Off/DD Ops/NEA Ops/NED Egypt Branch, Records re: EARIS, Box 1. "Community Organization Project for the EARIS Program as Suggested by A. I. Tannous for Discussion by EARIS Committee on Community Organization." 2 July 1953. It is worth mentioning that no other

committee mentioned including settlers in the decision-making process at this early date.

47. Ibid.

48. The rural population in the Nile Delta is overwhelmingly Muslim and thus the EARIS communities always included plans for mosques but never for churches.

49. RG 469 TCA/NEADS/Egypt Branch, General Records 1950–53, Box 4, "Report on TCA-Task Force Activities."

50. RG 469 TCA/NEADS/Egypt Branch, General Records 1950–53, Box 4, Harry Carr to Si Fryer, 1 June 1953.

51. Ibid.

52. Ibid.

53. The agreements were signed April 25, August 25, September 24, and November 30, respectively. For a brief description of the agreements, see RG 469 FOA/DDO/NEA/NE Central Files Egypt 1953–55, Box 6, "Briefing Book for Norman Paul visit, February 5–11, 1954."

54. Egyptian sensitivity over sovereignty had some basis in fact. On February 4, 1942, British tanks surrounded Abdin Palace and demanded that the king remove the Prime Minister and replace him with one more compatible with British interests. The king complied, and his action left a mark on Egyptian politics in subsequent years.

55. Interview with Aziza Shukri Hussein (Ahmed Hussein's widow), Cairo, Egypt, 19 August 1995.

56. RG 59 1950–54, 874.00 TA/11–953, Cairo to Washington, 9 November 1953.

57. The American embassy in London suggested that the "British would regard it as a gross breach of faith if we went ahead with economic aid to Egypt without prior consultation [with] UK." RG 59 1950–54, 874.00 TA/11–1053, London to Washington, 10 November 1953.

58. RG 59 1950–54, 874.00 TA/11–1353, Washington to London, 13 November 1953.

59. "Bermuda" was a reference to an upcoming conference of the heads of state of the United States, Great Britain and France in early December. RG 59 1950–54, 874.00 TA/11–1853. London to Washington, 18 November 1953.

60. See generally, Peter L. Hahn, *The United States, Great Britain and Egypt, 1945–1956: Strategy and Diplomacy in the Early Cold War* (Chapel Hill: University of North Carolina Press, 1991), pp. 166–169, and specifically, Washington to London, 28 January 1953 and London to Washington, 10 February 1953, reprinted in FRUS 1952–54, vol. IX, pp. 1971–1973 and pp. 1986–1987, Dulles to Eden, 13 November 1953 and Ambassador in UK to Dulles, 18 November 1953, reprinted in ibid. pp. 2165–2166, and Churchill to Eisenhower, 19 December 1953, reprinted in ibid., p. 2177–2178.

61. Egyptian intelligence picked up some reports of Anglo-American squabbling over aid to Egypt. See Egyptian National Archives, Foreign Ministry Archives, Box 1558, Memorandum from the Director of the Reports Office, 18 November 1953.

62. RG 469 DD Ops/NEA Ops/Admin Office/Egypt Project Files, 1953–58, Box 8, Memorandum of Conversation with Mr. El Kouni and Robert Carr, 19 November 1953.

63. Translation in RG 84 Cairo, Box 247, Cairo to Washington, 22 November 1953.

64. Reprinted in Egyptian National Archives, Foreign Ministry Archives, Reports of the Egyptian Embassy in Washington/Politics, Box 701.

65. Ibid.

66. The rising and declining fortunes of foreign aid in congressional deliberations is recounted in chapter 2, above.

67. The Egyptians seem to have learned that the figure of $27 million was the working figure in the State Department, although such information remained classified. See RG 469, USOM/E, CSF (CGF) 1951–56, Box 4. Harold Jorgenson to Byron Denny, 11 January 1954.

68. RG 469, USOM/E, CSF (CGF) 1951–56, Box 3. TCE Country Program for FY 1954. Egypt. No date, but appears to have been presented by Stevens in Istanbul in December 1953.

69. RG 469, USOM/E, CSF (CGF) 1951–56, Box 1. Technical and Economic Assistance Programs and Opportunities for Private Investment. Statement of Harold R. Stevens, Istanbul, Turkey, 11 December 1953.

70. The province was known in English as "Liberation Province," "Tahrir Province," and "Mudiriyat Tahrir," presumably depending on the Arabic knowledge of the foreign officials involved. I have adopted the middle position because it seems to have been the most common in English-language documents. The creation of EARIS was the lead story in *Al-Ahram* on March 20, but was relegated to page 5 in the Wafdist *al-Misry* on the same date.

71. Magdi Hassanein, *The Desert . . . The Revolution and the Wealth: The Story of Tahrir Province* (Cairo: al-Hayah al-Misriyah al-Ammah lil-Kitab, 1975, Ar.), pp. 102–104.

72. Hassanein wrote, "The work in Tahrir Province was built on exclusively Egyptian experience and exclusively Egyptian ideas and exclusively Egyptian implementation, all with the sole goal of determining the best results." Ibid., p. 123.

73. "The agricultural revolution will not be fulfilled without the modern farm, which depends primarily on different size farms than are found in Egypt. . . . The large farm is the foundation of making possible an agricultural revolution in Egypt." Ibid., p. 74.

74. Ibid., p. 103.

75. Ibid., p. 139.

76. Ibid., pp. 166–167.

77. Ibid., p. 168.

78. Ibid., p. 168.

79. According to an embassy official who spoke with Sidky in July 1953, "It is quite evident that his plans are an effort to apply in Egypt the planning principles he was taught at Harvard." Ironically, Sidky's dissertation argued for industrially led development in Egypt, judging "The chance of increasing the area of the cultivable land is limited." For the embassy official's

view, see RG 84, Cairo Box 252, Cairo to Washington, 27 July 1953. The quotation from the dissertation can be found in Aziz Sidky, "Industrialization of Egypt and a Case Study of the Iron and Steel Industry," Ph.D. Dissertation, Harvard University, May 1951, p. 24.

80. Doreen Warriner, *Agrarian Reform and Community Development in the U.A.R.* (Cairo: Dar al-Taawon, 1961), p. 54.

81. Hassanein, *The Desert,* p. 124.

82. Ibid., p. 134.

83. RG 469, NEA Ops/NED/Egypt Branch, Subj. Files 1954–57, Box 3, Cairo to Washington, 17 April 1954.

84. Each village contained 30 families, with an average of 5 people per family; thus each cluster of villages (or *nuqta*) contained 900 persons and had the services of a social expert and agricultural expert.

85. RG 469, NEA Ops/NED/Egypt Branch, Subj. Files 1954–57, Box 3, Cairo to Washington, 17 April 1954.

86. Hassanein, *The Desert,* p. 115.

87. RG 469, DD Ops/NEA Ops/NED/Egypt Branch, Subj. Files 1954–57, Box 3, Cairo to Washington, 17 April 1954.

88. Phase One had a budgeted cost of 4.7 million £E ($13.5 million) to benefit 20,000 settlers, or 235 £E for every man, woman, and child resettled. This was due in part to initial capital expenditures like a 1 million £E power plant, and in part to the utilization of superior irrigation methods. For example, irrigation lines were buried, which limits evaporation but sharply raises costs. See, generally, RG 84, Cairo Box 252, Cairo to Washington, 27 July 1953. Comments on higher cost of irrigation from, *inter alia,* interview with Ambassador Tahseen Bashir, Cambridge MA, 20 October 1995.

89. RG 469, NEA Ops/NED/Egypt Branch, Subj. Files 1954–57, Box 3, Cairo to Washington, 17 April 1954.

90. The settlers were to arrive November 1, 1954, although the first settlers appear to have arrived in March 1955. The Egyptian staff apparently took the decision to commence settlement without consulting the American staff of EARIS, which led to a shouting match and the eventual resignation of the Community Development Adviser in the American mission. See RG 469, USOM/E, Subject File/H Stevens, Box 2. Charles A. Wright to File, "One Incident in EARIS Operations," 21 March 1955.

91. RG 469, FOA/DDO/NEA Ops/NEA Central Files, Egypt 1953–55, Box 6. EARIS (no date), p. 3.

92. RG 469, DDOps/NEA Ops/NED/Subj Files re: Egypt, Box 1. "Land Reclamation and Resettlement," March 1955.

93. Interview with Dr. Rifky Anwar, 24 October 1994.

94. RG 469, DD Ops/NEA Ops/NED, Subject Files Re: Egypt, Box 1. "Land Reclamation and Resettlement," March 1955. See, for example, the caption on p. 20.

95. Recall that the competing Tahrir Province featured communal ownership and collective farming; stressing that EARIS settlers were "new landown-

ers" may have been intended to highlight this difference between the two programs.

96. RG 469, DDOps/NEA Ops/NED/Subj Files re: Egypt, Box 1. "Land Reclamation and Resettlement," March 1955, p. 21.

97. Ibid., p. 23.

98. Ibid., p. 14.

99. RG 469, USOM/Egypt/Executive Office/CSF, Box 6. Seager to Stevens, 4 April 1955.

100. Warriner, *Agrarian Reform,* p. 61.

101. *Permanent Council for Social Services, October 1953-March 1957* (Cairo: Matba'at Nahdat Misr, 1957) p. 336.

102. The programs are described in some detail in ibid., pp. 268–303.

103. A *mudiriya* is roughly equivalent to an American state. Its subunit is the *markaz,* which is roughly equivalent to an American county. Under the terms of the plan, each markaz was to be divided into units of 15,000 inhabitants, and each smaller group would be served by a social center.

104. Permanent Council, pp. 315–316.

105. Eva Garzouzi, *Old Ills and New Remedies in Egypt* (Cairo: Dar al Maaref, 1958), p. 147.

106. Interview with Dr. Rifky Anwar, Cairo, Egypt, 24 October 1994. Anwar received his Ph.D. in soil science from Cornell, and in the course of earning his degree spent some five years in the United States. Dekmejian's interviews suggest that Anwar won the trust of his American collaborators much more successfully than his predecessor, Dr. Azzouni.

107. Interview with Dr. Rifky Anwar, 24 October 1994.

108. Ibid. The cooperative movement existed in Egypt before the revolution, with modern roots beginning just after World War I and serving a population encompassing perhaps 20 percent of the total rural population in Egypt by the end of World War II. Cooperatives were not established in EARIS areas until 1959, coinciding with a period in which cooperatives were both spreading in Egypt and coming under fire for being too tightly controlled by the central government. See, respectively, Gamal-Eddine Heyworth-Dunne, *Egypt: The Cooperative Movement* (Cairo: Renaissance Bookshop, 1952), p. 11; Gabriel S. Saab, *The Egyptian Agrarian Reform, 1952–1962* (London, New York: Royal Institute of International Affairs [by] Oxford U.P., 1967) p. 214; and Keith Wheelock, *Nasser's New Egypt: A Critical Analysis* (New York: Praeger, 1960), p. 83.

109. For example, the Minister for Local Administrative Affairs during this period was Wing Commander Abdel Latif al-Baghdadi, one of the original Free Officers.

110. Garzouzi, *Old Ills,* p. 152.

111. Dr. John Swanson of the American University in Cairo made this point to me more persuasively than I have heard it elsewhere.

112. The classic presentation of the argument for geography's effect on Egyptian life is Gamal Hamdan, *Egypt's Character* (Cairo: Maktabat al-Nahda al-Misriya,

1970, Ar.) This argument is distinct from Wittfogel's argument about hydraulic societies, in which he suggested that Egypt has a tradition of strong governments because of the need to coordinate and regulate waterworks during the annual flood of the Nile. See Karl Wittfogel, *Oriental Despotism* (New Haven: Yale University Press, 1957).

113. RG 469, USOM/E, Subj File/H Stevens, Box 2. Charles Wright to Admiral Stevens, 30 April 1955.

114. The technicians' signed memorandum was dated June 4, but a copy with the same text found in the Washington files was dated May 27. Norman Paul, head of NEA Operations in Washington, wrote across the top of his copy, "This is up to mission to work out." RG 469 NEA Ops/NE Division/Egypt Branch/Subj Files 1954–57, Box 3 and DDOps/NEA Ops/Office of the Chief/Subj Files Re: Egypt 1953–61, Box 1, respectively.

115. Ibid.

116. Ibid.

117. RG 469 USOM/E/Subj Files/H. Stevens, Box 2, Roscoe Bell to Stevens, "Expediting Administration of EARIS," 31 August 1955 and "EARIS Organization," 21 December 1955.

118. Bell, in his December 21 memo cited above, suggested that in fact EARIS had shifted from a technical assistance project to a development assistance project, and thus mostly required American funding with little ongoing involvement by technically skilled American personnel.

119. Ibid.

120. The head of the EARIS division in the American aid mission judged years later that "Azzouni was reasonably effective," suggesting that someone with a clearer understanding of Azzouni's constraints was more understanding. A program officer in the aid mission recalled later too that "A serious problem was the attitude of superiority on the part of some American personnel." Interviews with Roscoe Bell, Ed Felder.

121. Interview with Dr. Rifky Anwar, Cairo, Egypt, 5 December 1994.

122. Ibid. Dr. Anwar notes that his basic government salary as a soil engineer in the early 1950s was 35 £E/month, and he received a premium of 25 £E/month for working with EARIS.

123. Engineer Abd al-Azim Shawqi al-Saidi interview, Cairo, Egypt, 8 November 1994.

124. RG 469, NEA Ops/NE Div/Egypt Branch/Subj Files 1954–1957, Box 3, Comptroller General of the United States, "Audit Report to the Congress of the United States. U.S. Assistance Program for Egypt," 30 June 1955, p. 49.

125. This program, which still exists, was also known as "Food for Peace." The law provides for the distribution of surplus agricultural commodities to poor countries at no cost to them. In 1955 and 1956, total shipments under this program were valued at $37 million. Yet Egyptian government officials complained that program cost them $150 million, because it delivered surplus American cotton to worldwide markets, thereby severely weakening demand

for Egyptian cotton. Although their figures were likely wrong, cotton did represent almost one third of the total value of agricultural products exported in the first months of the program. See RG 469 USOM/Egypt/CSF 1955–56, Box 6. Evaluation Report on ICA Program for Egypt, August 10, 1955, p. 3, and RG 469 NEA Ops/NE Division/Egypt Branch/Subj Files, 1954–57, Box 3, Egypt Evaluation Team Briefing Meetings, 19 and 20 May 1955, Meeting with State Department Group.

126. RG 469, NEA Ops/NE Division/Egypt Branch/Subj Files, 1954–57, Box 3. Egypt Evaluation Team Briefing Meetings, 19 and 20 May, 1955. Meeting with O/NEA Staff.

127. Ibid.

128. Such reference is replete in interviews conducted by myself and Professor Dekmejian.

129. RG 469, NEA Ops/NE Division/Egypt Branch/Subj Files, 1954–57, Box 3. Egypt Evaluation Team Briefing Meetings, 19 and 20 May, 1955, Meeting with Office of Public Services Personnel.

130. Ibid., Meeting with Mr. Dimick.

131. One official estimated that $20 million of new direct investment would have been required annually simply in order to maintain a constant standard of living in Egypt. This amount would have been over and above any funds required for the Aswan High Dam. Mr. Warden in meeting with Office of Trade, Investment and Monetary Affairs, ibid.

132. Ibid., Meeting with State Department Group, Mr. Gay.

133. Ibid.

134. RG 469 USOM Egypt/C Subj Files 1955–56, Box 6. Evaluation Report on ICA Program for Egypt, Washington, 10 August 1955. Their evaluation may only partly have been based on EARIS's failures in the community development field. EARIS reduced its goals from resettling 16,000 families to resettling 5,000 with no change in the overall budget.

135. RG 469 USOM/Egypt/Subj Files (Directors), 1954–56, Box 2. Evaluation Team—USOM Report. July 1955.

136. Ibid.

137. Ibid.

138. RG 469 USOM/Egypt/CSF, 1955–56, Box 6. Evaluation Report on ICA Program for Egypt.

139. Ibid.

140. Ibid.

141. Ibid.

142. RG 469, NEA Ops/NE Div/Egypt Branch/Subj Files 1954–1957, Box 3, "Summary of [ICA/W] Staff Comments on Recommendations in the Egypt Evaluation Report" (no date).

143. Dr. Rifky Anwar gave the land value as 1.8 £E/feddan at the time of reclamation and 50,000 £E/feddan currently. Interview with Dr. Rifky Anwar, 24 October 1994. According to extant documentation, EARIS land was sold to settlers at a cost of 30 £E/feddan. An AID evaluation of EARIS in 1983

placed the value of an average holding in Abis (presumably 5 feddans) at 15,200 £E, or 3,040 £E/feddan. An appendix notes that average land values in 1981 ranged from 4,000 £E/feddan in interior areas to 20,000 to 30,000 £E/feddan along the Alexandria Agricultural Road. See Pamela R. Johnson, et al., *Egypt: The Egyptian American Rural Improvement Service, A Point Four Project, 1952–1963* (Washington: U.S. Agency for International Development, 1983), p. 5 and p. E-2.

144. Johnson et al., *Egypt,* p. 7.

145. Eng. Shawqi interview. Eng. Shawqi worked in EARIS from 1955–1966, and then worked for the Ministry of Agriculture and Land Reclamation in Tahrir and other governmental land reclamation projects through 1980.

146. Shawqi interview, and interview with Engineer Badr Badawi, Abis, Egypt, 18 November 1994. In an Arabic conversation, Badawi recalled that whenever he asked Americans about trying something a new way, they said (and here he broke into English), "Why not?"

147. A settler who arrived in 1959 and went on to serve as a member of the Egyptian parliament, said many sons of settlers—including his own—were able to gain an education and make better lives for themselves in other parts of Egypt. Interview with Hagg Rashad 'Omran, Abis, Egypt, 19 November 1994. Johnson et al., note that "the manager of a small cheese factory in Abis is . . . the son of a settler, who was educated and has returned to the village to work." *Egypt,* p. 10.

148. Johnson et al., *Egypt,* p. 9.

149. Ibid., p. F-2.

150. EARIS cost a total of approximately $1,400 per reclaimed feddan, once housing, roads, schools, sanitation, and other costs are figured in. See Richard H. Dekmejian, "An Analytical History of EARIS," in Johnson et al., *Egypt,* p. D-34.

151. Recall that the only land to be resettled in the first six years of the EARIS project was land in Abis that the Egyptian government had reclaimed without any American assistance whatsoever.

152. Top Egyptian officials tended to be bilingual, while very few Americans spoke any Arabic at all. Americans often complained that they couldn't follow meetings among the Egyptian staff because they were conducted in Arabic.

153. Recall that the idea of jointly administered development projects got its greatest boost during World War II, when the United States established "*servicios cooperativos*" or "cooperative service organizations" in several Latin American countries.

154. A. O. Hirschman's observation about the importance of the "hiding hand" is pertinent here—if individuals or countries understood in advance how high the costs of certain projects would prove to be in the future, they might never undertake the projects in the first place, and the pace of innovation and progress would be significantly slowed. See Albert O. Hirschman, *Development Projects Observed* (Washington: Brookings Institution, 1967), ch. 1.

155. The AID report suggests that Egyptians who participated in the "EARIS School"—some of whom came to the United States for training missions in the early 1960s—went on to contribute mightily to Egyptian land development and to the larger Egyptian economy as a whole. While the individuals undoubtedly continued to work in land reclamation, the report left unclear how their contribution was materially changed by their participation in a project such as EARIS, as opposed to a routine career in Egyptian government service. See Mohey Khattab, "The EARIS School," in Johnson et al., *Egypt*, appendix G.

Chapter 5

1. For the first figure, see Ali al-Gritly, *The Economic History of the Revolution, 1952–1966* (Cairo: Dar al-Ma'araf bi-Misr, 1974, Ar.), p. 73 ff. For the second figure, see, H. E. Hurst, *The Nile: A General Account of the River and the Utilization of its Waters* (London: Constable, 1957), p. 296. H. E. Hurst, R. P. Black, and Y. M. Simaika, *The Nile Basin*, vol. X, *The Major Niles Projects* (Cairo: General Organization for Government Printing Offices, 1966), p. 97 gives the average discharge from 1870 to 1959 as 92.6 billion m^3, with a standard deviation of 19.8 billion m^3.
2. "The High Dam Project is Greater Than the Pyramids," *al-Ahram* (Ar.), 7 October 1955, p. 8.
3. Hurst, *The Nile*, p. 38.
4. On the latter point, see Roger Owen, *Cotton and the Egyptian Economy, 1820–1914* (Oxford: Clarendon Press, 1969).
5. Hurst, *The Nile*, p. 46.
6. A barrage is a dam intended to raise the level of the water behind it. Without a barrage, the level of the river could easily fall below the levels of the intakes of the irrigation canals, the canals would dry out, and the land dependent on those canals would become parched.
7. Recall that British troops invaded Egypt in 1882 to secure debts and exercised control over domestic affairs in Egypt to varying degrees until after World War II. Improvements during the time of the British occupation were significant. In 1886, 2 million feddans of Egyptian land were irrigated through a basin system and 2.9 million were irrigated perennially. Sixty years later, only one million feddans were irrigated by basin irrigation and five million were irrigated perennially. The net gain, then, is both an additional one million feddans of agricultural land and the opportunity to grow two or three crops a year instead of just one on two million feddans of land. See Hurst, *The Nile*, p. 284.
8. An account of the various plans to systematically control the Nile is contained in H. E. Hurst, R. P. Black and Y. M. Simaika, *The Nile Basin*, vol. IX, *The Hydrology of the Blue Nile and Atbara and of the Main Nile to Aswan, with Some Reference to Projects* (Cairo: General Organization for Government Printing Offices, 1959), pp. 117–120. Aswan was selected as an appropriate

site for the dam because the river walls at that point are granite and thereby relatively impervious to water seepage.

9. The original reservoir capacity of the dam was approximately 1 billion cubic meters. Subsequent heightenings raised the capacity to approximately 2.25 billion m^3 and 5.25 m^3 respectively. See Hurst et al., *The Nile Basin*, vol. IX, p. 120.

10. H. E. Hurst, R. P. Black, and Y. M. Simaika, *The Nile Basin*, vol. VII, *The Future Conservation of the Nile* (Cairo: S.O.P. Press, 1946), passim.

11. The name derives from the fact that the calculations were computed to account for a century's worth of variation in water flow.

12. Hurst et al., *The Nile Basin*, vol. X, p. 96. The years Hurst uses run from August 1 to July 31, beginning with the start of the flood each year.

13. Hurst et al., *The Nile Basin*, vol. VII, pp. 25–26.

14. Hurst, *The Nile Basin*, p. 297.

15. Hurst et al., *The Nile Basin*, vol. VII, p. 63.

16. Ibid., p. 4.

17. Ibid., p. 55. The irrigation scheme contemplated total reservoir capacities of something on the order of 195 billion m^3 outside Egypt's borders, in addition to an 8 billion m^3 reservoir at Aswan for flood prevention in Egypt. Ibid., p. 4.

18. Quoted in RG 469 USOM/Egypt/CSF (CGF), 1951–56, Box 5. Harold Jorgenson to John Nichols, "Daninos' views on Egypt's reclamation program," 13 September 1952.

19. Reprinted in Hurst et al., *The Nile Basin*, vol. X, p. 164. (original in English)

20. The memorandum was reprinted in Hurst et al., *The Nile Basin*, vol. X without any indication of authorship. It likely was written by Samir Helmy, an engineer and Free Officer whom Daninos approached in August 1952 and who shepherded the proposal through the Egyptian government. See John Waterbury, *Hydropolitics of the Nile Valley* (Syracuse: Syracuse University Press, 1979), pp. 100–101. Helmy's view of Egyptian development is described above in chapter 3.

21. Hurst et al., *The Nile Basin*, vol. X, p. 168 (original in Arabic).

22. Ibid. Waterbury asserts that the RCC tentatively approved the High Dam scheme "in principle" in September 1952. According to Waterbury's account, Samir Helmy and Anwar al-Sadat approached Minister of Public Works Murad Fahmy only after this decision. Fahmy's analysts accurately perceived the winds of change and thus gave cautious approval to the project. See Waterbury, *Hydropolitics*, p. 101. At the time preliminary approval was given, the RCC estimated that the Dam would cost a mere 30£E million, or about $100 million. As will be seen below, the World Bank estimated costs for the Dam (excluding generators) at approximately 110£E million, with a total required investment for the Dam and related projects of 470£E million. RG 469 HQ Off/DD Ops/Economic Aid to Egypt, 1952–55, Box 1. "Preliminary Views of Egyptian Military High Committee on Possible U.S. Economic Assistance," Cairo to Washington, 13 November

1952. *The Economic Development of Egypt*, World Bank Report #A.S. 40a, 25 August 1955.

23. Tom Little, *High Dam at Aswan: The Subjugation of the Nile* (London: Methuen & Co., 1965), pp. 30–31.

24. Ibid., p. 31, 32. A State Department cable to the U.S. Operations Mission in Egypt in November 1952 advised the mission to consult the Embassy "regarding [the] eccentricities [of] this man who has tried in [the] past to obtain the support of the Department and other US agencies on [a] plan to develop [the] Nile Valley. Department . . . suggests TCA/Egypt proceed with caution in dealing [with] Daninos and his plan." RG 84, 874.00TA/10–3152, Washington to Cairo, 19 November 1952.

25. World Bank Archives, Hector Prud'homme to files, 27 January 1953.

26. RG 469 DD Ops/Office of Near East, South Asia and Africa/Administrative Office/Egypt Project Files 1953–58, Box 8, Memorandum of Conversation between I. Cleveland Steele, consulting engineer and James Rives (TCA/NEADS), 20 August 1953.

27. For example, the popular weekly magazine *Akher Sa'a* profiled him on 12 January 1955, p. 6.

28. An article in *Akher Sa'a* pointed out that Daninos proposed the High Dam plan under the old regime, "And they accused him of insanity. . . . Then the New Era arrived." The month before, a brief profile of the General Secretary of the PCDNP, Dr. Muhammad Ahmed Selim, pointed out that Dr. Selim received his Ph.D. from the University of California and had experience in irrigation from the United States, but the pre-revolutionary government opposed all his proposals to create a council to develop national production. Selim's pleas for the efficacy of such organizations, claiming that there were 32 such councils in the U.S., fell on deaf ears. "And finally the New Era adopted Dr. Selim's proposal, implemented it and Dr. Selim became the General Secretary of the Production Council." "First Photographic Investigation of the High Dam," *Akher Sa'a* (Ar.), 22 April 1953, p. 30; "The Development of Production," *Rose al-Yusef* (Ar.), No. 1291 (9 March 1953), p. 2.

29. RG 469 HQ Office/DD Ops/Economic Aid to Egypt, 1952–55, Box 1. Cairo to Washington, 20 November 1952.

30. Described above in chapter 3.

31. RG 84, 874 00TA/12–1152, Cairo to Washington, 11 December 1952.

32. Little, *High Dam*, p. 41.

33. Ibid.

34. This includes Little and Waterbury (who states on p. 260 ff. of *Hydropolitics* that he relies on Little's study). The account contained in Edward S. Mason and Robert E. Asher's *The World Bank since Bretton Woods* (Washington: The Brookings Institution, 1973) suggests that it was the World Bank which sold the United States on the plan (p. 631 ff.), although American records suggest it was the other way around, and I found no indication in the World Bank records I saw to indicate otherwise.

35. American involvement is made clear in the section of the PCDNP's annual report for 1955 which dealt with the dam.

36. The firm awarded the contract, Jack Amman, won the contract for the aerial survey in part because no other firm bid on it. Their first plane crashed, and the camera broke in the second. When a replacement camera was shipped to Egypt, it broke in transit from Cairo to Aswan. When the film was finally shot, it was sent by diplomatic pouch from Cairo to Washington, driven by an FOA officer to the Army Map Service for developing, and then pouched back to Cairo. The finished maps surveyed 9,000 square miles. Interview with Harry Hemmerich, 25 July 1994, Washington, DC, RG 469 DD Ops/NEA Ops/NE Central Files/Egypt Project Files, 1953–1958, Box 8. Memorandum from Perry Ellis to the Ambassador, "Views of Various Americans on the Proposed Aswan High Dam," 4 August 1953, and USOM/Egypt/Subject Files, 1955–56, Box 44, "Egypt and Point Four" (pamphlet, n.d.).

37. RG 469 DD Ops/NEA Ops/NE Central Files/Egypt Project Files, 1953–58, Box 8. Nichols to Andrews, 3 April 1953.

38. Mason and Asher, *The World Bank,* p. 629.

39. Nichols to Andrews, 3 April 1953.

40. Ibid.

41. John Nichols was removed as director of the American aid program in Cairo not specifically because of his endorsement of the High Dam project, but because his administrative skills were thought to be lacking. His aide, Joseph LaRocca, was a controversial figure who clashed with many in the aid mission. Nichols's removal is discussed in RG 469 TCA/NEADS/Egypt Branch/General Records, 1950–53, Box 4. Andrews to Nichols, 4 May 1953. His weak administrative skills and the problems with LaRocca are discussed in veiled terms in RG 469 TCA/NEADS/Egypt Branch/General Records, 1950–53, Box 4, Hartman to Andrews, 27 January 1953.

42. News of the High Dam did not appear on the front page of the leading Cairo daily newspaper, *al-Ahram,* until October 1955, when the paper cited American reports that the Soviet Union had offered to finance construction.

43. American records identify these individuals as L. F. Harza of Chicago, I. C. Steele of Piedmont, CA, two unnamed Swedes, and an unnamed Italian. RG 469 DD Ops/NEA Ops/NE Central Files/Egypt Project Files, 1953–53, Box 8. Perry Ellis to the Ambassador, "Views of Various Americans on the Proposed Aswan High Dam," 4 August 1953. An Egyptian magazine listed them as Harza, Steele, Gallioli of Italy, Dr. Kintch of Germany, an unnamed Swede, and a leading German scientist from Switzerland. "First Photographic Investigation," p. 31. This is a different group than the one which passed judgment on the final feasibility study in November 1954, discussed below.

44. Permanent Council for the Development of National Production, 1955, pp. 146–48.

45. RG 469, DD Ops/Office of Near East, South Asia and Africa/Administrative Office/Egypt Project Files, 1953–1958, Memorandum of Conversation, I. Cleveland Steele and James Rives, 20 August 1953.

46. RG 469 DD Ops/NEA Ops/NE Central Files/Egypt Project Files, 1953–58, Box 8. Cairo to Washington, 28 August 1953.

47. "First Photographic Investigation," p. 31.

48. RG 469, DD Ops/NEA Ops/NE Central Files/Egypt Project Files, 1953–58, Box 8. Cleared draft of cable, Washington to Cairo, 11 September 1953 (cleared by FitzGerald, Seager 14 September).

49. RG 469, DD Ops/NEA Ops/NE Central Files/Egypt Project Files, 1953–58, Box 7. Memorandum of Conversation, Amb. Hussein, el-Emary, Sayed, A/S Byroade, Gardiner, 16 September 1953.

50. This point was not lost on the Egyptians. See "The World Bank and the High Dam Project," *al-Ahram* (Ar.), 15 Jan 1955, p. 5, which cites an article to the same effect in *Fortune* magazine.

51. The total aid allotment to Egypt was $27.5 million, with the largest portion—$15 million—going toward road construction. RG 469 HQ Office/DD Ops/Economic Aid to Egypt, 1952–55, Box 1. Cairo to FOA, 23 September 1953, "Justification of Special Economic Aid for Egypt."

52. The total economic aid requested for Egypt was $20 million, with an additional $5 million if and when they reached a settlement with the British on Suez. The annual request for Iran, by comparison, was $50 million, and for Israel between $40 and $50 million. The "desk study" referred to was a study of the Nile Basin to be executed with available information and not involving a field study in Egypt. RG 469 HQ Office of DD Ops/Economic Aid to Egypt, 1952–1955, Box 1, 10 November 1953, "FOA Special Economic Assistance Near East and Africa FY 1955 Request."

53. Described in chapter 4, above.

54. See, for example, Abdullah Imam, *Ali Sabri Remembers* (Beirut: Dar al-Wahda al-Arabiya, 1988, Ar.), p. 12–13. Mohamed Hassanein Heikal described the mission in *The Cairo Documents* (Garden City: Doubleday, 1973) pp. 37–39, although his dates for the mission do not coincide with those given both by Sabri and the American documents. He also claims that Churchill phoned Eisenhower to discourage the president from supplying Egypt with arms, although there is no indication in the American files that such a phone call took place.

55. DD Ops/Office of Near East, South Asia and Africa/Administrative Office/Egypt Project Files, 1953–58, Box 8. Carr to Caffery, 21 November 1953.

56. Hassan Fathy Ragab, "How Has Turkey Benefited from American Aid?" *al-Musawwar* (Ar.), 12 June 1953, p. 25.

57. RG 469 DD Ops/NEA Ops/NE Central Files/Egypt Project Files, 1953–58, Box 8, Cairo to State, 21 December 1953, Memorandum of Conversation between Muhammad Selim and Robert Carr.

58. RG 469 DD Ops/NEA Ops/NE Central Files/Egypt Project Files, 1953–58, Box 8, Box 7. Cairo to Washington, 11 January 1954.

59. RG 469, USOM/Egypt/CSF (C Central Files) 1951–1954, Box 4. Kenneth Platt to Admiral Stevens, 24 May 1954.

60. RG 469 USOM/Egypt/Subj Files (Director's Files), 1954–56, Box 3. Preliminary Assessment of Egypt's Economic Potential, 16 October 1954.

61. Ibid.

62. RG 469, HQ Office/DD Ops/Records Relating to Economic Aid to Egypt, 1952–55, Box 1. Cairo to State, 22 October 1954.

63. RG 469, HQ Office/DD Ops/Records Relating to Economic Aid to Egypt, 1952–55, Box 1. J. Evans to N. Paul, 27 October 1954.

64. Ibid.

65. William J. Burns, *Economic Aid and American Policy toward Egypt, 1955–1981* (Albany: State University of New York Press, 1985), p. 16.

66. The Egyptian objection to American advisers is made passionately in Anwar al-Sadat, *My Son, This Is Your Uncle Gamal* (Cairo: Dar al-Hilal, 1958), pp. 113–15.

67. The CIA messages are reprinted in FRUS 1952–54, vol. IX, pp. 2315–2323. Two American participants in the talks give their accounts in Wilbur Crane Eveland, *Ropes of Sand: America's Failure in the Middle East* (New York: W.W. Norton, 1980), pp. 100–104, Miles Copeland, *Game of Nations: The Amorality of Power Politics* (London: Weidenfeld and Nicholson, 1969), pp. 123–126. A well-informed Egyptian account of the negotiations, apparently based on records of Egyptian intermediary Hassan al-Touhami, can be found in Muhammad al-Tawil, *The Game of Nations and Abdel Nasser* (Cairo: al-Maktab al-Misri al-Hadith, 1986, Ar.), pp. 110–125.

68. "Aswan High Dam: There's been nothing quite like it," *Engineering News-Record,* 9 February 1956, p. 44. Spellings of names and nationalities given here differ slightly from accounts by Mason and Asher and Waterbury, which differ from each other.

69. Ibid., p. 46. See also "Egypt Plans Large Aswan Dam," *Electrical World,* 3 January 1955, p. 43 for a description of the dam and an account of the American tour of Egyptians leading the dam effort.

70. Mason and Asher, *The World Bank,* p. 631, who state that one of the engineers, Gail Hathaway, was "borrowed from the office of the Chief of Engineers of the US Army."

71. RG 469 USOM/Egypt/Central Subject Files, Box 9. Memorandum of Conversation, John de Wilde and G. M. Bennsky, Jr. 28 February 1955.

72. RG 469, DD Ops/NEA Ops/Administrative Office/Egypt Project Files, 1953–1958, Box 7. Cedric Seager to Harold Stassen, 4 March 1955. Seager suggested in a letter to Stevens in July that Egypt was likely to fund construction with a $100 million IBRD loan and $200 million out of extant sterling reserves, making U.S. aid nonessential. The proposal under discussion the following fall, however, required a heavy U.S. investment. RG 469 USOM/E/C Subj Files (C FS), 1955–56. Box 9. Seager to Stevens, 25 July 1955.

73. Many officials in the Department of State doubted that the Government of Israel sincerely desired peace with the Arabs, especially because a settlement would likely require the return of territory Israel seized in 1948. When Israeli troops attacked an Egyptian army post in Gaza on February 28, 1955,

the American Ambassador in Egypt speculated that the Israelis had heard something about Alpha and struck a particularly strong blow to dissuade the Egyptians from seeking peace. See Letter from Byroade to Allen, 27 March 1955, reprinted in *Foreign Relations of the United States, 1955–57, vol. XV: The Arab-Israeli Dispute, 1955* (Washington: U.S. Government Printing Office, 1989), pp. 120–22.

74. See, for example, Memorandum from Francis Russell to Secretary, 18 May 1955, reprinted in ibid., pp. 204–205.

75. RG 84, Byroade Eyes Only to Dulles, 3 April 1956. Document obtained as a consequence of Freedom of Information Act request.

76. The list of requested items is reprinted in FRUS, 1955–57, vol. XV, p. 274. The Department of Defense's initial response is reprinted in ibid., pp. 337–338.

77. RG 469, DD Ops/NEA Ops/Administrative Office/Egypt Project Files, 1953–58, Box 7. USOM/E to ICA, 18 July 1955. "Program Analysis Nile High Dam, Sadd El-Aali."

78. When initial intelligence reports reached the State Department on September 19 that a Soviet-bloc arms shipment might be imminent, Byroade refused to caution the Egyptians against accepting the weapons. Byroade protested he had delivered the same message countless times before, and further fumed that he found it "impossible to understand why I have not been informed of Department's reasoning in turning down repeated and increasingly urgent recommendations that we make [a]financial arrangement which would permit Egypt to take advantage [of] our offer (in response its request) [to] sell arms. . . . To this Embassy it is crystal clear that by our unwillingness [to] manipulate a few million dollars we are permitting [the] situation [to] deteriorate to [a] point where [a] chain reaction of [a] nature that will constitute a major defeat for US policy in Middle East . . . is highly probable." Byroade's policy isolation would, in fact, continue. Byroade to Hoover, 20 September 1955, reprinted in FRUS 1955–57, vol. XV, pp. 483–484.

79. "Russia Will Fund the Dam," *al-Ahram* (Ar.), 11 October 1955, p. 1.

80. RG 469 DD Ops/NEA Ops/NE Division/Egypt Subj Files, 1955–59, Box 2. Cairo to ICA, 13 October 1955, "FY 1957 Program Submission." According to American documents, Ambassador Hussein announced in Washington on October 17 that the Soviet Union had offered over the previous two months to extend a 30-year loan for High Dam construction, to be repaid in agricultural commodities. RG 469 DD Ops/NEA Ops/Administrative Office/Egypt Project Files, 1953–58, Box 7. "Report on the High Dam–Sadd el-Aali," 20 October 1955. Ambassador Hussein's account of his subsequent meeting with Secretary Dulles is reprinted in Muhammad Hassanein Heikal, *The Suez Files* (Cairo: Markaz al-Ahram lil-Tarjama wal-Nashr, 1987, Ar.), pp. 774–6.

81. RG 469 DD Ops/NEA Ops/Administrative Office/Project Files, 1953–58, Box 2. Cairo to State, 15 October 1955.

82. Ibid., Box 7. Washington to Paris, 25 October 1955. The entirety of the $134 million American contribution was to be spent in the United States.

83. In the years after the Egyptian revolution, British troops agreed to leave the Sudan and Egypt, and the Sudan was allowed to choose unity with Egypt or independence. In the event they chose the latter, leading to sharp tensions in the Egyptian-Sudanese relationship in the late fall of 1955. See Waterbury, *Hydropolitics,* ch. 2.

84. On the British side of these negotiations, see Diane B. Kunz, *Economic Diplomacy of the Suez Crisis* (Chapel Hill: University of North Carolina Press, 1991), pp. 48–53.

85. RG 469 DD Ops/NEA Ops/Administrative Office/Project Files, 1953–58, Box 7. Dorsey through FitzGerald to Stassen, "Quotations from Briefing Paper for Hoover for Conversation with Dr. Kaissouni," 23 November 1955.

86. RG 469, DD Ops/NEA Ops/NE Central Files/Egypt Project Files, 1953–58, Box 7. Cairo to Washington, 25 November 1955.

87. RG 469 DD Ops/NEA Ops/NE Central Files/Egypt Project Files, 1953–58, Box 7. Cairo to Washington, 28 November 1955.

88. RG 469 DD Ops/NEA Ops/Administrative Office/Egypt Project Files, 1953–58, Box 7. Cairo to State (for Hoover). 30 November 1955.

89. RG 469 DD Ops/NEA Ops/NE Central Files/Egypt Project Files, 1953–58, Box 7. USOM/E to ICA, 16 December 1955.

90. Ibid., Circular Cable from Washington to Middle Eastern embassies. 16 December 1955.

91. Mason and Asher, *World Bank,* p. 635.

92. RG 469 USOM/Egypt/Subj Files (Director's), 1954–56, Box 9, Carr to Ambassador, 28 December 1955. "Reaction of Helmy and Selim to Results of Washington Discussions Regarding the Financing of the High Dam."

93. RG 469 DD Ops/NEA Ops/NE Central Files/Egypt Project Files, 1953–58, Box 7. Cairo to Washington, 29 December 1955, section 1.

94. Ibid., Cairo to Washington, 29 December 1955, section 2.

95. See, for example, the cable from Dulles to Anderson on 27 January 1956, reprinted in FRUS 1955–57, vol. XV, pp. 82–83.

96. The agreement is summarized in Cairo to Washington, 24 January 1956, reprinted in FRUS 1955–57, vol XV, pp. 60–63. The December agreement is referred to in several other messages (for example, Anderson's message of January 19 [reprinted ibid., pp. 28–36], and likely included "the idea we have continuously discussed that Egypt assume the position of leadership in the Arab world and of having the national prestige and courage to make proposals which the other Arab states could be induced to adhere to." See Anderson to Secretary of State, 6 March 1956, reprinted in ibid., pp. 302–307. According to a document reproduced (in English) in Tawil, Kermit Roosevelt first broached the topic of a face-to-face meeting between Egyptian and Israeli leaders—the ultimate goal of the Anderson mission—with Abdel Nasser in December 1954, fully a year before. Tawil, pp. 399–400.

97. Eisenhower wrote of Anderson in his diary, "He is one of the most capable men I know of. . . . His capacity is unlimited and his dedication to this country is complete." Reprinted in FRUS 1955–57, vol. XV, p. 23.

98. Memorandum of Conversation drafted by Dulles, 11 January 1956, reprinted in ibid., pp. 20–22.

99. Ibid.

100. Recall that Zakaria Mohieddin's cousin, Khaled Mohieddin, was also active in the Revolution and a member of the RCC until his exile in 1954. To avoid confusion, American documents generally refer to Zakaria Mohieddin by his first name.

101. See Anderson's cable to Secretary Dulles, 29 January 1956, reprinted in FRUS 1955–57, pp. 94–95. Adding to difficulties, Anderson said, Mohieddin and Sabri were fully occupied with their regular duties during the day to maintain the secrecy of Anderson's operations, and thus arrived unprepared for meetings with him which stretched into the early hours of the morning. On the Israeli side, the State Department did not inform the U.S. Embassy in Israel of Anderson's mission until three weeks after its inception. See Washington to Tel Aviv, 14 February 1956, reprinted in ibid, p. 170. The Anderson Mission remained so secret in Egypt that Ali Sabri denied its existence in 1990 to an Egyptian academic and continued to do so until the academic showed him the declassified American documents concerning the mission. See Gamal Mu'awwad Shaqra, "The Political Movement in Egypt, from the March 1954 Crisis to the Issuance of the Decisions of July 1961," Doctoral Dissertation, Ain Shams University [Egypt], 1992, p. 366.

102. The State Department notified the Tel Aviv Embassy of the mission on February 14, 1956, almost a month after Anderson began it. See FRUS 1955–57, vol. XV p. 170. Ambassador Byroade was informed during a consultations in Washington in January 1956. Burns, *Economic Aid*, p. 59.

103. The U.S. Embassy in Cairo appears to have had a security problem. One official, probably Kermit Roosevelt, appeared to regard as fact Abdel Nasser's complaint "that several times in the past we had given sensitive info to [the] American Embassy and that it has subsequently leaked to his and often our extreme disadvantage." See Message from Cairo to Washington, 24 January 1956, reprinted in ibid., p. 62.

104. Roosevelt was Washington based. See Burns, pp. 61–62.

105. Message from Robert Anderson to the Department of State, 19 January 1956, reprinted in FRUS 1955–57, vol. XV, pp. 28–37.

106. Message to Washington, 24 January 1956, reprinted in ibid., pp. 56–58.

107. Anderson to Department of State, 28 January 1956, reprinted in FRUS 1955–57, vol. XV, pp. 88–91.

108. Hoover to Cairo, 31 January 1956, reprinted in FRUS 1955–57, vol. XV, p. 117.

109. On January 28, Eleanor Roosevelt issued a statement on behalf of herself, Harry Truman, and labor leader Walter P. Ruether urging the United States to sell significant arms to Israel. In February, 40 Republican Congressmen and 86

of their Democratic counterparts sent letters to Secretary Dulles urging arms for Israel. *New York Times,* 29 January 1956, p. 1 and 7 February 1956, p. 1.

110. See Message from the Ambassador in Egypt to the Acting Secretary of State, 22 February 1956; Message to the DCI, 22 February 1956; and Letter from the Ambassador in Egypt to the Secretary of State, 23 February 1956, FRUS 1955–57, vol. XV, pp. 207–212.

111. RG 469 USOM/Egypt/CSF (CFS), 1955–56, Box 9. USOM to ICA, 20 February 1956.

112. RG 469 DD Ops/NEA Ops/NE Central Files/Egypt Project Files, 1953–58, Box 6. Solomon Silver to Cedric Seager, 8 March 1956. "Obligation of Funds for High Aswan Dam."

113. Anderson to Secretary of State, reprinted in FRUS 1955–57, vol. XV, pp. 302–307.

114. Ibid.

115. Ibid.

116. Ibid.

117. Anderson to Acting Secretary of State, 7 March 1956, reprinted in ibid., pp. 320–322.

118. Dulles to Department of State, 8 March 1956, reprinted in ibid., pp. 325–326.

119. Diary entry by President Eisenhower, 13 March 1956, reprinted in ibid., p. 342–343.

120. Memorandum for the Director of the Office of Near Eastern Affairs, 14 March 1956, reprinted in ibid., pp. 352–357.

121. Attachment to a note from the British Ambassador to Secretary of State Dulles, reprinted in ibid., pp. 384–387.

122. Egyptian National Archives, Foreign Ministry Archives, Box 698. Memorandum. 17 March 1956.

123. Ibid.

124. Egyptian National Archives, Foreign Ministry Archives, Box 397. Hussein to Cairo, 29 March 1956.

125. Message to Washington, 3 April 1956, reprinted in FRUS 1955–57, vol. XV, pp. 448–449.

126. Ibid., p. 461. W. Scott Lucas, *Divided We Stand: Britain, the US and the Suez Crisis* (London: Hodder & Stoughton, 1991), p. 113, follows Eveland, *Ropes of Sand,* p. 180 in asserting that future American Ambassador to Egypt Raymond Hare ran the Omega operation, although a memorandum reprinted on p. 896 of the above-mentioned volume suggests he was not part of the Omega group. Hare's possible involvement in efforts to isolate Abdel Nasser is important, because he replaced Byroade as U.S. Ambassador to Egypt on August 14, 1956.

127. Unpublished memoirs of Lord Sherfield (formerly Sir Roger Makins) in the Bodleian Library, Oxford. The British government generally agreed with the American goals, but expressed impatience at Washington's desire to keep Britain at arm's length in public.

128. Ray Takeyh, *The Origins of the Eisenhower Doctrine: The US, Britain and Nasser's Egypt, 1953–1957* (New York: St. Martin's Press, 2000), pp. 110–115.

129. See, for example, Memorandum from the Secretary of State to the President, 28 March 1956, reprinted in FRUS 1955–57, vol. XV, p. 419–421.

130. The Embassy sent the proposal on February 23, and appealed for guidance on March 8. See ibid., pp. 227–233 and 330–331.

131. Byroade to Dulles, 27 March 1956 and Dulles to Byroade, 29 March 1956, reprinted in ibid., p. 403.

132. Department to Byroade, 3 April 1956, reprinted in ibid., p. 454.

133. Anwar, who was only 31 at the time, went on to become Minister of State for Foreign Affairs and Ambassador to the United Kingdom and the Soviet Union.

134. Egyptian National Archives, Foreign Ministry Archives, Box 397. Handwritten memorandum by Samih Anwar, 4 April 1956.

135. Egyptian National Archives, Foreign Ministry Archives, Box 373. Washington to Cairo, 12 April 1956. Reprinted in Muhammad Hassanein Heikal, *The Suez Files* (Cairo: Markaz al-Ahram lil-Tarjama wal-Nashr, 1986, Ar.), pp. 790–791. Heikal repeats an error contained in the original reporting memorandum that renders the name "Duber."

136. Egyptian National Archives. Foreign Ministry Archives, Box 397. Handwritten memorandum, 15? April 1956. Shortly thereafter an unnamed visitor delivered a message strictly along the lines Anwar described. Hussein to Cairo, 19 April 1956. Heikal identified the visitor as Charles Bohlen in *Cutting the Lion's Tail* (New York: Arbor House, 1987), p. 105, but Ahmed Hussein's widow suggested it was much more likely to have been Harry Kern. Personal correspondence, 2 January 1997.

137. Memorandum Prepared in the Bureau of Near Eastern, South Asian and African Affairs, 28 March 1956. Reprinted in FRUS 1955–57, XV, p. 410.

138. From President Eisenhower's diary entry, 28 March 1956, reprinted in ibid., p. 425.

139. Lucas, p. 117.

140. American and British experts on the Middle East at the time saw no smoking gun in Egypt, though this was of little consolation to Eden.

141. Nutting later claimed to one author that the actual phrase was "I want him *murdered.*" Cited in Lucas, *Divided We Stand*, p. 347.

142. Eveland, *Ropes of Sand*, p. 168, 171–2, 194.

143. Ibid., p. 137.

144. Ibid., p. 159.

145. Miles Copeland, *The Game Player: Confessions of the CIA's Original Political Operative* (London: Aurum Press, 1989), p. 168. A similar quotation appears on p. 161.

146. Ibid., p. 168.

147. Ibid., p. 167.

148. See, for example, Cairo to Washington, 26 May 1956 and 16 June 1956, reprinted in FRUS, 1955–57, vol. XV, pp. 680–682 and 731–734.

149. State to Cairo, 28 June 1956, reprinted in ibid., pp. 759–60. Dulles first told Byroade he would likely leave Egypt in January 1956, i.e., at the beginning of the Omega operation.

150. State to Cairo, 9 July 1956, reprinted in ibid., pp. 793–797.

151. Cairo to State, 13 July 1956, reprinted in ibid. pp. 832–834.

152. See Cairo to State, 12 July 1956, reprinted in ibid., p. 822.

153. Rountree to Dulles, 6 June 1956, reprinted in ibid., pp. 717–719.

154. How much contact Hussein had with Abdel Nasser is unclear. Heikal asserts that Hussein did not see Abdel Nasser until July 8 (just before the latter left for Yugoslavia), meaning he spent seven weeks in Cairo before he could see the Prime Minister. Hussein told Secretary Dulles that he met with Abdel Nasser "a number of times" during his trip to Egypt and discussed the High Dam. See Heikal, *Suez Files,* p. 448, and Memorandum of Conversation with Dulles, Hussein et al., 19 July 1956, reprinted in FRUS, 1955–57, vol. XV, pp. 867–873.

155. "America Confirms its Readiness to Fund the High Dam," *al-Ahram* (Ar.), 7 July 1956, p. 1.

156. Heikal, *Suez Files,* p. 448.

157. Heikal reports the conversation in three of his books: in Arabic in *Suez Files,* p. 449, in *The Cairo Documents,* p. 65, and in *Cutting the Lion's Tail,* p. 110. Despite a liberal use of quotation marks, each of Heikal's accounts is different, although they all portray Hussein as something of a starry-eyed rube, which he certainly was not.

Bibliography

Archival Sources

Bodleian Library, Oxford, UK. Unpublished memoirs of Lord Sherfield (Sir Roger Makins)

Egyptian National Archives, Cairo, Egypt. Foreign Ministry Archives.

Georgetown University Library, Washington, DC. Foreign Affairs Oral History Collection.

    Henry Byroade

    Parker Hart

    Wells Stabler

Ahmed Hussein Diary. Private collection.

International Bank for Reconstruction and Development (World Bank), Washington, DC. Archives.

US National Archives, Washington, DC.

    RG 59, General Records of the Department of State

    RG 84, Diplomatic Post Records

    RG 286, Records of the Agency for International Development and its Predecessor Agencies.

    RG 469, Records of U.S. Foreign Assistance Agencies, 1948–1961.

Foreign Relations of the United States, 1952–1954, vol. IX: The Near and Middle East. Washington: Government Printing Office, 1986.

Foreign Relations of the United States, 1955–1957, vol. XIV: Arab-Israeli Dispute, 1955. Washington: Government Printing Office, 1989.

Foreign Relations of the United States, 1955–1957, vol. XV: Arab-Israeli Dispute, January 1-July 26, 1956. Washington: Government Printing Office, 1989.

Public Papers of the Presidents of the United States: Harry S. Truman, 1949. Washington: Government Printing Office, 1964.

Newspapers and Periodicals

In Arabic

al-Abhath
al-Ahram
al-Ahram al-Iqtisadi
al-Akhbar
Akher Sa'a
al-Gumhuriya
al-Misri
al-Musawwar
Rose al-Yusef
al-Tahrir

In English

American Mercury
Atlantic
Congressional Quarterly Weekly Report
Economic Bulletin (National Bank of Egypt)
Egyptian Gazette
Electrical World
Engineering News-Record
Harpers Magazine
Life
Nation
New Republic
New York Times
Newsweek
Reader's Digest

Books, Articles, and Manuscripts in English

"Aid for Economic Development and the Objectives of United States Foreign Economic Policy." *Economic Development and Cultural Change* IV (1 1955):

Abdel-Fadil, Mahmoud. *Development, Income Distribution and Social Change in Rural Egypt, 1952–1970.* Cambridge: Cambridge University Press, 1975.

Abdel-Malek, Anouar. *Egypt: Military Society.* Trans. by Charles Lam Markmann. New York: Vintage Books, 1968.

Abdel Meguid, Ahmed R. "The Keynesian Economics Once More." *L'Egypte Contemporaine* XLIV (274 1953): 21–28.

Abdel Nasser, Gamal. *The Philosophy of the Revolution.* Buffalo: Economica Books, 1959.

Abramovitz, Moses. *The Allocation of Economic Resources: Essays in Honor of Bernard Francis Haley.* Stanford: Stanford University Press, 1959.

Aciman, Andre. *Out of Egypt*. New York: Farrar, Straus & Giroux, 1994.

Addison, Herbert. *Sun and Shadow at Aswan: A Commentary on Dams and Reservoirs on the Nile at Aswan, Yesterday, Today, and Perhaps Tomorrow*. London: Chapman & Hall, 1959.

Agarwala, Amar Narain and Sampat Pal Singh. *The Economics of Underdevelopment*. Bombay and New York: Oxford University Press, 1958.

"Aiding Underdeveloped Areas Abroad," *Annals of the American Academy of Political and Social Science*. Vol. 268 (April 1950).

Alcalde Cardoza, Xavier and White Burkett Miller Center. *The Idea of Third World Development: Emerging Perspectives in the United States and Britain, 1900–1950*. Lanham: University Press of America, 1987.

American Academy of Political and Social Science and Berthold Frank Hoselitz (eds). *Agrarian Societies in Transition*. Philadelphia: Annals of the American Academy of Political and Social Science 305 (1956).

American Christian Palestine Committee. *Problems of the Middle East: Proceedings of a Conference Held at the School of Education, New York University, June 5th–6th, 1947*. 1947.

Aronson, Geoffrey. *From Sideshow to Center Stage: U.S. Policy toward Egypt, 1946–1956*. Boulder, CO: Lynne Rienner, 1986.

Asad, Talal, ed. *Anthropology & the Colonial Encounter*. London: Ithaca Press, 1973.

Ayrout, Henry Habib. *The Fellaheen*. Cairo: s.n., 1954.

Ayubi, Nazih. *Bureaucracy and Politics in Contemporary Egypt*. London: Ithaca Press, 1980.

Badawy, Helmy Bahgat. "Technical Assistance Programmes: Their Role in Stimulating Our Economic Development." *L'Egypte Contemporaine* XLII (263 1951): 13–22.

Baer, Gabriel. *A History of Land Ownership in Modern Egypt, 1800–1950*. London: Royal Institute of International Affairs [by] Oxford University Press, 1962.

Baker, Gladys. *The County Agent*. Chicago: University of Chicago Press, 1939.

Baker, Raymond William. *Egypt's Uncertain Revolution under Nasser and Sadat*. Cambridge: Harvard University Press, 1979.

Baldwin, David A. *Economic Development and American Foreign Policy, 1943–1962*. Chicago: University of Chicago Press, 1966.

Baran, Paul. "On the Political Economy of Backwardness." *The Manchester School of Economic and Social Studies* 20 (January 1952): 66–84.

———. *The Political Economy of Growth*. New York: Monthly Review Press, 1957.

Barawy [Barrawi], Rashed. *Economic Development in the United Arab Republic (Egypt)*. Cairo: Anglo-American Bookshop, 1970.

Elbrawy [Barrawi], Rashid. "Some Problems of Economic Planning in the Middle East with Special Reference to Egypt." *Middle East Economic Papers* 1954.

Barrett, Edward W. *Truth is Our Weapon*. New York: Funk and Wagnalls, 1953.

Bauer, P. T. *Economic Analysis and Policy in Underdeveloped Countries*. Durham, N.C.: Published for the Duke University Commonwealth-Studies Center [by] Duke University Press, 1957.

———and Basil S. Yamey. *The Economics of Under-developed Countries*. Chicago: University of Chicago Press, 1957.

Beattie, Kirk J. *Egypt During the Nasser Years: Ideology, Politics and Civil Society.* Boulder, CO: Westview Press, 1994.

Berger, Morroe. *Bureaucracy and Society in Modern Egypt: A Study of the Higher Civil Service.* Princeton: Princeton University Press, 1957.

Bernstein, Barton J., ed. *Politics and Policies of the Truman Administration.* Chicago: Quadrangle Books, 1970.

Bianchi, Robert. *Unruly Corporatism: Associational Life in Twentieth-century Egypt.* New York: Oxford University Press, 1989.

Bingham, Jonathan. *Shirt-sleeve Diplomacy: Point 4 in Action.* New York: John Day, 1954.

Black, Cyril E. and Woodrow Wilson School of Public and International Affairs. Center of International Studies. *The Dynamics of Modernization: A Study in Comparative History.* New York: Harper & Row, 1966.

Black, Jan Knippers. *Development in Theory and Practice: Bridging the Gap.* Boulder: Westview Press, 1991.

Blackman, Winifred Susan. *The Fellahin of Upper Egypt.* London: G. G. Harrap, 1927.

Bock, Edwin A. *Fifty Years of Technical Assistance: Some Administrative Experiences of U.S. Voluntary Agencies.* Chicago: Public Administration Clearing House, 1954.

Bonne, Alfred. *The Economic Development of the Middle East.* London: K. Paul, Trench, Trubner & Co., 1945.

————. *State and Economics in the Middle East.* London: K. Paul, Trench, Trubner & Co., 1948.

Botman, Selma. *The Rise of Egyptian Communism.* Syracuse: Syracuse University Press, 1986.

Brands, H.W., Jr. "The Cairo-Tehran Connection in Anglo-American Rivalry in the Middle East, 1951–53." *International History Review* 11 (3 1989a): 434–456.

————. *The Specter of Neutralism: The United States and the Emergence of the Third World, 1947–1960.* New York: Columbia University Press, 1989.

Brown, William Adams and Redvers Opie. *American Foreign Assistance.* Washington: Brookings Institution, 1953.

Buchanan, Norman S. and Howard S. Ellis. *Approaches to Economic Development.* New York: Twentieth Century Fund, 1955.

Burns, William J. *Economic Aid and American Foreign Policy toward Egypt, 1955–1981.* Albany: State University of New York Press, 1985.

Campbell, John C. *Defense of the Middle East: Problems of American Policy.* New York: Council on Foreign Relations [by] Harper & Brothers, 1960.

Castleberry, H. P. "The Arabs' View of Postwar American Foreign Policy." *Western Political Quarterly* XII (March 1959).

Chamber of Commerce of the United States of America. *The Point Four Program: A Business Viewpoint on the President's Plan for Economic Advancement of Underdeveloped Areas. Report of Special Committee Approved by Board of Directors.* Washington: 1949.

————. Foreign Commerce Dept. *The Middle East and Its Development.* Washington: 1951.

Clark, Colin. *The Conditions of Economic Progress.* London: Macmillan, 1951.

Cleland, Wendell. *The Population Problem in Egypt: A Study of Population Trends and Conditions in Modern Egypt.* Lancaster, PA: Science Press Printing Co., 1936.

Commission on Organization of the Executive Branch of Government. *Overseas Economic Operations: A Report to the Congress.* Washington: Government Printing Office, 1955.

———. *Task Force Report on Overseas Economic Operations.* Washington: Government Printing Office, 1955.

Committee for Economic Development. *Economic Development Abroad and the Role of American Foreign Investment.* New York: 1956.

Conteh-Morgan, Earl. *American Foreign Aid and Global Power Projection: The Geopolitics of Resource Allocation.* Aldershot, Hants., England: Dartmouth Pub. Co., 1990.

Cooke, Hedley Vicars. *Challenge and Response in the Middle East: The Quest for Prosperity, 1919–1951.* New York: Harpers, 1952.

Cooke, M. L. *Nasser's High Aswan Dam.* Washington: Public Affairs Institute, 1956.

Copeland, Miles. *The Game of Nations: The Amorality of Power Politics.* London: Weidenfeld and Nicolson, 1969.

———. *The Game Player: Confessions of the CIA's Original Political Operative.* London: Aurum Press, 1989.

Crouchley, Arthur Edwin. *The Economic Development of Modern Egypt.* London: Longmans, 1938.

Curti, Merle Eugene and Kendall Birr. *Prelude to Point Four: American Technical Missions Overseas, 1838–1938.* Madison: University of Wisconsin Press, 1954.

Darling, Sir Malcom. "Land Reform in Italy and Egypt." In *Yearbook of Agricultural Cooperation.* Oxford: Basil Blackwell, 1956.

DeNovo, John A. *American Interests and Politics in the Middle East, 1900–1939.* Minneapolis: University of Minnesota Press, 1963.

Dillick, Sidney. *Community Organization for Neighborhood Development: Past and present.* New York: William Morrow, 1953.

Domar, Evsey D. *Essays in the Theory of Economic Growth.* New York: Oxford University Press,

Douglas, William O. *Strange Lands and Friendly People.* New York: Harpers, 1951.

Egypt (Kingdom of), Ministry of Social Affairs. *Second Social Welfare Seminar for Arab States of the Middle East.* Cairo: SOP Press, 1950.

Egypt (Republic of), Ministry of Commerce and Industry, *Opportunities for Industrial Development in Egypt* [Report to U.S. Government Foreign Operations Administration Under Contract SCC-21504 C-58780] Cairo: Government Press, 1955.

Egypt (Royal Government of), Ministry of Social Affairs. *Social Welfare in Egypt.* Cairo: 1950.

Egypt. Ministry of Agriculture. "Estimates for Agricultural Features." Cairo: 1955.

Egyptian Information Bureau. *Egypt in Two Years.* Washington: 1954.

Eisenstadt, Shmuel Noah. *Modernization: Growth and Diversity.* Bloomington: Department of Government, Indiana University, 1963.

Elder, Robert Ellsworth. *The Information Machine: The United States Information Agency.* Syracuse: Syracuse University Press, 1968.

Eveland, Wilbur Crane. *Ropes of Sand: America's Failure in the Middle East.* New York: W.W. Norton, 1980.

Ezzat, M. A. W. "The Land Tenure System in Egypt." In *Land Tenure*, ed. K. H. Parsons et al. Madison: University of Wisconsin Press, 1956.

Fahim, Hussein M. *Dams, People, and Development: The Aswan High Dam Case.* New York: Pergamon Press, 1981.

Feinberg, Richard E. and Rachik Mamikonovich Avakov. *From Confrontation to Co-operation?: U.S. and Soviet Aid to Developing Countries.* New Brunswick, USA: Transaction Publishers, 1991.

Feuer, Lewis Samuel. *Imperialism and the Anti-imperialist Mind.* Buffalo, N.Y.: Prometheus Books, 1986.

Fisher, Sydney Nettleton, (ed.) and Social Science Research Council (U.S.). Committee on the Near and Middle East. *Social Forces in the Middle East.* Ithaca: Cornell University Press, 1955.

Frankel, S. Herbert. *The Economic Impact on Under-Developed Societies: Essays on International Investment and Social Change.* Oxford: Blackwell, 1953.

Gaddis, John Lewis. *Strategies of Containment: A Critical Appraisal of Postwar American National Security Policy.* New York: Oxford University Press, 1982.

Gallagher, Nancy. *Egypt's Other Wars: Epidemics and The Politics of Public Health.* Syracuse: Syracuse University Press, 1990.

Gamal al-Din, Said. "An Appraisal of the Classical Theory." *L'Egypte Contemporaine* XLV (275 1954): 17–27.

Garzouzi, Eva. *Old Ills and New Remedies in Egypt.* Cairo: Dar al Maaref, 1958.

Gendzier, Irene L. *Managing Political Change: Social Scientists and the Third World.* Boulder: Westview Press, 1985.

Gerschenkron, Alexander. *Economic Backwardness in Historical Perspective: A Book of Essays.* Cambridge: Belknap Press of Harvard University Press, 1962.

Gershony, Israel and James Jankowski. *Egypt, Islam and the Arabs: The Search for Egyptian Nationhood, 1900–1930.* New York: Oxford University Press, 1986.

Ghali, Boutros Boutros. "Middle East Security Pacts." *Revue Egyptienne de Droit International* XIII (1957): 31–39.

El-Ghazali, Abd-el-Hamid. *Planning for Economic Development: Methodology, Strategy and Effectiveness.* Cairo: Modern Cairo Bookshop, 1971.

El-Ghonemy, M.R. "The Investment Effects of the Land Reform in Egypt." *L'Egypte Contemporaine* (278 1954):

Gordon, Joel. *Nasser's Blessed Movement: Egypt's Free Officers and the July Revolution.* New York: Oxford University Press, 1992.

Greene, Graham. *The Quiet American.* London: W. Heineman, 1955.

El-Gritly, A.A.I. *The Structure of Modern Industry in Egypt.* Cairo: Government Press, 1948.

Haar, Charles, Benjamin Higgins, and Lloyd Rodwin. "Economic and Physical Planning: Coordination in Developing Areas." *Journal of American Institute of Planners* 24 (3 1958).

Hagen, Everett E. and Massachusetts Institute of Technology Center for International Studies. *On the Theory of Social Change: How Economic Growth Begins.* Homewood, Ill.: Dorsey Press, 1962.

Hahn, Peter L. "Containment and Egyptian Nationalism: The Unsuccessful Effort to Establish the Middle East Command, 1950–53." *Diplomatic History* 11 (1 1987): 23–40.

————. *The United States, Great Britain, and Egypt, 1945–1956: Strategy and Diplomacy in the Early Cold War.* Chapel Hill: University of North Carolina Press, 1991.

Hall, Harvey P. (ed.) *The Evolution of Public Responsibility in the Middle East.* Washington: Middle East Institute, 1955.

————(ed.) *Middle East Resources: Problems and Prospects.* Washington: Middle East Institute, 1954.

Halpern, Manfred. *The Politics of Social Change in the Middle East and North Africa.* Princeton, NJ: Princeton University Press, 1963.

Hamed, Osama Ahmad. "The State as an Agent of Economic Development: Egypt 1952–1970." Ph.D. Dissertation, UCLA, 1987.

Hansen, Bent. "Egypt Decolonialized." *Journal of Economic History* 45:3 (1985): 716–718.

————and Marzouk A. Girgis. *Development and Economic Policy in the UAR (Egypt).* Amsterdam: North-Holland Pub. Co., 1965.

Harper, John Lamberton. *America and the Reconstruction of Italy, 1945–1948.* Cambridge [Cambridgeshire]; New York: Cambridge University Press, 1986.

Harrod, Roy Forbes, Sir. *Towards a Dynamic Economics: Some Recent Developments of Economic Theory and their Application to Policy.* London: Macmillan, 1948.

Hassan, Abd al-Rizak Mahmoud. 'A Socio-Economic Analysis of the Keynesian Theory." *L'Egypte Contemporaine* XLIV (279 1953): 19–33.

Headrick, Daniel R. *The Tentacles of Progress: Technology Transfer in the Age of Imperialism, 1850–1940.* New York: Oxford University Press, 1988.

Heikal, Mohamed H. *The Cairo Documents.* Garden City, NY: Doubleday, 1973.

————. *Cutting the Lion's Tail: Suez Through Egyptian Eyes.* New York: Arbor House, 1987.

Heyworth-Dunne, Gamal-Eddine [James]. *Egypt: The Cooperative Movement.* Cairo: Renaissance Bookshop, 1952.

————. *Select Bibliography on Modern Egypt.* Cairo: Renaissance Bookshop, 1952.

Heyworth-Dunne, James. *Religious and Political Trends in Modern Egypt.* np: Washington, 1950.

Higgins, Benjamin. *Economic Development of Underdeveloped Areas: Past and present.* 1955.

————. "The 'Dualistic Theory' of Underdeveloped Areas." *Economic Development and Social Change* IV (2 1956): 99.

————. *Economic Development.* New York: Norton, 1959.

————. *United Nations and U.S. Foreign Economic Policy.* Homewood, Ill.: R. D. Irwin, 1962.

Hirschman, Albert O. *Development Projects Observed.* Washington: Brookings Institution, 1967.

Hla Myint, U. *The Economics of the Developing Countries.* New York: F. A. Praeger, 1965.

———and University of Oxford. Institute of Colonial Studies. *An Interpretation of Economic Backwardness.* London: 1954.

Hobsbawm, E. J. and T. O. Ranger. *The Invention of Tradition.* Cambridge [Cambridgeshire]; New York: Cambridge University Press, 1983.

Hoselitz, Berthold Frank, ed. *The Progress of Underdeveloped Areas.* Chicago: University of Chicago Press, 1952.

———. "Generative and Parasitic Cities." *Economic Development and Cultural Change.* 3 (3 1955).

———. "Noneconomic Factors in Economic Development." *The American Economic Review* XLVII (May 1957): 28–71.

Hoskins, Halford L. *The Middle East: Problem Area in World Politics.* New York: Macmillan, 1954.

———. "Some Aspects of the Security Problem in the Middle East." *American Political Science Review* XLVII (March 1953).

Hosseinzadeh, Esmail. *Soviet Non-capitalist Development: The Case of Nasser's Egypt.* New York: Praeger, 1989.

Hourani, Albert. *Arabic Thought in the Liberal Age, 1798–1939.* Cambridge: Cambridge University Press, 1962.

Hunsberger, W. S. *New Era in the Non-Western World.* Ithaca: Cornell University Press, 1957.

Hurewitz, J. C. *Middle East Dilemmas: The Background of United States Policy.* New York: Council on Foreign Relations [by] Harper & Brothers, 1953.

Hurst, H. E. *The Nile: A General Account of the River and the Utilization of its Waters.* rev. ed. London: Constable, 1957.

Hurst, H. E., R. P. Black and Y. M. Simaika. *The Nile Basin.* Vol. VII. *The Future Conservation of the Nile.* Cairo: SOP Press, 1946.

Hurst, H. E., R. P. Black and Y. M. Simaika. *The Nile Basin.* Vol. IX. *The Hydrology of the Blue Nile and Atbara and of the Main Nile to Aswan, with Some Reference to Projects.* Cairo: General Organization for Government Printing Offices, 1959.

Hurst, H. E., R. P. Black and Y.M. Simaika. *The Nile Basin.* Vol. X. *The Major Nile Projects.* Cairo: General Organization for Government Printing Offices, 1966.

Hussein, Ahmed. *Rural Social Welfare Centers in Egypt.* Washington: Embassy of Egypt, 1954.

Hutchison, William R. *Errand to the World: American Protestant Thought and Foreign Missions.* Chicago: University of Chicago Press, 1987.

Ismail, Tarek and Rifaat Said. *The Communist Movement in Egypt* Syracuse: Syracuse University Press, 1993.

Issawi, Charles. *Egypt.* London: Oxford University Press, 1947.

———. *Egypt at Mid-century.* London: Oxford University Press, 1954.

———. *Egypt in Revolution: An Economic Analysis.* London: Oxford University Press, 1963.

———. "A Note on the Conditions of Economic Progress in the Middle East." *Economic Development and Cultural Change* I:4 (December 1952).

Iverson, Kenneth. "The 'Servicio' in Theory and Practice." *Public Administration Review.* Autumn 1951.

Jacoby, Neil H. *United States Aid to Taiwan: A Study of Foreign Aid.* New York: Praeger, 1966.

Johnson, Pamela, et al. *Egypt: The Egyptian American Rural Improvement Service: A Point Four Project, 1952–63.* A.I.D. Project Impact Evaluation No. 43. Washington: Agency for International Development, 1983.

Johnston, Eric. *We're All in It.* New York: E. P. Dutton, 1948.

Johr, Walter Adolf and Hans Wolfgang Singer. *The Role of the Economist as Official Adviser.* London: Allen & Unwin, 1955.

Kamil, M. *Tomorrow's Egypt.* Cairo: Eastern Press, 1953.

Kaufman, Burton Ira. *Trade and Aid: Eisenhower's Foreign Economic Policy, 1953–1961.* Baltimore: Johns Hopkins University Press, 1982.

Keen, Bernard. *The Agricultural Development of the Middle East.* London: H.M. Stationery Office, 1946.

Kendall, Patricia L. "The Ambivalent Character of Nationalism Among Egyptian Professionals." *Public Opinion Quarterly* XX (Spring 1956): 277–289.

Khallaf, H. "Financing Economic Development in Egypt." *Middle East Economic Papers* (1955):

Killick, Tony. *Development Economics in Action: A Study of Economic Policies in Ghana.* London: Heinemann, 1978.

Kingston, Paul W. T. *Britain and the Politics of Modernization in the Middle East, 1945–1958.* Cambridge: Cambridge University Press, 1996.

Knorr, Klaus E. and Gardner Patterson. *A Critique of the Randall Commission Report on United States Foreign Economic Policy.* Princeton: International Finance Section, Princeton University, 1954.

Koestner, N. "Some Comments on Professor Nurske's Capital Accumulation in Underdeveloped Countries." *L'Egypte Contemporaine* XLIV (283 1953): 1–18.

Kolko, Joyce and Gabriel Kolko. *The Limits of Power: The World and United States Foreign Policy, 1945–1954.* New York: Harper and Row, 1972.

Krämer, Gudrun. *The Jews in Modern Egypt, 1914–1952.* Seattle: University of Washington Press, 1989.

Krueger, Anne O. and The Brookings Institution. *Economic Policies at Cross-purposes: The United States and Developing Countries.* Washington: Brookings Institution, 1993.

Kuniholm, Bruce R. *The Origins of the Cold War in the Near East: Great Power Conflict and Diplomacy in Iran, Turkey and Greece.* Princeton: Princeton University Press, 1980.

Kuntz, Diane B. *Economic Diplomacy of the Suez Crisis.* Chapel Hill: University of North Carolina Press, 1991.

Kuznets, Simon S. *Economic Growth.* Durham: Duke University Press, 1955.

———. *Postwar Economic Growth: Four Lectures.* Cambridge: Belknap Press of Harvard University Press, 1964.

———. *Modern Economic Growth: Rate, Structure and Spread.* New Haven: Yale University Press, 1966.

————. "Quantitative Aspects of the Growth of Nations." *Economic Development and Cultural Change,* vol. V (1956).

Lacouture, Jean, and Simonne Lacouture. *Egypt in Transition.* Trans. by Francis Scarfe. New York: Criterion Books, 1958.

Lederer, William J., and Eugene Burdick. *The Ugly American.* New York: W. W. Norton, 1958.

Leibenstein, Harvey. *Proposal for the Development of a Theory of Economic Growth.* Santa Monica: Rand Corporation, 1954.

————. *Economic Backwardness and Economic Growth: Studies in the Theory of Economic Development.* New York: Wiley, 1957.

Lerner, Daniel. *The Passing of Traditional Society: Modernizing the Middle East.* Glencoe, IL: Free Press, 1958.

Lewis, John P. and Norman T. Uphoff. *Strengthening the Poor: What Have We Learned?* New Brunswick, USA: Transaction Books, 1988.

Lewis, W. Arthur. *The Theory of Economic Growth.* London: Allen & Unwin, 1955.

Lilienthal, David E. *TVA: Democracy on the March.* New York: Harper & Brothers, 1944.

Little, Tom. *High Dam at Aswan: The Subjugation of the Nile.* London: Methuen & Co, 1965.

Louis, William Roger. *The British Empire in the Middle East, 1945–1951: Arab Nationalism, the United States, and Postwar Imperialism.* Oxford: Clarendon Press, 1984.

————. *Imperialism at Bay: The United States and the Decolonization of the British Empire, 1941–1945.* New York: Oxford University Press, 1978.

Lucas, W. Scott. *Divided We Stand: Britain, the US and the Suez Crisis.* London: Hodder & Stoughton, 1991.

Lumsdaine, David Halloran. *Moral Vision in International Politics: The Foreign Aid Regime, 1949–1989.* Princeton, NJ: Princeton University Press, 1993.

Mabro, Robert. *The Egyptian Economy, 1952–1972.* Oxford: Clarendon Press, 1974.

————and Samir Radwan. *The Industrialization of Egypt, 1939–1973: Policy and Performance.* Oxford: Clarendon Press, 1976.

Mack, Robert Tandler. *Raising the World's Standard of Living: The Coordination and Effectiveness of Point Four, United Nations Technical Assistance, and Related Programs.* New York: Citadel Press, 1953.

Malenbaum, Wilfred and Massachusetts Institute of Technology. Center for International Studies. *Community Development and National Economic Growth.* Cambridge, Mass.: Massachusetts Institute of Technology, Center for International Studies, 1957.

Malin, Martin. "Entrepreneurial Statecraft: Egypt and the Superpowers, 1952–1967." Ph.D. Dissertation, Columbia University, 1995.

Mallalieu, W. C. *British Reconstruction and American Policy, 1945–1955.* New York: Scarecrow Press, 1956.

Mandelbaum, K. *The Industrialisation of Backward Areas. 2nd ed.* Oxford: Blackwell, 1955.

Marei, Sayyid. "The Agrarian Reform in Egypt." *International Labor Review* LXIX (2 1954).

————. *Agrarian Reform in Egypt*. Cairo: Impr. de l'Institut francais d'archeologie orientale, 1957.

Marrama, V. "The Relation Between Distribution of Income and Economic Development." *L'Egypte Contemporaine* XLVI (281 1955): 1–15.

Marriott, McKim. "Technological Change in Overdeveloped Rural Areas." *Economic Development and Cultural Change* I:4 (December 1952).

Marsot, Afaf Lutfi al-Sayyid. *Egypt's Liberal Experiment, 1922–1936*. Berkeley: University of California Press, 1977.

Mason, Edmund S. and Robert E. Asher. *The World Bank since Bretton Woods*. Washington: Brookings Institution, 1973.

McClelland, David C. "Community Development and the Nature of Human Motivation: Some Implications of Recent Research." Background paper, Conference on Community Development Sponsored by Center for International Studies (MIT), 1957.

————. *The Achieving Society*. Princeton: Van Nostrand, 1961.

McMahon, Robert J. *The Cold War on the Periphery: The United States, India and Pakistan, 1947–1965*. New York: Columbia University Press, 1994.

Mead, Donald C. *Growth and Structural Change in the Egyptian Economy*. Homewood, Ill.: R. D. Irwin, 1967.

Meier, Gerald M. and Dudley Seers (eds.). *Pioneers in Development*. New York: World Bank [by] Oxford University Press, 1984.

Meijer, Roel. *The Quest for Modernity: Secular Liberal and Left-wing Political Thought in Egypt, 1945–1958*. unpublished manuscript.

Merrill, Dennis. *Bread and the Ballot: The United States and India's Economic Development, 1947–1963*. Chapel Hill: University of North Carolina Press, 1990.

Meyer, Gail E. *Egypt and the United States: The Formative Years*. Cranbury, NJ: Associated University Presses, 1980.

Millikan, Max F., ed. *Income Stabilization for a Developing Democracy: A Study of the Politics and Economics of High Employment without Inflation*. New Haven: Yale University Press, 1953.

Millikan, Max F. and W. W. Rostow. *A Proposal: Key to an Effective Foreign Policy*. New York: Harper & Bros., 1957.

Mohi El Din, Khaled. *Memories of a Revolution: Egypt 1952*. Translated by TRIACC Translation Services. Cairo: American University in Cairo Press, 1995.

Monroe, Elizabeth. *Britain's Moment in the Middle East, 1914–1956*. Baltimore: The Johns Hopkins Press, 1963.

Moore, Clement Henry. *Images of Development: Egyptian Engineers in Search of Industry*. Cambridge: MIT Press, 1980.

Murden, Forrest D. *Underdeveloped Lands: Revolution of Rising Expectations*. New York: Foreign Policy Association, 1956.

Myrdal, Gunnar. *Development and Under-development: A Note on the Mechanism of National and International Economic Inequality*. Cairo: National Bank of Egypt, 1956.

————. *Economic Theory and Under-developed Regions*. London: G. Duckworth, 1957.

El Naggar, S. *Foreign Aid and the Economic Development of the U.A.R.* Princeton: Princeton University Program in Near Eastern Studies, 1964.

Neguib, Mohammed. *Egypt's Destiny.* London: Victor Gollancz, 1955.

Nash, Manning and Berthold Frank Hoselitz. *Essays on Economic Development and Cultural Change: In Honor of Bert F. Hoselitz.* Chicago: University of Chicago Press, 1977.

Nurkse, Ragnar. *Problems of Capital Formation in Underdeveloped Countries.* New York: Oxford University Press, 1953.

————. *Patterns of Trade and Development.* New York: Oxford University Press, 1961.

O'Brien, Patrick K. and The Royal Institute of International Affairs. *The Revolution in Egypt's Economic System: From Private Enterprise to Socialism, 1952–1965.* London, New York: Royal Institute of International Affairs [by] Oxford U.P., 1966.

Overseas Development Council. *The U.S. and the Developing World.* New York: Praeger, 1974.

Owen, E. R. J. *Cotton and the Egyptian Economy, 1820–1914.* Oxford: Clarendon Press, 1969.

Packenham, Robert A. *Liberal America and the Third World.* Princeton: Princeton University Press, 1973.

————and The California Arms Control and Foreign Policy Seminar. Working Group on U.S. Relations with Leftist Regimes. *The United States and Third World Development.* Santa Monica: The Seminar, 1973.

Palmer, Monte, Ali Leila and Sayed Yasin. *The Egyptian Bureaucracy.* Syracuse: Syracuse University Press, 1988.

Parsons, Kenneth H., et al. (eds.) *Land Tenure: Proceedings of the International Conference on Land Tenure and Related Problems in World Agriculture Held at Madison, Wisconsin, 1951.* Madison: University of Wisconsin Press, 1956.

Paterson, Thomas G. *Meeting the Communist Threat: Truman to Reagan.* New York: Oxford University Press, 1988.

Peretz, Don. "U.S. Aid in the Middle East." *Current History* XXXIII (August 1957): 55–100.

Perry, Glenn E. "United States Relations with Egypt." Ph.D. Dissertation, University of Virginia, 1964.

Peterson, Samiha Sidhom. "Elites and the Modernization of Underdeveloped Countries." Ph.D. Dissertation, University of Minnesota, 1972.

Platt, Raye R. *Egypt, A Compendium.* New York: American Geographical Society, 1958.

Pollard, Robert A. *Economic Security and the Origins of the Cold War 1945–1950.* New York: Columbia University Press, 1985.

Pye, Lucien W. "Community Development as a Part of Political Development." Background Paper, Conference on Community Development Sponsored by Center for International Studies (MIT), 1957.

Radwan, Samir Muhammad. *Agrarian Reform and Rural Poverty, Egypt, 1952–1975.* Geneva: International Labour Office, 1977.

Republic of Egypt, Ministry of Commerce and Industry. *Opportunities for Industrial Development in Egypt.* Cairo: Government Press, 1955.

Republic of Egypt, Ministry of Commerce and Industry. *The Population Problem of Egypt.* Cairo: Government Press, 1955.

Richards, Alan. *Egypt's Agricultural Development, 1800–1980.* Boulder: Westview Press, 1980.

Rizvi, Nihal H. "Political Organizations of a Revolutionary Regime: The Case of Egypt." *Indian Political Science Review* 16 (1 1982): 94–115.

Rockefeller Foundation. *Annual Report 1913–14.* New York, Rockefeller Foundation, n.d.

Rondinelli, Dennis A. *Development Administration and U.S. Foreign Aid Policy.* Boulder: L. Rienner Publisher, 1987.

Rostow, W. W. *The Process of Economic Growth.* New York: Norton, 1952.

———. *The Stages of Economic Growth: A Non-Communist Manifesto.* Cambridge: Cambridge University Press, 1960.

———. *Eisenhower, Kennedy, and Foreign Aid.* Austin: University of Texas Press, 1985.

Rubin, Barry. "America and the Egyptian Revolution, 1950–1957." *Political Science Quarterly* 97 (1 1982): 73–90.

Ruopp, Phillips. *Approaches to Community Development: A Symposium Introductory to Problems and Methods of Village Welfare in Underdeveloped Areas.* The Hague: W. Van Hoeve Ltd., 1953.

Rycroft, Robert W. and Szyliowicz, Joseph S. "The Technological Dimension of Decision Making: The Case of the Aswan High Dam." *World Politics* 33 (1 1980): 36–61.

Saab, Gabriel S. *The Egyptian Agrarian Reform: 1952–1962.* London, New York: Royal Institute of International Affairs [by] Oxford U.P., 1967.

Sadowski, Yahya. *Political Vegetables? Businessman and Bureaucrat in the Development of Egyptian Agriculture.* Washington: Brookings Institution, 1991.

Sale, Sara L. "Harry S. Truman, the Development and Operations of the National Security Council, and the Origins of United States Cold War Policies." Dissertation, Oklahoma State, 1992.

Sanders, Irwin T. *Community Development and National Change* [Summary of a conference sponsored by Center for International Studies (MIT) held at Endicott House] (Washington?: International Cooperation Administration, 1958.

Sanny, Lackany. "What is Underdevelopment?" *L'Egypte Contemporaine* XLIX (291 1958): 61–62.

Sayed-Ahmed, Muhammad Abd el-Wahab. *Nasser and American Foreign Policy, 1952–1956.* London: LAAM, 1989.

Joseph A. Schumpter. *The Theory of Economic Development: An Inquiry into Profits, Capital, Credit, Interest, and the Business Cycle,* trans. by Redvers Opie. Cambridge: Harvard University Press, 1934.

Seminar on Research Perspectives and Problems and North Central Land Tenure Research Committee. *Agrarian Reform & Economic Growth in Developing Countries: Papers.* Washington: Farm Economics Division, Economic Research Service, U. S. Dept of Agriculture, 1962.

Shalaby, Mohamed M. *Rural Reconstruction in Egypt.* Cairo: Soc. Art Graphique for the Egyptian Association for Social Studies, 1950.

Sharp, Walter R. *International Technical Assistance: Programs and Organization.* Chicago: Public Administration Service, 1952.

El Shazly, Hamdy. "Abis as a Pilot Project in Settlement" (lecture, no date). United Nations Development Programme. Integrated Development and Settlement of New Lands Irrigated by High Dam Waters. UNDP/UNOTC/ARE-71.

Shibl, Yusuf A. *The Aswan High Dam.* Beirut: Arab Institute for Research and Publishing, 1971.

Sidky, Abdel Razzaq. *The Agricultural Policy in the New Era.* Cairo: Government Press, 1953.

Sidky, Aziz. "Industrialization of Egypt and a Case Study of the Iron and Steel Industry." Ph.D. Dissertation. Harvard University, 1951.

Sinai, I.R. *The Challenge of Modernization.* London: Chatto & Windus, 1964.

Singer, H.W. "Obstacles to Economic Development." *Social Research* 20 (1953): 19–31.

Sjoberg, Gideon. *The Preindustrial City, Past and Present.* Glencoe, IL: Free Press, 1960.

Smith, Brian H. *More than Altruism: The Politics of Private Foreign Aid.* Princeton: Princeton University Press, 1990.

Spence, Jonathan D. *To Change China: Western Advisers in China, 1620–1960.* New York: Penguin Books, 1980.

Staley, E. *World Economic Development. 2d ed.* Montreal: International Labor Office, 1945.

———. *Creating an Industrial Civilization.* New York: Harper, 1952.

Stanford Research Institute, Stanford University and United States. International Cooperation Administration. *The Role of Small-scale Manufacturing in Economic Development: The Experience of Industrially Advanced Nations as a Guide for Newly Developing Areas.* 1957.

Stephens, Oren. *Facts to a Candid World: America's Overseas Information Program.* Stanford: Stanford University Press, 1955.

Syrquin, Moises and Hollis B. Chenery. *Patterns of Development, 1950 to 1983.* Washington: World Bank, 1989.

Takeyh, Ray. *The Origins of the Eisenhower Doctrine: The US, Britain and Nasser's Egypt, 1953–1957.* New York: St. Martin's Press, 2000.

Tansky, Leo. *U.S. and U.S.S.R. Aid to Developing Countries: A Comparative Study of India, Turkey, and the U.A.R.* New York: Praeger, 1967.

Taylor, Carl C. *A Critical Analysis of India's Community Development Program.* Community Projects Administration, Government of India, 1956.

Thweatt, W. "The Egyptian Agrarian Reform." *Middle East Economic Papers* (1956).

Tignor, Robert L. "Dependency Theory and Egyptian Capitalism, 1920–1950." *African Economic History* 9 (1980): 101–118.

———. *State, Private Enterprise and Economic Change in Egypt, 1918–1952.* Princeton: Princeton University Press, 1984.

Torres, James F. *New Directions for Development in Third World Countries: The Failure of U.S. Foreign Policy.* Aldershot, England; Brookfield, USA: Avebury, 1993.

True, Alfred Charles. *A History of Agricultural Extension in the United States.* Washington: Government Printing Office, 1928.

United Arab Republic, Aswan High Dam Authority. *Aswan High Dam.* 1964.

United Arab Republic, Ministry of Agrarian Reform and Land Reclamation. *Agrarian Reform and Land Reclamation in Eleven Years.* 1963.

United Arab Republic, Ministry of the High Aswan Dam. *The High Aswan Dam.* 1963.

United Nations. *The Development of Manufacturing Industry in Egypt, Israel and Turkey.* 1958.

United Nations, Department of Economic and Social Affairs. *Economic Developments in the Middle East.* (annual).

United Nations. Department of Economic Affairs. *Economic Development in Selected Countries: Plans, Programmes and Agencies.* 1947.

————. *Domestic Financing of Economic Development.* 1950.

————. *Measures for the Economic Development of Under-developed Countries.* 1951.

United Nations. Economic and Social Council. Mission on Community Organization and Development in Selected Arab Countries of the Middle East, Sir Oswald Allen, and United Nations. Technical Assistance Administration. *Report . . . Prepared for the Technical Assistance Administration of the United Nations.* 1953.

United States. Commission on Foreign Economic Policy. *Staff Papers Presented to the Commission on Foreign Economic Policy.* Washington: Government Printing Office, 1954.

United States. Commission on Foreign Economic Policy and Clarence Belden Randall. *Report to the President and the Congress.* Washington: Government Printing Office, 1954.

United States. Congress. Senate. Special Committee to Study the Foreign Aid Program. *Foreign Aid: Report.* Washington: Government Printing Office, 1957.

United States. Department of Agriculture Extension Service and Office of Foreign Agricultural Relations. *Committee Report on the Contribution of Extension Methods and Techniques toward the Rehabilitation of War-Torn Countries.* Washington: Government Printing Office, 1945.

United States. Department of State. Commercial policy series, 105. *The Development of the Foreign Reconstruction Policy of the United States, March-July 1947.* Washington: Government Printing Office, 1947.

United States. Department of State. Office of Intelligence Research. *Economic Problems of Underdeveloped Areas: External research, a listing of recent studies.* Washington: External Research Staff, Office of Intelligence Research, Dept. of State, 1956.

United States. International Development Advisory Board. *Partners in Progress: A Report to the President.* Washington: Government Printing Office, 1951.

Vatikiotis, P. J. *The History of Egypt From Muhammad Ali to Mubarak.* 3d ed. Baltimore: Johns Hopkins University Press, 1985.

Viner, Jacob. *International Trade and Economic Development: Lectures Delivered at the National University of Brazil.* Glencoe, Ill.: Free Press, 1952.

Vitalis, Robert. *When Capitalists Collide: Business Conflict and the End of Empire in Egypt.* Berkeley: University of California Press, 1995.

Warriner, Doreen. *Agrarian Reform and Community Development in the U.A.R.* Cairo: Dar al-Taawon, 1961.

———. *Land and Poverty in the Middle East.* London: Royal Institute of International Affairs, 1948.

Waterbury, John. *The Egypt of Nasser and Sadat: The Political Economy of Two Regimes.* Princeton, NJ: Princeton University Press, 1983.

———. *Hydropolitics of the Nile Valley.* Syracuse: Syracuse University Press, 1979.

Wheelock, Keith. *Nasser's New Egypt: A Critical Analysis.* New York: Praeger, 1960.

Wickwar, William. *The Modernization of Administration in the Near East.* Beirut: Khayats, 1963.

Wittfogel, Karl. *Oriental Despotism: A Comparative Study of Total Power.* New Haven: Yale University Press, 1957.

Zaki, Hashem. "Financing a Planned Process of Economic Development in Underdeveloped Countries." *L'Egypte Contemporaine* XLII (263 1951b): 33–50.

———. "Industrialization and the Decline of Agriculture in Under-developed Countries." *L'Egypte Contemporaine* XLIII (269 1952a): 1–15.

———. "Trade Pattern of Developing Countries." *L'Egypte Contemporaine* XLII (276 1952b): 21–34.

Books, Articles and Manuscripts in Arabic:

Abbas, Ra'uf (ed.). *Egyptian-British Relations, 1951–1954.* Cairo: Markaz al-Dirasat al-Siyasiya wal-Istratijiya bil-Ahram, 1995.

Abdel Fadil, Mahmoud. *The Egyptian Economy between Central Planning and Economic Opening.* Beirut: Ma'had al-Inma' al-Arabi, 1980.

Abdel Moneim, Ahmed Faris, "The Egyptian Decision to Make the Czech Arms Deal of 1955: A Study in Egyptian Foreign Policy." Master's Thesis, Cairo University, Faculty of Economics and Political Science, 1980.

Ali, Fatin Ahmed Farid. "Egyptian Diplomacy and the Suez Crisis up to the Aggression, 26 July–29 October 1956." Master's Thesis, Ain Shams University, 1989.

Amr, Abdel Ra'uf Ahmed. *The History of Egyptian-American Relations, 1939–1957.* Cairo: al-Haya al-Misriya al-Ama lil-Kitab, 1991.

Al-Baghdadi, Abdel Latif. *Memoirs, pt. 1.* Cairo: al-Maktab al-Misri al-Hadith, 1977.

Al-Barrawi, Rashed. *The Economic Philosophy of the Revolution.* Cairo: Maktabat al-Nahda al-Misriya, 1955.

Baybars, Diya al-Din. *On the Margins of the Story of Muhammad Hassanein Heikal.* Beirut: Manshurat al-Maktaba al-Asriya, n.d. (1975).

Al-Bishri, Tariq. *The Political Movement in Egypt, 1945–1952.* 2nd printing. Cairo: Dar al-Shuruq, 1983.

———. *Studies in Egyptian Democracy.* Cairo: Dar al-Shuruq, 1987.

Dar al-Mustaqbal al-Arabi. *The 23 July Revolution: Judgments of the Present and Challenges of the Future.* Cairo: Dar al-Mustaqbal al-Arabi, 1987.

Al-Dessouqi, Asim. *Large Agricultural Landowners and Their Role in Egyptian Society, 1914–1952.* Cairo: Dar al-Thaqafa al-Jadida, 1975.

Egypt. *Ministry of Social Affairs: Its Activities, Development and Services.* Cairo: The Ministry, 1955.

Egypt. *Permanent Council for Public Welfare Services, October 1953-March 1957.* Cairo: Matba'at Nahdat Misr, 1957.

Egyptian Society for Political Economy, Statistics and Law. *Studies for the Fiftieth Anniversary, 1909–1959.* Cairo: Sharikat al-A'alanat al-Sharqiya, 1960.

Fawzi, Mahmoud. *The Free Officers Talk.* Cairo: Maktabat Madbuli, 1990.

Al-Gritly, Ali. *The Economic History of the Revolution, 1952–1966.* Cairo: Dar al-Ma'araf bi-Misr, 1974.

Hamdan, Gamal al-Din. *Egypt's Character.* Cairo: Maktabat al-Nahda al-Misriya, 1970.

Hamrouche, Ahmed. *The Story of the July 23 Revolution, vol. 1: Egypt and the Military.* Cairo: Maktabat Madbuli, 1975.

———. *The Story of the July 23 Revolution, vol. 4: Witnesses to the July Revolution.* Cairo: Maktabat Madbuli, 1978.

Hamuda, Adel. *The Crisis of the Intellectuals and the July Revolution.* Cairo: Maktabat Madbuli, 1985.

Hassanein, Magdi. *The Desert: The Revolution and the Wealth: The Story of Tahrir Province.* Cairo: al-Haya al-Misirya al-Ama lil-Kitab, 1975.

Heikal, Muhammad Hassanein. *The Suez Files.* Cairo: Markaz al-Ahram lil-Tarjama wal-Nashr, 1986.

Ibrahim, Sa'ad al-Din, "The Social Project of the July Revolution." *The 23 July Revolution.* Cairo: Dar al-Mustaqbal al-Arabi, 1987.

Imam, Abdullah. *Ali Sabri Remembers.* Beirut: Dar al-Wahda, 1988.

Kishk, Muhammad Galal. *The American July Revolution: Abdel Nasser's Relationship with American Intelligence.* Cairo: al-Maktaba al-Thaqafiya, 1992.

Mattar, Fuad. *Frankly about Abdel Nasser.* Beirut: Dar al-Qadaya, 1975.

Mohieddin, Khaled. *And Now I Speak.* Cairo: Markaz al-Ahram lil-Tarjama wal-Nashr, 1992.

Al-Mursi, Fuad. *Egyptian-Soviet Relations, 1943–1956.* Cairo: Dar al-Thaqafa al-Jadida, 1987.

Ramadan, Abdel Azim. *Revolutionary Thought in Egypt before the July 23 Revolution.* Cairo: Maktabat Madbuli, 1981.

———. *The Social and Political Conflict in Egypt from the 23 July Revolution to the March Crisis of 1954.* Cairo: Maktabat Madbuli, 1989.

Republic of Egypt, Permanent Council for the Development of National Production. *Principal Production Projects.* Cairo: The Council, 1954.

———. *Report.* Cairo: The Council, 1955.

Al-Sadat, Anwar. *My Son, This is Your Uncle Gamal.* Cairo: Dar al-Hilal, 1958.

Al-Sa'id, Rifa'at. *History of the Egyptian Communist Movement, vol. 2: The Public Press.* Cairo: Sharikat al-Amal lil-Taba'a wal-Nashr wal-Tawzi', 1987.

Shaqra, Gamal Ma'awad. "The Political Movement in Egypt, from the March 1954 Crisis to the Issuance of the Decrees of July 1961." Doctoral Dissertation, Ain Shams University, 1992.

Tawil, Muhammad. *The Game of Nations and Abdel Nasser.* Cairo: al-Maktab al-Misri al-Hadith, 1986.

Toward an Educated Citizen: A Program to Educate Adults. Sirs al-Layan, Manufiya: Markaz al-Tarbiya al-Asasiya fil-Alam al-Arabi, 1956.

United Arab Republic, Information Department. *Collection of Speeches, Statements and Proclamations of President Gamal Abdel Nasser, pt. 1: 23 July 1952–1958.* Cairo: Information Department, n.d.

Yusuf, Amr Izz al-Rijal Muhammad. "The Role of the Egyptian Foreign Ministry in Foreign Policy Decision-making, 1952–1982." Master's Thesis, Cairo University. College of Economics and Political Science, 1988.

Interviews

Author conducted interviews in Arabic and English with Rifky Anwar, Badr Badawi, Tahseen Bashir, Salah Dessouki, Kamal al-Din Hussein, Aziza Shukri Hussein, William Lakeland, Ahmed Hamrouche, Hussein Fahmy, Harry Hemmerich, Mohey Khattab, Khalid Mohieddin, Rashad Omran, Abd al-Azim Shawqi al-Saidi, Hamdy El Shazly, Aziz Sidky, George Sweeny, and William Weathersby.

H. Richard Dekmejian granted the author permission to use interviews he conducted with EARIS veterans as part of an AID-sponsored evaluation of the EARIS program, including Roscoe Bell, A. B. Bonds, Albert Farwell, Ed Felder, Erwin Hannum, Kenneth Platt, and John Russell

Index